The War Diaries of
JOAN STRANGE
1939 – 1945

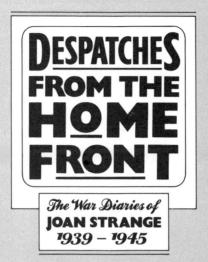

Joan Strange

Edited by Chris McCooey

MONARCH PUBLICATIONS
Eastbourne

Designed by Ron Bryant-Funnell

British Library Cataloguing in Publication Data

Strange, Joan
  Despatches from the home front.
  1. World War 2 – Biographies
  I. Title
  940.54′8
  ISBN 1-85424-049-8

Printed in Great Britain for
MONARCH PUBLICATIONS LTD
1 St Anne's Road, Eastbourne, E Sussex BN21 3UN by
Richard Clay Ltd, Bungay, Suffolk.
Typeset by CST, Eastbourne, E. Sussex.

Contents

CARRY YOUR GAS MASK

Realistic gas tests are being held in different parts of the country and on March 27 the Minister of Home Security spoke in the Commons about the possibility of enemy gas attacks. 'This country', he said, 'will in no circumstances be the first to employ the gas weapon', but if the Germans thought gas would be of military advantage, they would use it.

ACKNOWLEDGEMENTS

Numerous photographs and some cartoons appear in this book. Where it is possible to identify the sources and dates, this has been done. However, after fifty years it has proved simply impossible to trace some sources, and apologies are offered where omissions have occurred.

The author and publishers would specifically like to acknowledge the following sources: The Daily Telegraph, The Sunday Times, The Evening Standard, The Evening News, Punch, The Chicago Daily Tribune, Picture Post and The Worthing Herald.

I wish to thank Christopher McCooey for his encouragement
in getting this book published and for the care with which he
has abridged the twelve volumes. Thanks, too, to my sister,
Kathleen Strange, and to Muriel Thomas and my other friends
who have urged me to go ahead with publishing what I wrote
in those far-off black-out evenings of 1939 to 1945.

Joan Strange

'My sister Joan kept a diary all through the Second World War,' said Kathleen. It was the monthly meeting of the Tunbridge Wells Writers' Circle journalism group and we were discussing the upcoming fiftieth anniversary of the outbreak of hostilities in Europe. As a freelance writer and journalist I was interested. 'She also kept one throughout the First World War,' added Kathleen. Joan sounded quite a lady. I was *very* interested.

A week later Kathleen and I were merrily motoring through the Weald and up and over the South Downs. We dropped down into the seaside town of Worthing and pulled up in front of a house in Langton Road. The front door was open and a grey haired lady with chuckling eyes and wearing an apron was waiting there to greet us.

Joan had prepared a huge lunch. Fresh grapefruit, roast shoulder of lamb with mint sauce, roast potatoes with carrots, leeks and cabbage. There was a choice of two puddings: rhubarb crumble and a whipped fruit dish. The mint for the sauce, the leeks, cabbage and rhubarb were freshly picked from among the flowers that bordered the lawn in the sheltered back garden. I ate my crumble with a silver spoon that Joan had won in a tennis tournament in the Thirties. We three ate heartily, talked animatedly and laughed a lot. Both Joan and Kathleen have mastered the art of conversation: topics ranged from the Grocer's Daughter and whether Edwina Currie was a good egg, to double yellow parking lines, back pains (Joan was a physiotherapist for many years), the price of oranges (in the kitchen a batch of marmalade had just been made for the church sale), and how the Strange family had been adept at making up words – the family dog was said to be 'numningating' when it put its leg over its shoulder to clean itself.

After lunch we took our coffee and went and sat in the lounge. 'Now Joan, Chris would like to see the diaries,' Kathleen said, with a former civil servant's due regard for time and not wasting it. 'They're under the bed,' said Joan, 'where they've been since the war ended. It was such a relief to stop writing them.' Joan returned with a smallish leather suitcase. Inside were twelve hard-backed notebooks; the insertions of newspaper cuttings made each volume bulge like a well-filled sandwich.

I began to read the diary for 1939. On the first page the Archbishop of Canterbury had made a broadcast in which he urged people 'to hope for the best and prepare for the worst'. A couple of pages later Joan is reading *Mein Kampf* in bed – an

Austrian pen friend (with whom she still keeps in touch) had sent her a copy. Over the page Mother is making eighty sausage rolls for the Church of England's Men's Society Whist Drive and Mr Chamberlain, the Prime Minister, is off to Paris for talks aimed at giving moral support to the French who are having a territorial dispute with Mussolini. By 10th January 1939 I was convinced that the diaries were a remarkable social and historical document and that they should be published. Kathleen enthusiastically agreed. Joan demurred. She couldn't believe anyone would be interested in what she had written so long ago; she said she was thinking of throwing them away!

I was born in 1949. My only knowledge of the war prior to working on these diaries was the bare outline of events gleaned from history books and the recognition of a few famous names of ships, airmen, soldiers and battles. All that has now changed. I now feel as if I actually lived through those fateful war years of 1939 to 1945. Joan not only recorded the events as they unfolded, but she wrote about how war, with all its gallant and ugly deeds, all its hopes and expectations and lies and hatreds, affected her and her family, her neighbours in Worthing, the people in London. Indeed, how the war affected and fashioned the British national character.

Now, having been so intimately involved in these years and these lives through editing these diaries, I can only add that I have the greatest admiration for Joan and those like her who won through in the end. Please God that I and my family should have half her solid truthfulness, her stubborn common sense, her depths of Christian compassion and charity, her strength of faith and character. And, please God, that I and my family and all of us passengers on this planet are never put to the test by such madness on such a massive scale ever again.

Chris McCooey

DRAMATIS PERSONAE...

FAMILY

Mother – Mrs E M Strange, wife of Worthing draper George Nevill Strange, who died in 1919 at the age of 47. Mrs Strange was the mother of Mollie, Joan, Kathleen, and Ken. Mother was born in 1868 and died in 1968 after receiving two telegrams from the Queen congratulating her on her hundredth birthday (Kit, her daughter, noticed that in the first telegram the word 'hundredth' had been mis-spelt).

Mollie Strange, the eldest daughter, married Jack Lasseter and during the war they lived in Godalming, Surrey with their two sons, Michael and Roger. Mollie died in 1978 at the age of 80; Jack remarried and still lives in Godalming.

Kathleen Strange, known as Kit, was born in 1904 and now lives in Tunbridge Wells, Kent. During the war she was a housing manager in Chelsea.

Ken Strange, married Helen Wenban-Smith and they had three sons – John, Richard and Simon. During the war Ken was a teacher at Worthing High School for boys and a part-time air raid warden. He died in 1981.

Nevill Strange, Joan's cousin, being the son of Uncle Will who lived in Bournemouth. He was a POW for many years and after the war could not settle into civilian life and committed suicide.

Aunt Alice Colebrook was Mrs E M Strange's sister who went to study music in Germany before the war at Hildesheim near Hanover. Being an alien, she was summoned before the Gestapo when war looked inevitable. She was very rude about Hitler and suggested he didn't come from good stock as he was only a corporal, whereas British generals came from much better stock. Mildly eccentric, she escaped from Germany in 1939 and returned to Britain.

Mrs Wenban-Smith, mother of Ken's wife Helen; she lived in Worthing all during the war. She died in 1971.

FRIENDS

Captain and Mrs Albrecht and son, Hans. They were Austrian Jews who managed to escape to Britain in 1939. Before this Captain Albrecht was in charge of oil tankers on the Danube. During and after the war, he captained Dutch and British merchant ships and retired to Worthing in 1962 and died there in 1976. His son, Hans, still lives in Worthing, the only one to do so out of over 300 refugees who were helped by Worthing Refugee committee in 1939.

The Beermann family with JS & Eva Rabl – 1939.

Mrs & Elizabeth Chlumecky with Mother
at 13 Langton Road – 1940.

Mrs D Thornycroft, Hon
Secretary of Worthing Refugee
Committee 1939-40.

Dr Fleischmann and family.

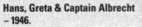

Hans, Greta & Captain Albrecht
– 1946.

Miss Bache, art mistress at Worthing High School for girls and very active in helping the refugees.

The Beermann family – Austrian Jews from Vienna. Mr and Mrs Beermann with son Heinz, known as Henry, and daughter Lisl, known as Elizabeth. Being 'trans-migrants' they were not allowed to work in Britain and were sponsored by Mrs E M Strange and Mrs Wenban-Smith. They arrived in February 1939 and left for America in November of the same year.

The Chlumecky family left Austria before the war as they were very anti-Nazi. There were three sons and one daughter, Elizabeth. The father and three sons were interned in Australia and were sent there on the same boat as Nazi sympathisers; they had a terrible passage with physical intimidations and their personal possessions destroyed. Elizabeth now lives in New York and still keeps in touch with Joan.

Eric Davis was Ken Strange's closest friend from school and university days. He joined the BBC in 1935 and was known as David Davis. During the war he served four years in the RNVR. After the war, when head of BBC's Children's Hour, he was known as Uncle David.

Dr and Mrs Fleischmann with daughter Susi (16 years old) and Martin (11) left Prague in 1939. Dr Fleischmann, a leading anti-Nazi in Czechoslovakia was a Rotarian and lawyer but died soon after his arrival in Worthing from ill-treatment by the Nazis in a concentration camp. Susi and Martin both attended Worthing High Schools. Susi and Mrs Fleischmann distinguished themselves after the war as professional doll makers and their dolls are collectors' pieces. Martin became a professor at Southampton University in electro-chemistry. He became an FRS in 1988 and announced jointly with an American colleague in 1989 a scientific breakthrough by claiming to produce cold nuclear fusion in a test tube.

Mr Harold Frampton, known as Frammie, a former mayor of Worthing and brother-in-law of Dr Gusterson; he was a well known local grower of tomatoes, grapes, etc. He formed the Worthing branch of the League of Nations Union at the end of World War One and was a very enthusiastic member of the Worthing United Nations Association after World War Two.

Dr Gusterson, local GP who served in India during the war. The moving spirit in the building and subsequent opening of the St Barnabas Home (hospice) in Worthing.

Frau Elvira Littna escaped from Czechoslovakia in the 1930s and came to live in Worthing. She was a lawyer and later a teacher. Like all aliens at the beginning of the war she had to leave the coastal areas and she went to Carlisle with her two daughters. She joined the ATS and eventually became a Lieutenant Colonel and was sent to Europe to help relocate displaced persons of many different nationalities. Married to an Englishman, Mrs Powell, as she's now known, lives in Hove.

The Moses family was the first German-Jewish family that the Stranges got to know in the early thirties. Ruth Moses, the first to arrive in England, taught German to Joan's brother Ken who went over to Germany before the outbreak of war and 'smuggled' back various pieces of jewellery, etc belonging to the family and their friends.

Mr Ritter, or Gottfried von Rittersheim, was an Austrian who managed to get to England in early 1939 by his own means. He was engaged to be married to Mrs Beermann's sister who had escaped from Austria and was living in Australia. He tried to get to Australia to marry her but was unable to because of his internment. After the war, his fiancée having died of cancer, he married an English woman and they had a small shop in London.

Mr Herbert Smith, known as Uncle Bert, was Mr George Strange's partner in the draper's business and Joan's godfather.

Mr and Mrs Steinhart were one of the first couples to be sponsored by Worthing Refugee Committee. They had three daughters, now all married to English men. One of them, Madeline, married Eric Joyce, who used to work for the *Worthing Herald* and is now a freelance journalist.

Josef Strasser, known as Sep, an Austrian teacher of English who came on holiday to Worthing before the war. Joan corresponded with him until letters to enemy aliens were banned, but after the war they renewed their correspondence and still keep in touch at Christmas and at other times.

The Thornycrofts, Oliver and Dorothy, were very active in refugee work with Mrs Thornycroft taking over the job of Honorary Secretary of the Worthing Refugee Committee after Mr Sunshine (formerly Zonnenschein) resigned in 1939. She was very persistent, on occasions refusing to leave the Home Office before her business on behalf of refugees was dealt with.

Mr and Mrs Weingarten (they later changed their name to *Ward*) escaped from Czechoslovakia. Mr Ward enlisted in the Pioneer Corps and saw active service in Europe. On Mr Ward's retirement they went to Austria and both died there in the early 1980s.

1939

January 1st An uneventful first day of the year. Had a chat with the Cooks outside church and Mr Cook said he'd rather trust the weather than politics during the year! Everyone's wondering what can happen next. Hitler and Goebbels have broadcast New Year messages to their people, dwelling on their 'harvest' of 1938. The *Sunday Times* is quite moderately optimistic.

January 2nd The Archbishop of Canterbury broadcast last night a New Year's Sermon telling all 'to hope for the best and prepare for the worst' — not very encouraging.

January 3rd Had a long letter from Sep Strasser in the five o'clock post. Did not show it to Mother as it would infuriate her so. Mostly eulogies on 'our glorious Führer' and his accomplishments, derogatory remarks on Jews and telling me he'd sent Hitler's *Mein Kampf* in English, and begging me to read it! He knows I will become an 'ardent National Socialist' if I do read it!

January 4th Read a few pages of *Mein Kampf* in bed — much as I'd imagined. *No* possibility of Sep's prophecy coming true! Busy day at work. At 3.30 helped chauffeur three blind people to the Old Folks' Dinner at Warnes. All must be over seventy. There were over 260 there, total ages reached nearly 23,000 years. The four eldest received £1 each (eighty-nine, ninety-one, ninety-two and ninety-four). All the others had tea or cigarettes to bring away. At 6 pm President Roosevelt broadcast his speech to Congress: I heard some of it — it came over well. Directed very much against the dictator states.

January 5th The Nazis furious at Roosevelt's speech according to the nine o'clock news bulletin. It is difficult to know how to foster international good-will when there are such divergent political systems.

January 7th Four of us to tea at the Odeon and at six o'clock in to see *Sixty Glorious Years*. An excellent show. It is in colour which makes it much more life-like — Anna Neagle as Victoria is wonderfully good and her love for Albert (Anton Walbrook) is well shown. With all the royal ties between England and Germany it is incredible that we have become such bad friends politically with Germany nowadays.

January 8th   In the afternoon we called at the Spanish Refugees at Lancing with 43/– left over from Christmas fund.

January 10th   Mother made her usual eighty sausage rolls for the Church of England Men's Society's whist drive and later went to it.

Mr Chamberlain started for Rome visit, calling in at Paris on his way. He promises to uphold France against the Italian claims for Tunis, Corsica and Jibuti.

January 11th   I am getting excited about Mrs Moses, Ellen and Richard 'escaping' from Germany. Richard has been in a concentration camp but has been released but with frost bitten feet. He's twenty-two. They have to send to Stuttgart for a doctor as there's no doctor in Esslingen allowed to treat a Jew. He's had to sign a declaration that he will not divulge what goes on in a concentration camp. Mr Chamberlain and Lord Halifax have arrived in Rome this afternoon. Accorded a great welcome. Should we welcome Mussolini in like manner I wonder? The totalitarian politicians keep on telling their people democracy is a worn out doctrine but the people persist in acclaiming us! All quite mad!

January 12th   So far Mr Chamberlain seems to be getting on non-committedly well!

January 14th   Up to London by the 12.33. We walked along and put down stools for *The Flashing Stream* by Charles Morgan. We'd fifty minutes to spare so we went to the News Theatre. It's 'Stage and Screen' day today, ie all cinemas and theatres give 10% of their takings and actors and actresses give part of their salary and the public are asked to subscribe to Lord Baldwin's Fund for Refugees. The Fascists are furious and are trying to hinder people giving by standing near the theatres and giving out leaflets against it.

Ken arrived and we had tea together. He's brought back from Germany two watches, one gold chain, one diamond pin, one ring and one typewriter from the Moses and friends. No trouble at all at the Customs. He saw Aunt Alice and had numerous conversations with Germans of all types. Hitler's popularity is *not* 100% and people there are full of fears and are living on their nerves. Everyone expects some 'affair' in the Spring.

January 18th   Franco steadily advancing. A lot of people have hoped he will not but it now looks an assured 'victory'. Anyhow it will *end* the war in Spain. Meanwhile in England Sir Arthur Geddes, advisor to Sir John Anderson, Civil Defence Minister, issues advice to all housewives to begin food-storing. An ominous and disquieting portent.

January 24th The news is all bad — seven St Ives lifeboat-men drowned at 3 am yesterday morning in a rescue attempt — the distressed boat managed to get to land safely.

Premier's appeal to us for 'National Service' (broadcast last night) reported in the papers as most important. In Spain the government's defence of Barcelona is giving in rapidly. Hitler and Mussolini are reported to be preparing their manifesto on their colonial demands for January 30th. Can war possibly be avoided?

January 25th Rained all day long and heavily too! Had five German and Austrian Jewish people to tea — a sorry tale but all of them courageous. Later Annie Margot, Mother and I went to the Odeon to see *Pygmalion* with Leslie Howard and Wendy Hiller in the cast.

January 26th In the paper was the case of a woman who brought back jewels, etc belonging to Jewish friends abroad who was fined £500 for avoiding Customs. Glad Ken got through alright. The evening papers report the fall of Barcelona to Franco — bad. Chile has been devastated by a terrific earthquake.

January 28th Worthing High School for Girls had an Old Girls' reunion in the evening and a very good one too. The new dances — Lambeth Walk, Palais Glide, Chestnut Tree — are extremely ugly.

January 29th Several surprise changes in the cabinet. PM wants new and younger blood. Lord Winterton (MP for Worthing) relinquishes his post as Chancellor of Duchy of Lancaster — good! Not a popular figure in his constituency although we always return him with a safe majority. PM made good speech in Birmingham yesterday, calling for peace moves by other powers.

January 30th While all Germany was listening to Hitler's broadcast on the sixth anniversary of the Third Reich, Worthing held a most interesting meeting in connection with the Jews. A Mr Davidson from Woburn House, London gave a talk on the work of the refugee problem and a committee was formed to co-ordinate efforts being made here in Worthing — I got on!

February 1st Peace Pledge Union meeting. Dr Crow from Brighton read a paper on the Pacifist attitude to ARP (Air Raid Precautions) and suggested that if we *were* to have 'shelters', why not plan underground roads to be used in peace as roads and in war as shelters. He stresses very much the psychological reaction of people in relation to ARP saying that he'd found by observation that it created *fear* rather than confidence.

4

February 2nd A voluntary national service worker came round to see about the billeting of children in case of war — we are liable to have five!

February 3rd In all the evening for once! Very nice. Washed hair and telephoned Kit (nine minutes). Listened to excellent broadcast 'Children in Flight', a series of sound records of the German child refugees. Peter Laufer, five and a half, was one of the refugee boys interviewed — the Laufer family is now living in Worthing. His father told me that Peter asked him if it were true that when he came to England he would be allowed to go into a garden again. In Austria and Germany Jews are not allowed in public gardens.

February 5th Peter Laufer and three other boys had a lovely time together on the beach. The news of the IRA is bad — plans for blowing up Buckingham Palace and Windsor found. Explosions have been effected in several places already.

Franco's army still advancing rapidly and the refugees' plight is *terrible*. The HQ of the Foster Parents Scheme have sent a heartrending appeal for more funds.

An advertisement out of the *Radio Times* for this week. We shall all be taking this for granted in a year or two I suppose!

February 6th   On the news at ten o'clock we heard that our unemployed have risen to the unprecedented figure of over two million and yet there are all sorts of works which could be put into operation — agriculture, road improvements, new level crossings with underground roadways, etc. In evening to Workers Education Association on Norway — to my surprise the country has only three and a half million people and no empire so there is comparatively little of the war fear there. In the last war though they lost a tremendous amount of sailors and shipping even though they were neutral.

February 8th   Invited Reverend Battersby, the vicar of St Paul's, and his wife, Misses Duncan and Brangwyn, Ken and Herr Laufer to tea to discuss the refugee problem. Upshot (we hope) St Paul's going to financially guarantee a family Herr Laufer knows very well. In the evening went to the Dick Sheppard Club at Brighton with two Austrian girls.

February 9th   Henshaw the twenty-four-year-old pilot has set up still another record to and from the Cape — 39 hours 25 minutes getting there and coming back 39 hours 33 minutes.

February 10th   Pope Pius XI died this morning — aged eighty-one. Was to have delivered an important speech tomorrow.

Mother, Helen, Ken and I motored over to Brighton to see *Goodbye Mr Chips* at the theatre. Very good but not so moving as the book.

France has opened her frontiers absolutely and refugees from Spain pour in by the thousands. The war cannot last longer than next week, the papers say. But how can Franco rule such a disunited people?

February 15th   Mother busy making cakes and scones in the morning for the tea at Parish Room after the meeting about the Jewish Refugees. The three Laufers there and at least we've fixed up their friends with temporary hospitality. Mrs Wenban-Smith's having two and we two. Lots of people turned up and much interest shown.

February 22nd   I'm reading *I Was Hitler's Prisoner* by S. Lorant, a former editor of a non-political illustrated paper in Munich, in the sixpenny Penguin edition. The Nazi régime is *loathly* to the last degree of the word.

February 23rd   Fred Payne and Norah Howden have just taken their ARP wardens' exam. One question was: how would you treat someone suffering from a centipede bite! I heard that someone in a First Aid Class was asked how he'd treat someone bleeding from the head and answered: 'Tie a tight tourniquet around the neck.' The victims of an air-raid are going to have a tough time!

6

February 25th At 6.30 called for Hanna, the refugee from Berlin, staying with Mr Sunshine, to hear Backhaus at the Dome. She was so excited as she's musical and has not been allowed to visit concerts recently in Germany because of being a Jew.

February 26th Today we hear that the British government proposes to recognise Franco — blow! There have been several demonstrations in London against the recognition of the Socialists.

February 27th All the cinemas here have granted free passes to all refugees. At the Refugee Committee meeting the Treasurer reported already over £4 definitely (pledged) weekly, ie enough to support an aged couple, and our leader wired off to the two old people who have been chivied from Germany, Austria, Jugoslavia and now Italy (by March 4th) to say we can have them. So we've done something concrete at last.

FEBRUARY 26, 1939

FIRST ISSUE OF AIR RAID SHELTERS

Sunday Times,
February 26th

March 6th Mother to Parochial Church Council and bravely pressed for St Paul's to support financially the Refugee Appeal (Jews from Germany mostly) but no-one supported her. The Vicar is cowed by his church warden.

March 7th Reported at Beach House for my gas mask. Quite footling but thought I'd better. Discovered Mother and I were not even registered! Luckily the first one fitted all right (shouldn't fancy having to try more than the one, especially as someone else may have breathed hard into it). The room is humorously labelled: this way → to Chamber of Horrors. Gas masks. And so it was! Mother wouldn't even look at mine and is not proposing to go.

March 8th Managed to get to the Industrial Christian Fellowship with the Bishop of Chichester as chairman and speaker on 'The German Church Conflict'. I'd no idea how awful things are there in the conflict between church and state. Over 700 ministers have been imprisoned.

March 10th Had a letter from Josef Strasser — he's about to go in for an exam in English — he is certainly writing well and is reading a lot of good English literature. He wants Chaucer's *Canterbury Tales* which I've ordered at W H Smith's. He cannot resist some propaganda against Jews and quotes some Shakespeare — Shylock in the *Merchant of Venice*. A pity.

March 15th Another wretched crisis in Czechoslovakia. Hitler appealed to and off to Prague immediately. The whole state built up by Masaryk completely disrupted and Hitler snaps up all the valuable pieces.

March 16th The whole world aghast at Hitler's arrogance. His flag hoisted on the wonderful old palace of Hungarian royalty. The Czechs humiliated to the dust — suicides, imprisonments, the Gestapo and all manner of dreadful doings.
   To badminton for an hour then to Lancing Choral practice.

March 17th Mr Chamberlain broadcasts speech from Birmingham — points out how he trusted Hitler when he said he had no more territorial demands to make in Europe and how he has gone back on his word. The whole European situation looks almost as black as it was last September. To Refugee Committee Meeting (Welfare Sub-Committee). Will have to consider more and more refugees now.

March 24th Rumania now gives in to Hitler over wheat and oil. Had a letter from Strasser — still so ardently 'Nazi', it's pathetic. Wants me to give him an *honest* account of the last day's doings in Europe! I must think it out!

March 28th Madrid surrenders to Franco after two and a half years. Mr and Mrs Balch to lunch and tea to meet the Laufers to give them more help for the USA.

March 31st Mr Chamberlain made important announcement to the Commons which was specially broadcast at four o'clock, committing us definitely to Poland. To Welfare Committee at six o'clock — work going well ahead and on to

Evening Standard, March 25th

MR. C. BURNS HIS UMBRELLAS
Mr. C. is, of course, following a firm policy of delaying specific commitments. In this way it is hoped to confuse Hitler so much that he won't know which country to pinch next.

LOW'S TOPICAL BUDGET

A bit mean I think.

Executive Committee at 8.15. Pathetically grateful letter from the Steinharts (old couple that Worthing adopted) read out.

April 1st Cambridge won the Boat Race by four lengths. Turned very warm and some good tennis in the afternoon. Took Dorothy Macpherson and the two Laufers to last Symphony Concert at Brighton with Myra Hess playing Beethoven's Pianoforte Concerto No 4 in G. All enjoyed it.

April 2nd In the afternoon took Helen and John and two Czech refugees, Frau Weingarten and Frau Lettna awfully nice young women, for a drive. Frau Lettna flew from Prague on Thursday with the twelve who were in much fear at the thought of being sent back and threatened to jump out if that happened. She expects her first child in two months time — she's twenty-five and a lawyer. Her husband is in danger in Prague, so is the other's husband. It's all dreadful. Hitler's speech yesterday is in somewhat milder tone referring to Friday's statement from Mr Chamberlain on our commitment to Poland. Hitler only recognises 'forceful' statements.

April 3rd Met Fraus Laufer, Lettna and Weingarten and Herr Weingarten has arrived most unexpectedly in England — great joy! He is a Jew and has suffered much. Frau Lettna has had a wretched domestic place for a month — a Dean's (Welsh) household and she has worked from 6 am to 10 pm. She looks ill but delighted with the news. Wrote to Josef Strasser to reassure him that English people 'do not send out waves of hatred to Germany'! I'm afraid they do to Hitler though — but I didn't tell him this — he'd never get the letter to begin with.

April 7th Good Friday. In the afternoon called for the Weingartens and Frau Lettna and took them to the bungalow that Miss Page is lending them for a month at Salvington. To tea here with the Laufers. A lot of talking and exchange of experiences (all grim). Herr Weingarten tells us that in Prague now anyone listening to English news on the wireless has twenty years' imprisonment and death if caught listening to Moscow. On an extra news bulletin at one o'clock heard that Italy has 'smashed and grabbed' Albania. Just like Hitler and his methods — what will result? The nine o'clock news reports fighting there.

April 9th The Laufers sailed for the USA — Mr Thornycroft took them down to Southampton, a very sad farewell he said it was. Poor things and they are some of the few 'lucky' ones out of millions.

April 11th International situation looks very bad. Everyone wonders if the war clouds can possibly be dispersed. I called on Mr Watts about getting refugees' shoes mended cheap — no luck — so called on humble Mr King and he will!

Build it NOW

Later on may be TOO LATE

NOW *your builder can erect this shelter speedily and cheaply*

LATER *both men and materials may be scarce*

NOW *it will serve you as a store, tool, bicycle or perambulator shed*

LATER *it will provide protection for you and yours against blast, splinters and falling debris*

NOW *is the time to act*

LATER *it may be impossible*

See your builder today! He will give you an estimate and you can then instruct him to commence work immediately.

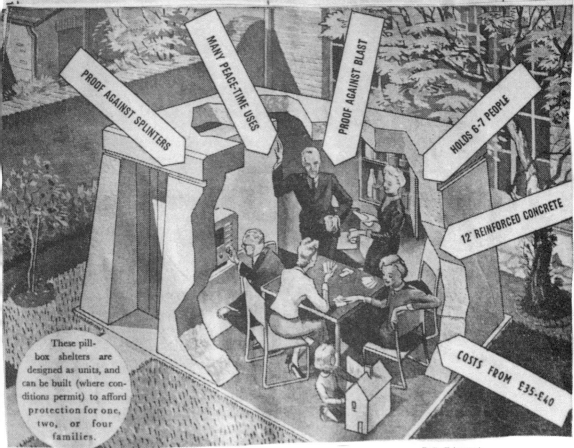

Daily Telegraph, March 29th

10

April 12th   Great interest in Mr Chamberlain's speech today — guarantees for Turkey, Greece and Rumania — but as Herr Weingarten says 'he guaranteed Czechoslovakia'. Kit writes to say all London very agitated about the prolonged crisis and should she go to the USA? Telephoned at 10 pm urging her to carry on.

April 14th   Refugee Welfare Committee at 5.45. A lot more work reported accomplished — had to leave early so missed hearing about the £500 and house.

April 15th   On wireless heard about President Roosevelt's message to the two dictators.

April 16th   Germany and Italy seem somewhat stunned by Roosevelt's proposal. There is a very bitter anti-British press campaign going on in the German press just now and now Roosevelt will be vilified too.
   Took kids and Mrs Porteous' grandchildren to a lovely primrose wood and picked hundreds. Heard that the Beermanns' permit has reached Vienna.

April 21st   Got a telegram announcing the time of our Beermanns' arrival here — six o'clock. They are even nicer than we had anticipated — Mr and Mrs Beermann, Henry and Lisl who is two years old.

April 22nd   Finished work at 12.15 and took the Beermanns to the Police Station to register. They really need not do so until they have been here three months. In the afternoon took Henry to the Free Library and got him fixed up in the Junior Department there! Then to the front and saw the boating and paddling pools. The Beermanns so impressed with English ways, for instance that we do not lock our front doors in the daytime — that our police are so friendly — that they are allowed free entry to cinemas, etc. For months fear has reigned in their hearts. Now — safety and self-confidence.

April 25th   Henry and I dashed round trying to track down a bicycle for him in the afternoon. The Beermanns got their cinema passes and we all went to see *The Citadel* in the evening. It's the first time they've been to a cinema for over a year. They enjoyed it all immensely — the film disappointing after the book.

April 26th   Mother, Mrs Beermann and I to the New Town Hall for important meeting at which Lord Winterton, Bishop of Chichester and a young German refugee pastor spoke. A good meeting but the appeal for money was poor. Conscription to be introduced into Great Britain.

£500 For Refugees

ON SUNDAY, the Rev. Rowland Smith, curate-in-charge of St Matthew's Church, made a pulpit appeal for funds for the Worthing Refugee Committee.

On Monday night, he found a cheque for £500 in his letter-box. It came from a Worthing woman who had given £50 for the committee at the end of last week.

Another woman has offered the committee an empty house.

April 27th Mrs Beermann, Elisabeth and I to St Matthew's to see the young Czech refugee couple married at 11.30. In the afternoon we went to the Thornycrofts (Henry cycled off) for the wedding breakfast! About thirty to forty refugees there and everything went off well.

Got back at 6.30 to find Henry still missing. Mrs Beermann and I motored to his lodging only to find an ambulance there — a broken leg — to Worthing Hospital and saw x-ray. He should be alright although it's a double fracture.

April 28th Managed to bring Henry home in a bath chair. Hitler made his two-and-a-quarter-hour speech in the Reichstag in answer to President Roosevelt's Peace Statement. He demands Germany's former colonies, denounces the Anglo-German Naval Treaty, makes demands on Poland. But on the whole the situation is no worse.

May 8th to May 17th Missed writing the diary because Mrs Lynes and I 'finished' the refugee house, 72 Canterbury Rd, and it took all my spare time. We got the stuff from all over Worthing and district and the finished product is really quite nice. Some people have been awfully generous, others have a very funny idea of refugees and quite a lot of stuff had to be burnt! The King and Queen have had a very adventurous time crossing the Atlantic in the *Empress of Australia*, the former German liner that belonged to the old Kaiser, as fog and ice and storms held them up for three days. They arrived late but amidst great welcome at Quebec on May 16th. Got a very good letter from Kit — she sailed from Montreal on May 11th — due here on the 19th.

May 19th Welfare Committee meeting but I had to meet the other four refugees for 72 Canterbury Rd. All seemed very nice and very pleased to be here. Two of them are brothers — formerly owners of a big dye factory in Czechoslovakia and the elder was a helper of refugees out there. They are Jewish.

May 23rd Mr Beermann had his first free haircut at Mr Chippings! Mrs B made him go as it was Mr Chippings' first free day offer and we felt someone should make use of it!

May 25th Nora Howden and I played second couple in tennis match against Bognor and won all three. Club won eight matches to one — good. Then to Refugee Committee Meeting 8.15 to 10.40!

May 26th Awoke to find Alice, the maid, telling me that our front step, path, wall and pavement outside had been written out in tar 'Jews get out', 'Britons before aliens'. Reported to police and Mrs Thornycroft who came early to help remove the marks with petrol and scrubbing. All off in half an hour. Very disgusting.

May 31st Had a lovely bathe in the morning — my first this season. In the evening the Beermanns, Mrs Wenban-Smith and we two to St Matthew's Hall to see concert in aid of the Refugee Fund. Quite good but a member of the audience took her *dog*. Most irritating.

King and Queen start back from Victoria (Canada) and half their journey done.

June 1st The refugees had their own social at the club room in the evening. Many there and all went off well. Mrs Beermann is quite overcome and overjoyed that everyone *laughs* again.

June 2nd The Littnas, Mrs Beermann and I to Bache's for supper and very interesting.

Terrible news of the sinking of a new British submarine and many feared trapped.

June 3rd Only four survivors of the submarine *Thetis* out of 101. A gloom is over *everyone* about it. If only 'civilisation' did not depend on such artificial devices.

Up to tennis in the afternoon, rather windy — home to tea. Later Mother and I took the Steinharts for a drive — everything was 'schöne'!

June 30th Everyone talking about Lord Halifax's speech last night. 'All Britain's might behind her pledges — unchallenge-able navy: air force to fear none.' It sounds like 1914 over again. Hitler is expected to snatch up Danzig — will this let loose the 'dogs of war'?

July 1st Busy all morning and arrived back to lunch to find Mother out with the Thornycrofts about the buying of my house! 37 Shakespeare Rd to be rented cheaply to the refugees — it will hold ten to twelve and is in good repair.

July 2nd In the afternoon went to Sydenham and discussed the Land Settlement Association's scheme there. Each family has a house — four acres of land, one greenhouse, one pigsty and one hennery. There are 159 families and all are unem-ployed miners from the North. It works well in the majority of cases but some of the wives are discontented and prefer a husband on the dole plus near neighbours, cinema, pub, fried-fish shop and Woolworths!

July 8th Called on Mr Moore, the bank manager, about my house and the finances. Having to borrow £200 from Mother and £200 from bank. My National Saving 500 units only came to £426!

Later to theatre to Shaw's *Doctor's Dilemma* with Mother, Ken, Mrs Beermann. Very good. The blackout started but neither heard nor saw anything of it!

July 10th Summer weather again. Very busy all day. Noticed the searchlights all round Worthing at midnight.

July 11th Dr Fleischmann very excited about his hoped for chicken farm at Castle Goring. He was telling me that his great friend Dr Otto Fleischner is now in Worthing as a guest of the Worthing Rotarians (he was and is now a Rotarian). He was in Dachau four months and nearly died as he was struck on the head — resulting in deafness — and made to stand with thousands of others in a shirt only, last December from 6 pm to 4 am. He got pneumonia.

Tennis for one hour at West Worthing.

July 14th Two Czech refugees moved into 37 Shakespeare Rd — they were married yesterday!

Dr Fleischmann was telling me why he was treated so badly last September — he was not a Nazi but a great social worker through the Oddfellows Society which was the chief charitable organisation in Czechoslovakia before Hitler's arrival there.

The news looks as bad as ever! Most depressing. The second leaflet on civil defence was delivered on the first post — about gas masks and blinds.

July 18th Mr Omega telephoned asking me if I could take four Spanish refugee children from Lancing to Newhaven to see seven of their compatriots off to Spain after nearly three years in England.

Tired and bewildered after the voyage, but clinging to her dearest possession. The publication of this picture brought in scores of offers of hospitality.

CANON CRITICISES ARCHBISHOPS

'TRIMMING TO THE WINDS'

Canon C. E. Raven, Master of Christ's College, Cambridge, at the Cromer Convention yesterday, said: "I would rather see Archbishops say frankly that Christianity is Utopian and cannot be seriously maintained as a practicable ethic than see them trimming their pulpits to the winds of political expediency and invoking Satan to cast out Satan.

"That is what they have been doing in the past 12 months," he declared.

All the bishops had denounced the Totalitarian State as Cæsar worship and blasphemy, "yet to-day, when our own nation is being mobilised on a Totalitarian basis for a war as an instrument of national policy, we see our fathers-in-God falling in obediently behind the recruiting officers and repeating without a blush the slogans and militarisms of 1914."

Daily Telegraph, June 27th

14

July 20th Mother and I to see *The Four Feathers* at the Odeon but so bloodthirsty and warry we came out (after Mother had had her nap!). 37 Shakespeare Rd looking quite decent now. Mrs Lynes and I had final talk on the furnishing of it. She does wish Mr Rowland Smith, the curate-in-charge at St Matthew's, was not a pacifist — I mentioned that he'd been through the last war, nearly got killed in it, and came out believing it could not be Christian to kill one's fellow men. She seemed rather surprised.

July 23rd Very busy all day and at six o'clock called for Hofer, Littna and Bache to go to the Dolmetsch Musical Festival at Haslemere. The whole affair very enjoyable specially the political conversations in the car coming back. H and L both communists! Of the right type. Back at 12.20.

July 26th How many things both international and personal will be related in this diary in the months to come? On which date shall I note down the departure of the Beermanns? For over three months they've lived with us and become part of our life and a very nice part too. Then there's Danzig — how will that knotty problem be solved?

August 10th Terribly wet all day — this is the wettest summer for years. To Refugee Committee meeting in evening and Mrs Lynes tried to get her 'reduced money payment' for refugees through, but with no luck! Rather a heated debate as Mrs Lynes feels so strongly that the refugees are living like fighting cocks and their total income is 15/– a week! The second blackout night.

August 11th Danzig events look ugly — Herr Forster has been to see Hitler and made violent anti-British and anti-French speeches to the Danzigians on his return.

August 13th Mother, Mr Beermann and I set off at two o'clock for Hayling — a lovely warm day. Mrs Beermann, Henry and Lisl all very brown and happy. Had a lovely tea outside the hut; at 6.15 set off for home again. For once the car behaved itself — it's had three punctures, one broken clutch and two broken springs in eight days! Met Mrs Lynes at 37 Shakespeare Rd and she's still *very* determined to reduce the refugees' allowance — very queer attitude.

August 14th At last the heat wave! Took lunch on the beach at Wenban-Smith's hut — about a dozen of us there. Up to tennis in the evening and had some good sets.
   The trouble in Danzig grows rather than abates but in the sunshine our anxiety is lessened.

August 15th Lunch and tea on beach with Ken and Co. — hot and lovely. Organised a tennis tournament (impromptu) and it went very well — about twenty-four up.

The IRA busy again — this time bombs have been found in seaside hotels.

August 20th In Italy there seems to be a 'no war' feeling and to quote the *Sunday Times* Rome Correspondent: 'There is no question here of the *solidarity* of the Rome–Berlin Axis on the Danzig question. . . . There are no unusual military activities, and the pursuit of peaceful activity is so manifold that apparently there is no time for the ordinary ARP.'

A glorious day. At 3.30 to Christ Church, to become a god-mother to Eva Joanna Littna.

August 22nd Crisis again. Amazing news of a Berlin–Moscow pact — sworn enemies but uniting in a non-aggression pact. 'World shocked' say the placards.

August 24th News blacker and blacker — Parliament re-called and Chamberlain made a momentous statement: the guarantee to Poland holds good. In this way the situation differs from that of last September over Czechoslovakia. Lord Halifax broadcast at 9.30 and Mrs Beermann remarked how very differently our men broadcast from the Germans.

August 25th News very bad but we are hopeful in this household that war will not come. Mother hasn't got any extra food in, any black stuff for blackouts or even a gas mask!

August 26th Our ambassador in Berlin flew to London and back to Berlin — our Cabinet met at six o'clock — great efforts being made to preserve peace, by the Pope, the Scandin-avian countries, President Roosevelt and King of the Belgians all doing what they can. We still feel all will be well. Hitler must feel on the horns of a dilemma specially as Japan's protested violently against the Russo–German pact and Italy does not look favourably on it either.

LONDON 'BUS of the Green Line service being converted into an ambulance at the Chiswick works of the L.P.T.B. during a mock gas attack. Some hundreds of such vehicles are being modified so that, in an emergency, they could rapidly be converted into ambulances.

August 27th Lovely day — Mother, Kit and I to Holy Communion at eight o'clock and then to St Matthew's Church for eleven o'clock service and then to the station to fetch Mr Ritter. He's had a more than adventurous six months in Switzerland and a terrible time getting to England — trains so full. Luckily he was allowed to land (he's an Aryan). We telegraphed to Mrs Beermann's sister (to whom he's engaged) in Australia — 5/10d for it. Had tea in the garden. We three to East Preston church for Evensong — we feel a great urge to go to a church where we know the parson is definitely against war in any form. After supper had a lovely moonlight bathe. News is as bad as ever — the Cabinet met this evening and our ambassador flies back to report to Hitler. What will the next three days bring forth? Mother still feels very strongly that it will be peace.

August 28th News worse and worse but the people feel everywhere that war will *not* come. The Mediterranean is closed to British shipping — Parliament to be recalled tomorrow, all merchant and fishing boats under government orders and so on.

August 29th Still lovely weather, bathed at 1 pm and 10 pm!
Many notes passing between British Cabinet and Hitler — we really feel war will be averted although preparations are still going on.
Worthing museum had a large van outside — presumably removing the treasures! Sugar is *very* scarce and people are making their houses light proof.

August 31st News as bad as ever — everyone very depressed and nowhere the feeling of hate towards the Germans but only hate of war.

September 1st Wireless news at one o'clock told us that the London school children would be evacuated tomorrow. Worthing is to expect 13,000 and we two! Terrible, as it makes war seem nearer. Surely it *can't* happen. It's dreadful to think that the 'victors' will be those who use most effectively the most diabolic instruments of death as quickly as possible.
The papers are very depressing — all the pictures are of soldiers, sandbags, ARP, city girls evacuating from their offices, guns, aeroplanes and so on. Mrs Jeffrey's neighbour has a £400 dug-out, bomb-proof (?) shelter erected in his garden disguised as a rockery but with two doors and two chimneys visible.

September 3rd I listened in the evening to the King's broadcast in company with Mr and Mrs Beermann, Mr Krausz and Mr Ritter (all Austrians and Germans who would have been our 'enemies' had they not escaped from the Nazis).

GREAT BRITAIN AT WAR

DESPATCHES
FROM THE
HOME
FRONT
1939

17

September 6th The first week of the war — it has been impossible to write daily for the last week as life has suddenly become very difficult under wartime conditions. Very few people felt this terrible blow would fall and right up to Sunday morning (September 3rd) there was a glimmer of hope. On Friday the Germans 'crossed the frontiers to resist the Poles' and the newspapers immediately declared 'war begins'. Everyone's spirits sank but rose again when Mr Chamberlain gave Hitler one more chance in a message sent on Saturday with a time limit up at eleven o'clock on Sunday morning. In the meantime the 'blackouts' have started, no one must show a glimmer of light anywhere. Cars have the merest glimmer left and have to be painted white in front, rear and on running boards — the roads have a white centre line and the kerbs whitened. Some food especially sugar is very scarce. Worthing, being a safe zone, has had over 10,000 evacuees from London billeted on the inhabitants. On Saturday afternoon Schofield and I helped billet some Bermondsey blind people. We both felt how terrible it was that so much money, time and trouble is taken to help these poor, old, ill, blind people while we send healthy, young, virile people to be killed. They were a really pathetic lot of people — mostly old (I took several over eighty),

*Daily Telegraph,
September 4th*

DAILY TELEGRAPH AND MORNING POST, MONDAY, Sept. 4

THE KING'S BROADCAST TO THE BRITISH EMPIRE

18

all dirty and several ill. Ken's been billeting school children and found it a strenuous job. I took Ken and family to a farm for a week's holiday on September 6th — the day the Beermanns should have had their USA visa granted them! What hard luck, after five months waiting here. But after the sinking of the *Athenia* on September 4th we feel relieved to think they are not going and besides they're so ripping we're glad to have them with us. We've had two air-raid warnings already — one on Sunday morning at about 11.35 (20 minutes after the declaration of war) and one at 8.15 this morning. I must try to write this daily now but so far I've not blacked out my bedroom — blow! That's where I do my reading and writing.

September 10th Exactly one week of the war between Germany and Britain and France and nine days between Germany and Poland. During these last four days we have all been cheered up by the five flights the RAF have taken over Germany dropping leaflets to the German people.

September 18th At last my bedroom is 'blacked out' and I can write my diary in bed! This last week has been sad as the papers prepared us gradually for Poland's collapse. The blow fell on Sunday when we heard on the wireless at 10.30 that Russia had marched into Poland. Poland is now being crushed by two great states and one can only hope that the two bullies will squabble among themselves. Actually Warsaw has not yet fallen but the cabinet has fled to Rumania. Our refugees were depressed about it but they were cheered up on Saturday morning when Mr Ritter heard a most interesting broadcast from a German woman belonging to a secret anti-Nazi society, urging women to prevent more bloodshed. She hopes to broadcast next Saturday. The end of the speech was jammed. On Sunday the Beermanns and I blackberried in the morning as Mother managed to get some preserving sugar. I took Mother and the Piltzers, a Czech refugee couple, for tea on the Devil's Dyke — they being 'friendly aliens' can go outside the five-mile limit from Worthing — not so the Beermanns who are 'enemy aliens'! They may leave only with police permission.

September 19th In evening Mother, Mrs Beermann, Lisl and I motored over to Lancing to see Mr Webb about the Lancing Choral Society — can it carry on amid 'blackouts', air raid warnings and so on? We hope so. Later had some folks in and played cards. News is bad — Poland is completely broken and our only hope is that Russia and Germany will quarrel over the spoils. Thousands of Polish refugees are pouring over the borders of neighbouring countries — now we can better imagine their plight — penniless, foodless, hopeless — and Hitler triumphant. The agony of modern warfare. Today Hitler has made a triumphant entry into Danzig and a boastful speech.

London Charivari,
September 13th

September 21st The Czechs in revolt — an organised rising took place yesterday and terrible suffering on both sides has resulted. Let's hope it will help to speed up the end.

September 23rd Mother slipped and fell (thanks to old Hitler and the blackout) and broke her collar bone. Petrol rationing really in this week and I've not had my extra ration allowance yet.

September 25th Received my extra grant of nine gallons per month of petrol.

September 26th Mother's arm seems much less painful. She had a lot of visitors (sixteen to tea!) plus flowers and sweets and Uncle Bert came for picquet in the evening while I and four 'enemy aliens'! walked to Bache's and spent the evening there. Lovely moon so no difficulty about getting there.
  The war budget! 2/– increase on income tax.

September 28th A glorious autumn morning when 'every prospect pleases and only man is vile' to quote the old hymn. Everyone is talking about the income tax but is taking it very calmly, 7/6d in the pound! Today Mr Ritter had his first job and earned 1/2d an hour by mowing Uncle Bert's lawn. Now all three have jobs — Mr Beermann cleans Dr Gusterson's car twice a week and Mrs Beermann 'chars' Bache's flat twice a week too! All thoroughly enjoy their work. I had my hair re-permed as it was so bad. Warsaw falls or 'dropped' as Fritz Krausz reported it! Terrible ordeal of the inhabitants. England to support the Save the Children Fund next Sunday at all churches. The *Daily Telegraph* reported that the pilot of one of our 'leaflet' planes reported back at headquarters two hours before he was due. His astonished CO asked for an explanation. 'Well, Sir,' the young officer replied, 'I flew over enemy territory as instructed and tipped out the parcels over the side.' 'Do you mean you threw them out still wrapped up in bundles?' said the CO in an anxious voice. 'Yes, Sir.' 'Good God, man, you might have killed somebody!' Then there was the pilot who turned up two hours *too late*. Explanation this time was that he'd been as quick as possible, pushing them under people's doors.

September 29th I called at the Police Office (now occupying the Art School) to retrieve Mr Ritter's camera. I'm 'buying' it so that it's back near him and ready to go to Australia. All the refugees are immensely struck with the good manners and humour of our police force and I don't wonder.

20

October 1st   England observes Day of National Prayer for Peace. To St Paul's and so crowded had to go to the gallery. Bought my first 'pool' petrol five gallons. Listened to Winston Churchill in evening on wireless — a typical product of the last war.

October 4th   Rained at last — the ground is very hard and dry. Many people are hoping to plant cabbages etc but so far the ground's been too hard. Had a tennis club committee meeting and heard that one of our members, 'Dutch' Linfield, the tomato grower, had been called up. No fresh news out yet. Once again we are all waiting for 'something'.

Picture Post

A Picture We All Remember—Wasn't It 25 Years Ago?
This is the nearest thing to a picture of British troops in action. You may see them entraining at station—but that is as far as it was permissible to follow.

If only we could beat Hitler without beating up his people.

October 5th   This war is certainly very different from the last one — the main differences being: (1) So far *no* hatred of the 'enemy'. (2) But much hatred for the Nazi leaders. (3) No knowledge of what's doing with our troops on the Western Front and now it's over *five* weeks since war started. (4) Series of leaflet air raids over Germany telling the people there a few facts — things they've forgotten ever existed. (5) No placards begging men to join up 'for King and Country'. (6) No talk of 'a war to end war'.

October 7th   Beermanns heard that after all they are to report at the USA consulate on the 18th. Great excitement. They will be off in November probably. A glorious morning and I set off with two Beermanns for the Tribunal for 'Enemy Aliens' set up in Chichester. It was a very pleasant interview for them and we were free by 11.15. Looked over the Cathedral — it was as lovely as ever but all the ancient tombs had been completely sand bagged.

Hitler's speech was much as expected — but he gives fourteen days in which to consider our reply. In the meantime nothing much is happening on the west front. Can it be peace?

October 13th   This is almost as if war has been declared for the second time. According to Berlin, Mr Chamberlain has insulted Hitler who says 'now that Britain so obviously wishes to wage war she shall feel the power of Germany's air, naval and military strength'. It's all so hateful as no doubt Hitler can justify (and does) his position as absolutely as Mr Chamberlain can justify his. Today Mr Ritter (von Rittersheim) appeared before the Tribunal and we are all very anxious about the result. His is a complicated case as he was counted an Aryan as his Polish Jewish grandmother's papers were lost at the time when everyone had to prove his purity! He's been an officer in the Austrian army and even held a state position. He also got out of Germany plus money! All he desires is to get to Australia and to marry Annie there! Will he be counted a 'friendly alien' and allowed to travel to Australia? Mother sponsored him and put his case very forcibly. Mrs Beermann also helped as his future Jewish sister-in-law.

October 14th   Mother and I set forth for our belated 'summer' holiday! By dint of cycling for my work I've saved some petrol for the trip up to Aunt Anne's at Cheltenham. I get only fourteen gallons a month.

October 15th   Rained all day! In the *Sunday Graphic* is a photo of B. Nichols' brother who is one of the saved men from the *Royal Oak*. Mrs Holland's son is also saved I see — but out of 1,200 men only 400 saved. Went to church at eleven o'clock and stayed in the rest of the day. Knitted and read and lazed — lovely!

October 16th   A lovely day. Shopped and coffee'd in the morning. Cheltenham very full of 'vacks' and the shops full of all the usual ARP goods. One gets sick of looking at black stuff, gas mask cases, identity card cases, buckets and shovels (for removing incendiary bombs), low powered bulbs, black shades, etc. The buses' windows are all blued over and give one a sick feeling whilst travelling. Heard at four o'clock the wireless message that German bombers had attacked the Firth of Forth but missed the Forth bridge. Four German planes were brought down. The *first* air-raid on Britain.

October 17th Several new aircraft factories are being built between here and Gloucester — hateful.

October 20th In the afternoon to the pictures where we saw *Knight Without Armour*, about the 1917 Russian Revolution and *The Return of the Scarlet Pimpernel* (French Revolution!). Mother slept most of the time! Turkey signs the Anglo-Turkish Treaty to our delight and Hitler's dismay. Still no battle on the Western front but another attempted air-raid on Scotland.

October 23rd Everyone is feeling elated because it looks as if old Hitler really is cracking up after all! He's dismissed two important generals (who must have dared to disagree with him) and Stalin has not acquiesced to Hitler's demand for 2,000 aeroplanes! Hitler now says the Russian–German pact was only a temporary one! Another glimpse of the obvious.

October 24th On the five o'clock post came a most important letter for Mr Ritter from the Government of Australia about his entry into Australia. They say they will have him but our side won't grant him his exit permit.

October 26th Mr Beermann up to town to get their exit permits! Turned very cold. Mother shopped in the afternoon and found difficulty procuring butter — none at Sainsburys, ½ lb at the Maypole but as much as she liked at the International! Dog meat is very scarce and sugar is erratic.

October 27th Lost my supplementary petrol ration vouchers! Blow. Hitler again! Got late for my first patient but found them later. Frightfully cold with bitter north-east wind. Mr Beermann has lumbago so we kept him here with a hot-water bottle (unknown in Austria owing to central heating) and grog (lemon, sugar, brandy and two aspirins). Welfare Committee at five o'clock and discussed the refugees' sale on November 13.

October 28th Still vilely cold, so no tennis. Shopped in afternoon. Couldn't help noticing the change in the shops — in Woolworths there are many things missing, eg notepaper and already toys and other articles are becoming war-influenced — dolls in Red Cross uniform for example. Butter could only be bought in ½ lbs today and meat, although plentiful, was limited to certain joints and it's goodbye to our tomorrow's pork!

October 29th Vicar preached a sermon on war as 'a judicial act of God'. It was a terrible shock to hear such things from a Christian pulpit.
    The town is full of evacuated children and their parents down from London.

October 30th Saw Mr Moore at the bank to tell him that I must overdraw again! I'd just paid off my overdraft on the refugee house when Mother ran out of money and so I've paid her back £50 of her £200 from my new overdraft! And there's the wretched new income tax waiting (£19) and the rates on 37 Shakespeare Rd (£14)!

October 31st The world waits to hear what Russia's Foreign Minister will say today — will Russia join Germany in a military alliance? The British Government has published a White Paper on German Concentration Camps — perfectly *horrible*. Is it a good thing to do at this time? After all we know the majority of Germans must hate the camps as we do. We must not work up hatred against the German people.

OLD BILL reappears in a poster designed to warn troops on leave against being too talkative.

November 2nd Nearly got summonsed for not blacking out my room but got let off with a 'caution'!

November 3rd The Beermanns had another nasty surprise this morning — their boat, the *Statendam*, does not sail till December 2nd and they'd expected about November 12th. If Holland is not involved in the war they really will get off on that date. Will this happen we are all wondering?

November 7th There is good news of a meeting between Queen Wilhelmina of Holland and King Leopold of the Belgians who jointly propose another peace effort. Mr Ritter had good news too — he had a letter from the Refugee Committee which is optimistic of his leaving for Australia this year.

November 8th Susan Fleischmann came at lunch time telling us her father had been taken ill and was in Worthing Hospital. He is pretty bad I'm afraid. There has been an attempt on the life of Hitler at Munich — a bomb exploded twenty-seven minutes after he'd left. Several people were killed. Is this the beginning of the end? His speech was as dreadful as ever.

24

Dr Fleischmann and family.

A WELL-PROTECTED fire-and-ambulance alarm at Ilford.

November 10th Everyone is talking about the attempt on Hitler's life. It seems only party men were at the hall and a most careful watch had been kept. Can it be that in the party itself there are dissidents? Poor Holland fears invasion and tonight's wireless gave details of the flooding of big areas with evacuation of the inhabitants. How terrible.

November 12th Dr Fleischmann died this afternoon at 3.30. Mrs Fleischmann, Susan and Martin came here to stay for a day or two.

November 16th Worthing feels little effects of the war so far. Feeling grows that it's all going to collapse before Christmas!

November 18th I shopped in the evening and found it very difficult especially at Woolworth's where I was having difficulty in getting past, as I thought, an *incoming* body only to discover it was myself in the glass reflection! 'Summer' time ends this evening six weeks overdue because of the war. German mine laying has begun in great earnest. They are magnetic and can be laid by aeroplane as well as by ships. The Dutch liner *Simon Bolivar* was the first big victim.

November 19th Beermanns sailing 'on or about' November 25th! We had a Christmas dinner, at least a Christmas pudding with a sixpenny piece in it and holly, so that the Beermanns should know what it's like.

November 20th Terrible Nazi mine sinking exploits going on — seven ships in the last two days — one is a Dutch liner, sunk in the North Sea and the 200-odd survivors were landed here in England. The Beermanns getting rather anxious.

November 23rd The Beermanns have found out they can leave at 6.33 on Saturday morning for Southampton. At six o'clock though there was a report that *all* Dutch shipping is cancelled. The nine o'clock evening news didn't mention the Dutch hitch. Maybe all's well. There are lots of neutral ships being sunk as the Nazis are laying tremendous numbers of mines.

November 25th Awoke and up at 5 am. All five slept here (Beermann family and Helle) and they started by the 6.30 am train for Southampton.

November 26th Kept wondering how the Beermanns were faring. A terrible day here — very stormy.

November 27th Had a letter from Mrs Beermann saying they'd spent all Saturday on the tender and then were ordered to disembark and stay the night in a hotel! This also happened on Sunday but I telephoned at 7 pm and the hotel porter reported that they'd sailed today. At 9 pm Mrs Fleischmann telephoned to say the news said the *Statendam* had been sunk! But it turned out to be another vessel with similar name. Mother had a big fright.

November 30th   The midday posters bore the news 'Russia invades and bombs Finland'. One more little country is succumbing to the big bully.

December 1st   Finland's Cabinet has resigned but the Russians are making sure they are going to get their own way and continue to bomb and machine gun the towns and cities. *Hateful.*

December 4th   Refugee Committee in evening — the work increases rather than decreases as since evacuation started there are over 1,000 aliens in West Sussex and Worthing is the only place with a committee — there are about 500 in Worthing — over 200 have registered at our office.

December 5th   Poor old Ritter heard from Australia House that no enemy aliens are allowed in Australia between the age of eighteen and forty-five. He is forty-three next month. He's seen the local Roman Catholics to see if they can help him as his money is running out. At five o'clock went to the Tivoli to see a Fred Astaire and Ginger Rogers picture. Really quite good — but the 'News' and 'March of Time' were too warlike and terrifying.

December 6th   Had a telegram from the USA so the Beermanns have had a safe voyage after all.

No Passion Play

The famous Oberammergau Passion Play will not be produced next year. Many of the actors are in the Siegfried Line, and the player who was to have taken the rôle of Christ is now an air-raid warden.

Daily Telegraph,
December 9th

December 11th   Called in at Refugee Office to say goodbye to the Weiss' who have been residents there and sort of caretakers. Found Mrs Weiss ill probably due to nerves and an awful upset about their emigration to the USA. So many are anxious to get off because of the mines and the sinkings and can't exchange their places.

December 13th   Had our third carol practice, about twenty-four here! It ought to go well we think. I phoned the police to see if there's any special restrictions this year — we'd heard there were but all's well. I wrote about eight letters to go abroad — they'll all be late for Christmas I'm afraid as the airmail rate's gone up so terrifically I can't send them by air. It's 1/3d to Janet in Australia.

December 15th A great naval battle has been fought in South American waters — a German raider has been chased into the neutral port of Monte Video, probably the *Graf Spee*.

December 16th Mother and I shopped vigorously all the afternoon in shops frightfully crowded owing to evacuees as well as the usual Christmas shoppers. Up to tennis club to see the Christmas Draw take place. Great excitement all over the world about the presence of the *Graf Spee* in Monte Video harbour. She has seventy-six hours allotted to her — will she scuttle or make a dash for it, or be interned?

December 17th At twelve o'clock switched on to hear news of the *Graf Spee* as the time limit expired at 11.30. Heard that she had scuttled. She was a very proud possession of Germany — her newest and best 10,000 ton pocket battleship costing nearly four-million pounds. Now a mass of twisted iron on the shallow sea bed near the Monte Video harbour.

December 19th Mr Ritter now officially a 'friendly alien', but still unable to proceed to Australia. Great interest still in the scuttling of the *Graf Spee*. Can it be a turning point in the war? It appears Hitler ordered the scuttling in a fury and the captain and men were furious. All are now interned in Argentina.

December 20th News reports the suicide of the Captain of the *Graf Spee*. Surely a very significant fact? And pathetic.

December 22nd Very 'seasonable' weather! I called round on the three refugee hostels and delivered a cake each, made by Mother. All very pleased. 37 Shakespeare Rd (my house!) is very cold. They can none of them get used to the cold bedrooms and lack of feather beds, poor things. The Finns are still keeping the Russians at bay in a wonderful manner. The cold is intense up there.

December 25th The usual excitement with the presents! Mr Ritter came and spent the day with us. Mother gave him a present in the shape of an invitation to spend a month here in January. The boys had long rides on Billy, the pony, in the morning after church and in the afternoon we walked the front and fed the seagulls. Played rummy in the evening.

December 30th Still very cold and in the afternoon seven of us to Patching Pond and skated — beautiful. Mr Ritter came to live a month with us. Letter from the Beermanns —

they are finding it *very* hard in the USA. I paid up my income tax. This was inside the demand note.

> "I well understand how heavy, under these "proposals, will be the weight of the "Income Tax and Sur-tax which will fall "due to be paid next January. Yet it is of "vital importance that the proceeds of the "tax should reach the Exchequer as soon "as possible after that date. I am "confident that we can rely on the great "army of taxpayers to carry us to success "in this part of the field just as we rely "confidently on the Armed Forces of the "Crown in the grimmer struggle which "they have to face."
>
> *The Chancellor of the Exchequer (Sir John Simon) in the House of Commons, 27th September, 1939*

December 31st The last day of this wicked old year! Mr Cook's prophecy that I reported on January 1st has come true. A lovely day — cold but not cold enough to skate. Mr Ritter and I to St Matthew's at 11.30 for Watch Night Service and then on to wish Canterbury Rd house a Happy New Year. The Archbishop of Canterbury broadcast on 'our righteous cause' — *awful*. War is never righteous. May 1940 see a quick and good end to this awful catastrophe.

Daily Telegraph, December 11th

January 1st Can 1940 bring us the blessing of a just European Peace? The year starts with Finland battling against Russia in a most extraordinary manner. After a whole month the Russians have scarcely gained anything except the disgust of the world. Turkey is stricken with an earthquake of great magnitude — floods, hungry wolves and so on.

January 2nd At five o'clock met Mother and Mr Ritter at the Odeon — had tea and then saw the film *Where's That Fire?* with Will Hay.

January 8th The 'marg and marm' breakfast of the last war now begins again!

January 11th More air-raids near Britain and Mr Chamberlain gave a warning of 'possible terrible times ahead'. But I saw in yesterday's *Worthing Gazette* that the Bishop of Chichester feels that there is a possibility of peace talks taking place before the terrible things happen. In the meantime we await in rather sheep-like fashion.

January 13th To Brighton in the afternoon to the Symphony concert, but owing to the war Orloff — the soloist — was not able to reach England in time. I suppose he's in the USA. Got into the car — the four of us — and blow me if the one headlight allowed would not light up! *Impossible* to drive in the dark with only the side lights so had to get it repaired.

January 17th Still *very* cold so took Mr Ritter and two others to Patching pond for skating. Mother heard that her money which used to bring in 5% then 3½% is now 2%! Everyone is grumbling about their drop in income and no wonder and for what? Other direct effects of war are the rationing of food and petrol, increase of the cost of living (it's gone up 12½% at least), unemployment among certain trades, especially among building and flower growing concerns in Worthing. Then we hear of Russians dying of cold by the hundreds, sailors being mined and torpedoed, airmen suffering big casualties, and —

the end? Many people are yearning for a just and lasting peace and are endeavouring to keep bitterness out of their minds at all cost.

January 21st   Colder than ever! Awful! The Framptons and I over to skate at Patching and then they helped us with our frozen pipes — no water upstairs at all!

January 22nd   Tomsetts the Plumbers sent a man early to see to our frozen pipes and all's well again. The intense cold in Europe may perhaps alter the course of the war — in Germany they depend very much on potatoes — these are easily spoilt by frost and we hear they are transporting them in warmed third-class railway trucks! Mrs Thornycroft is in Spain, having helped take another 100 Spanish refugee children back.

January 25th   The Archbishop of York's address, reported in *The Listener*, will be interesting later on. I'm afraid *State* comes first in many so-called 'Christian' clergymen's minds. He concluded by saying: 'One word more. I have spoken of a subtle change in our mood in the first months of the war, and of the special need of steadfastness of purpose. More ever than other wars, this war is a spiritual conflict. We shall best maintain our steadfastness and strengthen our determination to secure a truly just and not a vindictive peace if we can root our purpose ever more firmly in the righteous and loving God. We have no right to be engaged in war at all except so far as we believe that to be His will for us at this time.' How *awful*. How can any war be a 'spiritual conflict' or 'His will'. It's man's *ignorance* and *folly*.

January 26th   The bacon ration is to be doubled! Still no maid but I quite enjoy doing the early tea and breakfast. Had a continental one this morning — coffee, hot rolls and an omelette!

January 28th   Mr Ritter and I walked (or skidded) to Canterbury Rd Refugee Hostel. They dressed us up with old socks to come home with! Very slippery.

January 29th   Frightful weather again! Got chains fixed on my car and anti-freeze mixture in the radiator. Left car at Station Garage because my new bumper has come. The man told me that I was liable to a fine of £100 or three months in prison if I drove in the blackout without a whitened bumper and sides of running boards! Worst January for over fifty years!

Reminds me of the last war when we kept the top of the milk and whisked it up into the stuff we called butter mush!

30

February 1st To the Luncheon Committee meeting. We decided to see how much money we had in hand and send a big proportion to the minesweepers. Mrs Godden, the antique shop owner, says the two pleasure steamers, which used to call at Worthing, are now minesweeping.

February 2nd Took Mr Ritter up to Mrs Wenban-Smith's for his month there.

February 3rd Poor old Ritter had a telegram from Australia 'permit refused', and poor Annie (his fiancée).

February 6th The Weiss family have left Worthing at last. They are very sad at their departure for the USA to no friends, no money, no work. I said good-bye to them on Worthing Station and they looked so pathetic. Hitler, you brute!

February 7th The Finns are still resisting enormous Russian attacks in a wonderful way. Great excitement in Worthing today — a mine was seen being washed up at high tide. Police guarded it until seamen came and removed it. On the east coast a pier was partially destroyed by a mine exploding under it.

February 9th Mr Ritter had a very helpful letter from Miss Laura Livingstone, sister-in-law of the Bishop of Chichester, on the Refugee Committee; she holds out hope of Australia allowing him to enter after all. Mother made our allowance of marmalade today — she had to apply for the extra sugar — 6 lb I believe.

February 10th Heard that Lord Tweedsmuir (John Buchan), Governor General of Canada, is dangerously ill with concussion following a faint.
   The Finns still resisting terrific Russian onslaughts. Great shortage of firewood and firelighters in the town so Mother has ordered a gas poker to be fitted in the drawing room!

February 12th Lord Tweedsmuir died after third operation to try and save his life.

February 13th Mother seventy-two today! She had lots of flowers and letters. Finns still resisting Russians. Mother's Working Party are all working hard for the Finns — in *white* wool because of the weather conditions.

February 18th Up to the Downs — it snowed and we got a bit wet but the Downs looked lovely. Great excitement over the *Altmark*, the Nazi prison ship that had 303 British merchant seamen from ships sunk by the *Graf Spee*. The ship was cornered in a Norwegian fiord by the frigate *Cossack*.

Germany *furious*, Norway outraged and Britain triumphant!!

February 21st The first really spring-like day and two crocuses are almost out. Mother went to Miss Putt's whist drive in aid of knitting wool for soldiers. She and I went to St Matthew's 7.30 Lenten Mid-Week Service. 'Lord Haw Haw' broadcasts in a very Oxford voice from Germany every evening 'News in English' or rather 'Propaganda in English'! He is reputed to be Captain Stuart Baillie who was imprisoned in the Tower some years ago for espionage.

February 24th To a party in Gifford House in the evening — a success, we think. To think that these 1914–18 men have been disabled — some so badly they *never* go out — for over twenty years and now the world is busy doing the same again.

February 25th Lord Phillimore was quoted in the *Sunday Times*: 'I am optimistic about the war. I don't think that any nation really believes that peace can be achieved only by first killing five-million men. The best thing in the world today is the instinctive revulsion against mass slaughter.' One feels this revulsion growing among the people and it must be happening in Germany too surely? I believe war will eventually kill itself.

*Worthing Herald,
February 10th*

February 26th Mr Ritter went over to Littlehampton to see if it is suitable for a photographer's shop and he came back rather bucked with an empty shop in the Arcade there.

March 1st Finland still holding firm. Major Roosevelt, cousin to the US President, is taking over the 3,000 British recruits there.

March 4th To Worthing Youth Council evening — an organisation to co-operate all movements connected with youth.
    The sinking, preceded by bombings and machine gunning of fishing trawlers goes on apace by Nazi planes. There are thousands of Army Service Corps soldiers here with their hideous camouflaged lorries parked along the front — over 200 of them!

March 6th In the evening I went to a gardening lecture held to stimulate interest in 'digging for victory'! It was very good.

March 8th Up to London for weekend. Met Kit and she and I to see *The Corn is Green* with Sybil Thorndyke and Emlyn Williams acting in it — excellent. London in the blackout is much worse than Worthing and Kit forgot her torch! London seems remarkably full and it was difficult to realise a war was on except for the balloon barrage and presence of soldiers and the blackout. People appear fairly cheerful and confident though there is no great enthusiasm.

March 9th Kit took me to see some of her Kentish Town flats. The caretaker is worried that in the blackout each night hooligan boys come round breaking windows and stealing bricks being used for air-raid shelter construction. Tea in the Viennese café at Lyons Corner House, Piccadilly and then strolled up Regent and Oxford Streets. There are a few empty shops but on the whole they look much the same as before the war. Newspaper placards report a Finnish–Russian peace plan. Can it be possible? Also that Ribbentrop is rushing off to Rome to meet Mussolini and the Pope.

March 10th We walked through Hyde Park and Kensington Gardens. The orators *very* amusing. Hyde Park is also an anti-aircraft gun centre and ARP shelter centre — horrid. But the grown-ups still sail their boats on the Round Pond!

March 12th Mr Ritter and I to the Odeon but was called out to be interviewed by a Special Constable, Mr Lovesy, about the car! I'd committed two offences! *One*, I'd parked on the wrong side in the black out and *two* I shouldn't have parked at all at that particular spot!

March 13th The 'peace' inflicted by Russia is accepted by Finland. Everyone astounded at such a sudden ending. Everyone seems depressed by it and the ignorant blame Norway and

Sweden and then us for not being able to prevent it. Mr Ritter moved to 13 North St — the YMCA are letting the Refugee Committee use it.

March 15th   Dr Keele asked if I'd go up to Findon and photograph a baby saved from death from pneumonia by a rigged up oxygen tent ingeniously fixed up by the village nurse.

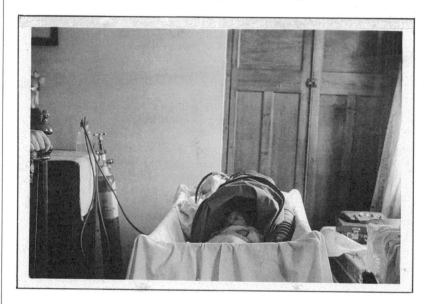

March 17th   We listened in to a seven o'clock service to the Forces and in the middle of a prayer someone in the congregation caused a disturbance by shouting out 'Pray for peace!' very loudly. Quite terrifying.

In the news heard that fourteen German planes had raided Scapa Flow and killed and injured some civilians in cottages near and also of the meeting of Hitler and Mussolini tomorrow.

March 20th   A very big RAF raid over Heligoland is reported — the biggest raid of the war so far. A reprisal for the German raid on Scapa Flow. Tons of bombs dropped and ammunition works were seen in flames.

March 22nd   Good Friday. Motor cars out in their thousands as there was a special Easter arrangement of petrol rationing.

March 26th   Butter ration doubled! Mr Ritter and I to Plaza to see *Mr Smith Goes To Washington*. Very good.

March 28th   Miss Goldsmith (the head of physiotherapy at Brighton Hospital who retired to Worthing) and I to Hove for lecture on the effect of gas on the lungs in wartime. A good lecture and demonstration but a horrid subject.

34

March 30th Dorothy and I over to Brighton to the last Dome Symphony Concert. Herbert Menges, the conductor, made a speech in the middle saying war or no war the Society would continue to play next season. War is shown by the use of force and force cannot last for ever but the arts will.

April 2nd To the First Aid class at three o'clock with Dorothy and Mrs Frampton. Mr Chamberlain made a statement today — the Allies are to tighten the economic blockade on Germany. Oh how hateful it all is. Our food supplies seem ample and some things like eggs and bacon are cheaper — eggs 1/8d a dozen and rashers 1/2d to 1/10d a lb. Cooked ham (to be had without coupons) 6d ¼ lb and very good too.

April 5th I should have turned up at the Police Court today in answer to my summons! The fine was 10/– only. I'd expected at least £1.

April 9th About 250,000 German troops have taken over the *whole* of Denmark and most of Norway. The beast has snapped again and gobbled up a very large couple of mouthfuls. Now Sweden is threatened. Germany says she is 'protecting' these countries from the democracies.

April 13th Our navy has fought a marvellous battle off Norway and sunk seven German destroyers. Also our boats have mined the Baltic. Surely this must augur well for the Allies?

April 17th British and Canadian troops land in Norway — Narvik is recaptured from the Germans who of course made light of it. It seems that Norway was betrayed from within a week ago today by Nazi agents and pro-Nazi Norwegians. I to Tennis Club Annual General Meeting. Only four 'men' there — one over seventy, one under eighteen, Mr Sams (over military age) and Mr Cushing (medically unfit). Home at 8.30. Mr Ritter and Mrs Langbank here and we played rummy.

April 18th Helped with the new refugee hostel for the Einhouses and Steinharts in Guildford Rd. This is Worthing Committee's sixth hostel. All newspapers are much smaller these days. For the last three days there have been no photos in the *Telegraph*.

April 21st Warm and sunny and clear. In the afternoon we primrosed and played telequoits, a good garden game using a ring instead of a ball and had tea. Later Mr Ritter and I walked along the front in the full moonlight — very warm and summery.

April 23rd The war budget announced today. Increases on tobacco, beer and spirits and postage and telephones. Letters now 2½d and postcards 2d from May 1st!

April 26th To the National Council of Women's meeting as Miss L. Baker-Beall was speaking on her experiences in Poland where she'd taught for thirty-three years and was there when the Germans invaded. She was detained in Berlin for two weeks and nearly interned but intervention by the American Embassy allowed her to get to Britain. Dwelt a lot on German atrocities (eye witnessed them) but also made stupid statement about all Germans being fundamentally bad.

April 28th Mother and I and Ritter and Riemer off at 8 am via Winchester to Oxford. Arrived 1 pm and had lunch in Addisons Walk then went around Magdalen Chapel and Hall, on to Christ Church kitchens and cathedral and lastly New College Gardens and Chapel. We hear several colleges have been taken over by the Government — Queens is now the Home Office and so on. Tea at a river garden. Home via Godalming where we stopped and saw the famous rabbits and fowls! Home by 9.30 — almost dark.

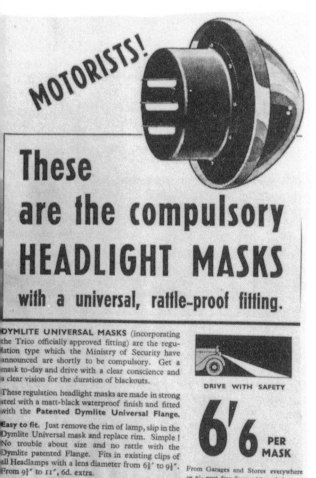

36

The shot-riddled wreckage of one of the many German planes shot down by British pilots during the past week's battle in Belgium.

THE END OF A NAZI BOMBER

Sunday Times,
May 19th

May 1st   A German mine-laying bomber crashed in Clacton last night — much damage.

May 3rd   It's gradually dawned on us (the general public) that we have had to *retreat* in south Norway. It seems we are out-numbered and have no ports and air-bases. Lord Haw Haw is triumphant but, in Asquith's last war phrase — 'wait and see'.

May 9th   Mr Chamberlain retained his government's majority by 281 to 200 votes — fairly close. It was a very stormy debate. Will he go? A glorious day and up to tennis. Mr Ritter seems much more cheerful after two long letters from Annie in Australia. Things are getting dearer. Mother bought some tea cloths today — 2/6d! instead of 1/3d. Tennis balls are 8/– a half dozen.

May 10th   I cycled out early before breakfast delivering notes and so saved 1/– or so. When I got to my first patient (a Londoner evacuated last September) I remarked on the weather and she said — 'but haven't you heard the news?' No. Holland and Belgium are invaded by the Germans. How *awful*. The usual tale of treachery.

Mrs Thornycroft had two trunk calls from London about possible refugees from Holland and Belgium. On the wireless we heard people are not to travel unnecessarily or to telephone but Kit did arrive for the Whitsun after all.

Mr Chamberlain resigns and Mr Churchill is now PM.

May 11th   Glorious day except for the news. The Allies have arrived in Holland and Belgium and the fighting is *terrible*.

May 12th   Mr Weingarten came at 10.30 to tell us Mr Ritter is to be interned together with all Austrian and German refugees between sixteen and sixty.

May 13th   Whit Monday. A perfect day for weather — most tantalising for banks and shops as the government has asked them to keep open. This is to ensure people keeping to their own towns and leaving the railways for military and other transport. No news of all our refugees. It is very sad hearing the wives' tales. The Czechs are all right and those Germans who came over on Czech passports. The Dutch Queen Wilhelmina and Princess Juliana and two daughters have arrived in England. The Queen did not like leaving Holland but the government persuaded her to as the Germans were trying to kidnap her. We were stopped twice on the road back from Arundel by soldiers. Parachute troops are the great bug-bear now.

May 15th   Holland capitulates — to prevent the complete destruction of the country the Commander-in-Chief ordered

'down arms'. News of our internees. After an anxious morning Mr Durst was released from Chichester and was re-united with his family and I saw them off at 3.30 from West Worthing station for Liverpool en route for the USA. He says about 100 men are all living together in Chichester in a large hall — food is good, beds are straw mattresses on the floor. All are in 'good humour' — we hope so!

May 16th News still terrible — terrific German onslaughts launched. All England is ready for invasion — we *can't* imagine the danger is so near. The wireless gave out to car owners to lock their garages and see that their cars cannot be used by strangers.

May 17th Belgian and Dutch refugees are arriving. Great care is being taken to ensure they are genuine. The 'fifth column' as it is called seems to be a most important feature of this war — the fifth column being traitors and spies. Holland was riddled with them. Heard that we may communicate with our interned refugees at Chichester, so I wrote to Mr Ritter.

May 19th The situation is still very serious though we are holding on better. I could not help feeling how true a verse in a psalm we sang in church was: 'a mighty man is not delivered by much strength' Psalm 33: 16. Hitler certainly has much strength but he won't win. Mr Churchill broadcast for the first time as PM this evening. He forecasts 'fiercer tactics, and furious and unrelenting assaults'.

May 21st Very grave evening news from France. The PM there M. Reynaud reports further German advances and the failure of the French to blow up some important bridges. The culprits are to be 'punished'. Mrs Thornycroft says the interned men are not to be allowed to write. Mother and I wrote to Annie, Ritter's fiancée, in Australia as she must feel worried. But parcels can be sent to internees so we sent some cigarettes, etc.

May 22nd I obeyed all orders today and took my gas mask, identity card, identity disc and removed my distributor business in car! Such is life!

May 23rd The wives of the interned refugees are *so* sad and upset, almost as if they were dead, as they are not allowed to write. Mr and Mrs Dornbusch are off to Bolivia tomorrow — they came to say good-bye and to bring me some apfelstrudel! On the six o'clock news we heard that Germans are in Boulogne — bad. I went to the ARP course at Beach House on high explosive and incendiary bombs — ugly! There was a picture of a Sussex poultry farmer who had been bombed in today's *Telegraph.*

May 24th Empire Day. The King broadcast very well at 9 pm. Our RAF are doing wonderfully well — over 1,500 German planes are known to have been brought down in the last fortnight. I heard guns very distinctly at 11.30 pm. Our pier has been closed by the military authorities and mined. No one is allowed to sit on the seats on the front near the pier.

May 28th M. Reynaud broadcast in French at 8.30 am and reported that King Leopold of Belgium had capitulated. Things go badly for us still but we can stick it. All the bathing huts have been trundled off the beach, filled with stones and put to block roads leading up from the sea! All boats have been removed from the beach and no bathing is allowed.

May 29th Criticism is very harsh on King Leopold's action but we are told to withhold it until later. It is a bitter blow though. His government continues to function and says Belgium will fight on in spite of the King whom they call a traitor. His sister, it must be remembered, is the Crown Princess of Italy. Italy still stands aloof but the press there is very anti-Allies. Two good bits of news — no three! We have definitely recaptured Narvik in Norway, the German workers are complaining of over-work and low wages and we have found homes for Mrs Chlumecky's valuable Persian cats! She and her four daughters have been interned on the Isle of Man. The family are not Jewish but could see danger ahead for those not obeying the Nazis and fled Austria early.

May 30th The British Expeditionary Force and the French are in desperate straits in Flanders and evacuation is essential. I signed on for a month's Land Army work in August. The front of Worthing is being cut up for 'pill-boxes', there is a look-out on top of County Café and people are leaving the coast hotels very rapidly and some residents with small children are going too.

June 1st Saturday. Up to tennis and quite a lot there. Very few go up during the week as many are working with the ARP or Observer Corps or 'digging for victory', etc. Everyone pretends not to be nervous but we can't resist noticing the aeroplanes very carefully and it is good to see the familiar RAF circles on the wings.

June 2nd The biggest item of war news is the brilliant evacuation of the BEF and Northern French Army from Dunkirk.

June 5th The Prime Minister made an important speech yesterday about the Dunkirk withdrawal and the events leading up to it. It seems miraculous that over 300,000 men were able to escape the *terrific* German onslaught. Some people

think it was God's answer to the National Day of Prayer last Sunday week. I feel very loath to draw God's name into this ghastly affair.

June 6th   Poor German population is being subjected to three days' bell-ringing to celebrate the victory of the Battle of the Ports.

June 7th   Awoke at 1.20 to hear the 'warbling' wail of the air-raid siren. I shot into Mother's room and she was still asleep! I stayed with her till the 'all clear' one and a quarter hours later. Our first alarm. Apparently there were several enemy planes about but very little damage done. Everyone very calm about it but a real raid must be very nasty. At last we've got Mr Ritter's first letter written eleven days ago — very poor food and poor furniture in their camp.

Daily Telegraph, June 3rd

DESTROYER'S DECK crowded with ...en of the B.E.F. who have been evacuated ...m Dunkirk. Craft of all sorts have been used.

40

June 10th Italy has declared war on Britain and France — ghastly. Mr Duff Cooper, Minister of Information, made a most scathing talk just before the 9 pm news. We've also brought our troops from Norway and King Haakon is in England.

June 11th Mussolini's words 'brotherhood of blood' and 'interpreting the *will* of the people' are nauseating. We are convinced the majority of Italians abhor war — certainly the Roman Catholics. The terrific German thrusts continue in France, and Paris is being evacuated. Princess Juliana and her two daughters have arrived in Canada. At tennis tonight noted a return flight of seventeen fighters — six groups of three except 'one of our fighters is missing' or as the BBC has it sometimes 'one failed to return'. What tragedy in those few words.

June 12th The office says that in all probability *all* Germans and Austrians must leave Worthing before the end of the week. Several of our hostels will have to close of course. The Germans are only 30 miles from Paris. Our RAF have got in first over Italy and have bombed many military and naval objectives. The RAF is magnificent. We heard of two local tragedies today. Young Lacey, married three weeks, has crashed and broken his back and other bones and young Blake is missing — he's left three babies (one set of twins) under two years. Mr Girdwood, the Congregational minister, is resigning, partly because of his extreme pacifism. I looked round the Public Art Gallery's War Photograph exhibition, which is really most wonderful. One photo I shall never forget 'Home on Leave' — a small child rushing to her soldier father at the station with outstretched arms and so excited — very pathetic.

June 14th Paris surrenders. This news came as a bombshell at one o'clock. It seems that rather than let it be a mass of ruins the French Cabinet — now at Bordeaux — ordered it to surrender quietly. Everyone anxious but calm. Uncle Herbert, Mother's half-brother in Canada, wrote sending me his allowance — for just £100 per year which I can use as I like! Mrs Schlichter came to say good-bye to Mother (all enemy aliens are to leave the coast) and she will receive the first sum as she is in a terrible plight.

June 16th A National Day of Prayer for France whose sufferings are terrible. Tremendous political activity is going on over there. What does it forebode? Mrs Thornycroft gave a farewell tea to our Austrian and German refugee departees — about forty there — very pathetic.

June 17th The worst blow of all — France has had to surrender, words cannot describe the situation. What can the future hold now? Mr Churchill broadcast at nine o'clock saying Britain and the Empire will fight on till victory is assured.

DESPATCHES FROM THE HOME FRONT

1940

June 18th The new immediate horror is invasion and air raids of great intensity. I went to Windlesham School in the afternoon. It is being evacuated to Glastonbury next Friday. They have cut their hay and stacked it bang in the middle of their cricket field as is being requested by the government.

June 19th Moll and Jack to tea to discuss possibility of Moll and boys going to Canada for the duration.

June 22nd The possible terms of the armistice between France and Germany are being discussed. Pétain says he will not agree to a 'shameful peace'.

June 23rd The armistice terms are terrible as everyone imagined they would be. The French colonies say they will not accept them and will fight on.

June 26th General de Gaulle broadcast from London that the armistice accepted by the Bordeaux government under the eighty-four-year-old General Pétain was a capitulation. He is marshalling all sorts of help from French people the world over and announced the formation of a French National Committee in England and said: 'The war is not lost, the country is not dead, hope is not extinct. Vive la France!' Mr Anthony Eden also broadcast and was most encouraging. We are getting used to hearing about 'the Battle of Britain', 'Britain is now a fortress', 'Britain in danger of invasion by sea and air' and so on. But *all stand firm*. Mollie is definitely off to Canada in a week or so with the boys.

Sandbags, Anderson ARP shelter, shovel (removal of bomb), stirrup pump, buckets of water, sand, paper on windows, barbed wire, gas mask, steel helmet, gun. 'Anything else you can think of, dear?' Yes — the 'first-aid'! adds Joan.

I found old Haw Haw at 11.15 but just as he was deriding something British his station went off the air which means our RAF over Germany again! Snubs to him.

June 28th From today onwards all cars must be rendered incapable of being driven away, ie when I stopped at each patient this morning and afternoon I had to remove ignition keys and lock doors. At night I must still continue to remove rotary gadget as well! Had a nice letter from Mr Ritter. He has a new commandant and things are better.

SMILING THROUGH . . . *By LEE*
[No. 1,815]   DESIRABLE RESIDENCE

" Anything else you can think of, dear ? "

*Evening News,
June 29th*

July 2nd   Will Hitler invade us tonight? The roads are well infested with anti-tank devices. Spent the evening with Bache and from her flat window watched the gun practice going on. No one is allowed to bathe at all now.

July 3rd   No invasion yet — but we live on tenter-hooks. People are still leaving Worthing. The summer sales begin this week. I listened in to Beethoven's seventh this evening — I believe from Germany. Very well played. I wondered if Hitler were listening too! One of Mother's letters to Mr Ritter was returned as she'd committed an offence under the Defence of the Realm! She'd mentioned France's armistice!

July 4th   Listened in at 8 am and heard exciting news about the French fleet — most of it seems to be in our possession but one Admiral at Oran objected and 'measures had to be taken'. Later this transpired to be a naval action between the British and French fleets in that part of the Mediterranean. Whoever would have felt this to be possible?

July 6th   I have cut out and pasted in this picture for no other reason other than I hope to be able to paste in the *opposite type* of picture at the end of this fourth volume 'a beating of swords into plough shares' one. One wonders — maybe it will be possible before the end of the book. One cannot be proud of a civilisation whose very existence depends on the amount possessed of deadly, death-dealing implements of destruction. Men have always held the reins of government. Is the solution in the hands of women? War *must* be destroyed or it will destroy civilisation.

Driving along Worthing front this morning I noticed how rapidly it had been converted into a battle front — machine guns hidden under shingle and sand-bags, ammunition dumps disguised as beach chalets and so on. The papers say we are now a 'defence area' which means no one can come here except with official permission. Worthing looks quite empty with no visitors and so many inhabitants moving inland.

July 7th   We'd just got out of church at 12 this morning when an air-raid siren sounded. Mother and I and the four Coads and Mrs Wenban-Smith all went into the Vicarage — but the all clear sounded after about ten minutes. We got home only to have a repetition. However the second all clear sounded just before 1 pm and we had our lunch in peace! We thought the invasion must have started. In the afternoon Mother and I invited eight Czechs in to a farewell tea. They are wonderfully cheerful in spite of hating the idea of leaving Worthing.

July 8th   Talks on the wireless about 'the Battle of Britain' are becoming more numerous but more reassuring. It's very difficult to visualise our land as a battlefield but with Churchill

The Great Speed-Up. By Herbert Morrison

ALUMINIUM for aircraft delivery at a Women's Voluntary Services centre.

as PM and so many well-trained troops here it's our duty as civilians to do as we are told. Our Worthing Women's Lunch Club had quite an interesting talk by V Arlett, of the Ministry of Information, this evening on our duty as civilians — we must not be a fifth columnist or a sixth columnist or a something else (can't remember what). But what with being told what we must not be: (a) too optimistic because it savours of complacency and this helped cause the war, or (b) pessimistic because that is playing into Hitler's hands, oh yes and not being full of fear, we've a good old job to know what to do and how to do it! The Food Controller broadcast this evening that tea is to be rationed to 2 oz per person from tomorrow! Also margarine. There is plenty of food but it must be stored as far as possible.

July 10th The Channel Islands have been evacuated during the last week. Re Lord Beaverbrook's appeal for aluminium, Mr McDonald next door asked if I would take his to the Women's Voluntary Service. I decided to comb Langton Rd for it and dropped a note in every door. Mother has started needle work at the Red Cross Centre in Liverpool Gardens! She has to wear a uniform! White overall and cap.

July 13th Mollie and boys definitely not going to Canada — good. For one thing the government can't spare the ships for convoying. I to farewell party at 37 Shakespeare Rd. About sixteen Czechs there.

July 14th The air war increases in intensity and Mr Churchill, who broadcast at 9 pm, predicts worse raids in the future and talks about the war possibly lasting another *two years*. Ken and family to tea and we had it in the garden — lovely day. Mr Graham, who lives opposite, came over and offered us the use of his air-raid dugout in case of need!

July 19th I was in the town at about six o'clock this evening, heard a plane, looked up and saw one with enormous black crosses underneath — a real German plane! No-one seemed unduly alarmed and as it flew out to sea three English fighters appeared. We heard it was brought down later.

July 22nd The town seems *very* empty as now the evacuated children have left us — 3,000 of them. Ex-Emperor Haile Selassie, after a most exciting journey, has reached his own country, Abyssinia, once more and will unite his peoples to fight against Italy. He lived here in Worthing in Warnes Hotel before he left England. Dr Benes has been recognised as the head of the new provisional Czech government in London. New war budget — income tax is now 8/6d! We can bathe in Worthing again now, the ban is lifted.

July 26th Twenty-eight German raiders were brought down by the RAF yesterday — the highest total of any one day yet.

To the long Refugee Committee meeting in the afternoon. Mrs Thornycroft and I wrote to the Home Secretary about Ritter's release from internment. I played singles with Mr Robinson at tennis — good fun. I couldn't help thinking how annoyed Hitler would be if he could see our recreation grounds — there were crowds bowling there. The Havant-Davieses to tea: they brought their own tea and sugar!

July 30th To ARP Report Centre at the Town Hall at 5.30 pm — I'm one of the volunteers who receive and pass on telephone messages when enemy aircraft are in the vicinity. A 'yellow' warning came through just after I went on duty. All clear came half an hour later. I was on duty again at five the next morning for three hours. Another yellow. Did a lot of knitting — so did Major Carlisle! He's deputy controller and looks very jolly.

July 31st A real hot day — got my first bathe in at last. Soldiers come and clear the beaches of people at 6 pm punctually.

August 2nd The Germans dropped leaflets over a large part of south-east England last night — they were devoted to Hitler's last 'peace offer' and appeal to common sense! One lady collected a lot of them and sold them as souvenirs for the Red Cross. Trouble seems to be brewing in the East. Japan has arrested several Britons — one of whom, a Reuters correspondent, has committed suicide. All were accused of spying.

August 4th The Japanese have released some of our men but we've now detained two of theirs in London! Situation looks slightly better. The whole affair in all probability engineered by Germany. Rumania seems very uneasy again.

August 11th On the nine o'clock news details of a further big defeat of German raiders over the South Coast today — fifty raiders are known to have been destroyed — we've lost nineteen fighters. The Weingartens say that the explanation of so many German bombs not exploding is that they were made by Czechs in the Skoda works and were filled with sand.

August 15th Hitler's day! 'By this date Britain would be brought to her knees.' And the RAF has had *its* day, having brought down 169 raiders over Britain in twenty-four hours. Croydon airport was attacked for the first time.

August 16th Mother and I went up to tea with Miss Goldsmith at High Salvington — she was senior lecturer at the Poulter School of Massage in Hove when I trained there in the 1920s. As usual the siren went off, at about five o'clock. We continued tea but planes got nearer and nearer. Suddenly firing broke out and planes seemed to be immediately overhead and *very* low — then a thud-thud and more firing. We adjourned to under the stairs while Miss Goldsmith pulled her blinds. She was very reassuring saying they often had it like that on the hill. Later she admitted she said that to calm Mother (who was not in the slightest upset!). Here we sat for about an hour and finally the all clear sounded at 6.45 — six raiders were brought down in and around Worthing and the thud we heard was one in Honeysuckle Lane on top of the hill. We got back to Worthing and called on Ken and family — Ken, as an air-raid warden, had been patrolling and had watched the various 'dog-fights' as they are called.

August 20th British Somaliland has been 'successfully evacuated'. Since the French collapse this has been a possibility as it is a desert colony completely surrounded by Italians in Libya and Abyssinia. It was not worth holding on to as it is a very difficult place to keep supplied and anyhow as the man told the children on the wireless (excellent five minutes 9.10 to 9.15 daily on 'Events of the Day') 'no-one bothers to rush out and cope with thieves in the orchard if you were also having to contend with burglars in your own house at the same time'!

August 28th If we are getting rather sick of the air-raid warnings so are the Germans. Mollie writes that they've spent several nights running into their cellar — she *hates* it but the boys rather enjoy it! We had a stirrup pump demonstration here in our back garden this evening. Every house in Langton Rd sent a representative. It *was* amusing. We are going to organise a fire-fighting squad. Let's hope we are never needed. There are only about half-a-dozen hale and hearty people here! A quiet day but at 10 pm 'mournful Mary' went off. Blow.

August 31st Visited the Huyton Aliens Internment camp and saw four of the Worthing refugees including Mr Ritter. It was a beautiful sunny day so the camp did not look so awful but the barbed wire is horrid. The men looked better than I'd anticipated but all so sad at lack of freedom.

September 4th We had a horrid air battle over Worthing today and eight raiders were brought down. I saw one come down and two men 'bale out', but it's all too awful. I hate even writing about it. The USA announced she was giving us fifty destroyers immediately in exchange for the use of island bases belonging to us — most excellent. Hitler shouted to the world that his 'patience' is now completely exhausted!

Ken visited the wounded German pilot in Worthing Hospital and found him very appreciative.

JUNKERS PILOT WHO BALED OUT

The pilot of a Junkers 87 who baled out when his aircraft was shot down during a recent raid, arriving under escort at a railway station in South-East England on his way to a prisoners' camp.

September 8th London had a terrific raid all last night — 500 raiders were employed and ninety-nine were brought down. But there was much damage in the dock area and hundreds of deaths — awful. I phoned Kit at 9.15 and found she was all right and had planned to come home for her week's holiday today. She arrived at 6.15 — it took her nearly four hours. Today was England's Second National Day of Prayer. I sold my gold bangle for the Red Cross and Spitfire Fund — £3 10s I got for it! Hector McLean gave it me in the last war!

September 11th London had its nightly visit again last night but during the day we brought down another eighty-nine raiders. There was a different method of attack at night — fewer search lights and more intense anti-aircraft fire. Of course we are bombing Berlin just as frequently. The King and Queen visited bombed areas yesterday. Would Hitler dare do a similar visit? A time bomb exploded at Buckingham Palace and did quite a lot of damage. The London and St Thomas's hospitals have been hit and Madame Tussaud's.

VIEWING THE BOMB DAMAGE TO THE PALACE

September 13th Everyone is a little apprehensive of an invasion attempt. We hear all coast towns in the south-east round to Seaford are pretty well evacuated. While I write at 11.30 pm I hear the drone of the Nazi bombers booming en route for poor London. Buckingham Palace was deliberately bombed again today.

September 14th Worthing's been bombed — whoever would have imagined it? At 6.30 am an aeroplane was heard circling about and suddenly all Worthing must have awakened to the sound of six bombs. We all got up and came downstairs and waited till the all clear. The postman came in good time and told us Mitchell's Bakery, Caffyn's Garage and Wells' Bird Shop had all been badly hit — minor damage to the Town Hall. What the targets are we can only surmise — probably the Post Office and Town Hall and the Gas Works and Hospital. Well, well. It's happened at last.

September 16th 185 raiders were shot down yesterday — this is the RAF's biggest victory so far. Many fell on London and its suburbs. Today is what is known as Invasion Day! Will it come? The weather seems to have broken and the Channel is very choppy for their barges, but . . . who knows? Our bombers are working hard against the invasion bases. St Paul's Cathedral in London had a narrow escape from destruction. A time bomb, measuring eight feet and weighing one ton was removed with great courage by a 'Bomb Disposal Section' under a Lt Davies after three days' work on it. It was driven to Hackney Marshes and exploded.

September 17th Mother and I have slept downstairs for three nights but it is so uncomfortable! And now the invasion is off so we've decided to retire upwards again! We've decided the only difference would be that a direct hit would (if we were upstairs) dispose of us at once, and if we were down it would bury us!

September 19th The awful air attacks against London continue — famous buildings, businesses, hospitals, galleries and so on — all are damaged badly. The poor in the East End are getting the worst of it. Why should these poor people, innocent of any war-like feelings, be subjected to such ghastly terror? Kit phoned to say she was all right — every night she spends in the public shelter and by day she tries to work between the raids. We sent her a paraffin cooking stove because London gas is a transitory commodity these days.

September 23rd Horrified at the eight o'clock news to hear that a child evacuee ship had been torpedoed in mid-Atlantic in darkness and in a gale. Only eight out of ninety-three children saved. How glad Mollie must feel she and the boys did not

take the risk of evacuating to Canada. Tea at Bache's. She told me a most exciting tale of her holiday in the New Forest a week ago. She was staying with a farmer and his wife. The farmer is in the Home Guard. One evening he was told that all the Home Guard were to stand to as there was trouble expected. He showed Bache how to fire a gun and told her she must shoot if someone called and could not answer the challenge. The farmer went off leaving the wife and Bache alone. They went to bed and to sleep but Bache woke up to the sound of *church bells*! We've been told that this denotes the presence of air-borne enemy troops. She flew down to find the farmer's wife there. Bombers flew overhead as usual but dropped no bombs — 'troop carriers' said the wife — five in all they counted. Then *footsteps*! Bache challenged — no reply. Challenged again and still no reply. Bache went out and found the culprit — a baby donkey! But the Home Guard farmer's version was that 250 of the enemy had been rounded up!

September 25th   Oh dear this diary! It's very little else but bombs, bombs, bombs. The whole world *is* mad. The Axis — Germany and Italy — are trying their best to drag both Spain and Japan in on their side. The USA remains very pro-British — will any country escape these awful times? We had a more cheerful letter from Mr Ritter today — he thinks it best to remain in camp if he can't get a transport to Australia.

September 30th   At five o'clock a big air battle took place over Worthing — the sky seemed to be teeming with glistening white butterflies very high up and the raiders puffed out white smoke screens. Our fighters forced them out to sea and later on the nine o'clock news we heard at least forty-five have been brought down. Sixteen of ours are lost, eight pilots safe.

October 3rd   At last rain all day. We got the first siren at five o'clock in the evening — nothing all day — a record! We have now had 120 siren warnings since May 9th. We get one *every* night at dusk which heralds the approach of German bombers en route for London — but London is holding its own in a most magnificent way. All the ARP services and others, such as the clergy etc are working magnificently. Some scarcely sleep at all during the twenty-four hours, Kit says. She helps at a 'Rest Centre' one night a week, a place where those bombed out of house and home go temporarily. There are changes in the War Cabinet, including the resignation of Mr Chamberlain, exactly two years after the Munich débâcle. Alys Battersby nearly suffered death from some bombs which did not explode. When examined they were found to contain *sand*, and were marked CZECH. Most significant. (I hope no one reads this till after victory!) Otherwise the placard 'She talked . . . this happened' may come true if a fifth column makes use of it!

October 5th   Apart from the usual four (or is it five?) warnings we've had a fairly peaceful day. Langton Rd's fire-fighting volunteers made a tour of inspection of their houses' fighting apparatus. Some have really good ladders — all have their buckets of water and sand ready — and there are three stirrup pumps in the road!

To tennis where the war-time teas would make Hitler's mouth water: bread, butter and two jams, great variety of cakes and tea and sugar — all for 7d!

October 8th   To the Report Centre as usual at 5.30. For a treat the ten of us had previously decided to have a hot supper sent in from a nearby cafe and it came at 6.50 — a jolly good mixed grill and all for 1/3d. We were all laughing and making a noise and suddenly we heard what we thought was someone tapping on the window but . . . it was bombs. We all shot out to the telephones and messages came in fast and furious — the Gas Works had been hit, houses in Park Rd and Lyndhurst Rd demolished, five people killed and several injured, some still feared trapped and so on. We worked hard till about 10 pm when everything was in good order. Later we heard that a lone raider had appeared suddenly, dropped its load and in flying off in a westerly direction machine gunned people walking in the road. I phoned up Mother and she was quite unperturbed and was playing picquet with Uncle Bert!

October 9th   Mr Churchill made a good speech in parliament yesterday, reviewing the whole war situation. He does not paint a glowing picture of sweeping victories but gives a well balanced account of our difficulties *and* our hopes.

October 12th   Kit came home for a short weekend. She says the spirit of the Londoners really is magnificent. Rumania is to all intents and purposes a vassal state to Germany. Troops have entered and taken over. Hitler will now have a good supply of looted oil and wheat.

October 14th   A very sad letter from Uncle Alfred at Eastbourne who's got the printing works there. The town has lost two-thirds of its population thanks to numerous awful air-raids and he is faced with ruin. Also a postcard from Ritter — he's been moved to the Isle of Man. There is a very vague hope of a transport to Australia for him. London had its worst air-raid last night. It must have been *awful*. Rumania is in Germany's hands completely.

October 18th   Silk stockings are now not to be sold to the public — they are needed for our export trade and also for war purposes. Kit phoned up about the London refugees we are hoping to place in Worthing. Helen's opposite neighbour is to have a thirteen-month-old baby, Aunt 'Flop' who used to be a

EVACUATING BABIES FROM BOMBED HOSPITAL IN LONDON

HOSPITALS BOMBED

CHILD PATIENTS VICTIMS

DAILY TELEGRAPH REPORTER

Four hospitals and a medical college, including the children's ward of a hospital, were among the London places hit by the Nazi raiders on Saturday night and early yesterday. The raids were on a somewhat wider scale than formerly, the chief attacks being on London, the Midlands and towns in the north-west.

Children who had been injured in previous air raids were among the casualties when their ward in the hospital was damaged. In the surgical...

Babies being removed from the maternity wing of a hospital in London which was damaged during a night bombing raid.

Daily Telegraph

sister at Brighton Children's Hospital another one, we an old lady of seventy-four and there are a few others. Our own people refugees now — hateful, hateful war.

October 19th Mollie had sent a beautiful fowl — home grown and fatted up specially for Sunday lunch and Ken and family came to help us eat it. Mother had tracked down a 5d lemon (very scarce just now) so she could stuff it. I'd already given her a fright over the price of onions — 9d a lb. Actually food prices are wonderful with very few exceptions. We are asked to make only one Christmas pudding this year but fruit is good and reasonable.

October 22nd Copper, a former colleague of mine when she worked at the Sussex County Hospital, phoned me to ask if I could possibly find rooms for five poor elderly 'bombed-out' people from London. I had to say yes after having had a letter previously from her telling me how simply pathetic and awful the devastation in London is.

October 23rd The five arrived today! All to tea here. Poor Mother — they arrived two hours earlier than was expected and Mother had to entertain them all. Two were stone deaf which wasn't to be wondered at as they were eighty-nine and eighty-five! The two others were very jolly seventy-nine and seventy-six and the other fifty-odd. After tea we dispersed them — four to Schofield's landlady and one to Dorothy Macpherson — with hopes that all would be well. The two very elderlies had not been out of their house for two years till they were bombed and the elderly gent looked like death. They are *very* old and helpless. Rev Wilkinson called and helped them with their ration and pension books.

October 25th 'Summer Time' is to remain with us throughout the entire winter, to enable city workers to get home in daylight. I started my YMCA canteen duty this evening six to ten and was awfully busy frying bacon, sausages, chips etc and washing up. There are many Scottish and Lancashire soldiers in Worthing now.

October 28th Italy has wantonly attacked Greece. Italy sent an ultimatum at 3 am and gave till 6 am for an answer. At *5.30* am Italy attacked. The CPR liner *Empress of Britain* bombed and sunk off Ireland. Over 500 saved.

October 29th Britain promises aid to Greece and so far she is resisting unexpectedly well. Jugoslavia is to 'remain neutral' she says. Will she be allowed to I wonder? Our RAF have got as far as Czechoslovakia and have bombed the famous Skoda works. The Czechs won't mind! They do their best for us by sending over dud bombs. There is still much correspondence about reprisals on Berlin, most newspaper correspondents are against it on various grounds — moral, Christian and strategic. Let's hope we *don't*.

October 31st A gale has blown for about twenty-four hours and the consequence is that mines have become dislodged and exploded on the beach. Several hotels (all empty) have had their windows broken by them. Greece is resisting well.

November 3rd Mrs Farringdon arrived — our 'bombed Londoner' from Kit — seventy-eight and somewhat talkative! But she's had a terrible time these last few weeks and her journey today took four and a half hours! A bomb was on the main London line and held up traffic. She was greeted by explosions here — mines bursting on the beach owing to the gale! No dusk siren tonight — whatever happened? Berlin was terribly bombed on Friday night for eight hours.

November 5th Guy Fawkes' Day! Too much gunpowder about all over the world these days. We bomb Germany and they bomb us. Lancing had awful bombs today — the evacuated convalescence home had a direct hit and is destroyed.

November 7th President Roosevelt is in for a *third* term of office. This is without precedent and England is *very* encouraged. We know him and although Wendell Wilkie sounds a good man too, he is unknown to us.

November 10th The Sunday nearest Armistice Day and ordered by the Archbishop of Canterbury to be a day of rededication — I went to St Matthew's in the morning. The Rev Rowland Smith, during his notices, reminded us of the BBC decision to record Big Ben at 9 pm nightly now so that all Britain can have a minute a day at least to remember our duty in this solemn time. The BBC announced the death of Mr Neville Chamberlain last night.

November 14th It really is good news from the Mediterranean. The Italians are very loath to leave their ports, so our Fleet Air Arm has attended to their ships there in Taranto with devastating effect. In the Atlantic too the Germans say they have sunk a convoy of *thirty-eight* but thanks to a wonderful effort from a small armed merchant boat, the *Jervis Bay*, which engaged the pocket-battleship *Scheer* and allowed the convoy ships to scatter, thirty-two of our ships escaped and reached port safely. Captain Fegen RN and over 200 officers and men went down with the *Jervis Bay*. A VC was awarded posthumously to the Captain.

November 15th Poor Coventry had an *awful* raid last night — the worst ever reported on the wireless. Mother's felt depressed all day about it. Over 200 killed and 1,000 injured; bombs were dropped every two minutes for over five hours.
To the YMCA and very busy frying all the time 6 to 9.30 pm.

November 16th Caught the eight o'clock to London, Victoria. Met Copper and had a coffee together and discussed bombs, etc the only conversation Londoners indulge in! One old news vendor had chalked up: 'houses down, shops down, churches down, but *we* are not down'. Good old Londoners. I tubed part of the way back to Victoria for the experience of seeing the tube life. The public are allowed down at 4.30 and I saw hundreds of bundles of rugs etc staking out the owners' claims! The sanitary arrangements are bad, but the people are good natured and stick their concrete beds well.

Chicago Daily Tribune

—BUT THEY ARE SUPPOSED TO SURRENDER!!! IF THAT HAD HAPPENED TO US, WE'D HAVE QUIT A LONG TIME AGO!

BRITAIN

HITLER

NAZIS

"THE BULLDOG BREED."   Chicago Daily Tribune.

SHIPPING LOSSES
Year's Balance Sheet
Mr. ALEXANDER, First Lord of the Admiralty, replying to Sir Ralph Glyn (Cons.): The number of merchant ships of all tonnages, including fishing vessels, lost by enemy action during the first 12 months of the war was:

		Gross tons.
British	406 of	1,611,842
Allied	103 of	474,816
Neutral	253 of	769,212
Total ..	762 of	2,855,870

The number of crews and passengers lost and saved was approximately: Lost, 3,327; saved, 15,635; taken prisoner, 1,100. Enemy losses for the first 12 months of the war as far as known: 261 ships of about 1,269,000 tons. The number of crews and passengers lost and saved in these ships is not known.

54

November 17th The King's visit to poor bombed Coventry has had a wonderful effect. It is now a question of bombing and counter bombing. We are hammering Germany — especially their oil, transport, and munitions supplies. The Italians too are paying the price of declaring war on their former friends.

November 18th Kit's two tenants arrive for their ten-day holiday. Mr Kipler is an alien — German but has lived in England fifty-nine years and has three sons in the Army — but we had quite a little affair at the police station registering them.

November 26th A land mine exploded near Wallace Avenue this afternoon and killed two soldiers and injured others. This is the sort of thing that is so awful in war — our own mine and our own soldiers. The Italians have been kept well on the run now and have been pretty well hustled out of Albania. Lovely! The old 1938 joke is coming true: Hitler to Chamberlain 'I have Italy on my side this time'. Chamberlain to Hitler 'Quite right too. We had them last time!'

Daily Telegraph,
November 27th

AN INVITATION THAT AMUSED THE KING

The King, with the Queen by his side, is holding the gold badge of the Trades Union Congress. He had just accepted it from Mr. George Gibson, the chairman of the T.U.C., at a mobile canteen presentation in the quadrangle of Buckingham Palace. "If your Majesty ever feels disposed to visit the Congress," declared Mr. Gibson, with sly humour, "this will be your Open Sesame." (Report on Page Five.)

November 27th I think this is a good omen for this fifth book! We've turned the corner! It's certain that this picture certainly could not have been taken between May and September this year.

November 28th Just before I came to bed Lord Haw Haw forced his way in to the English programme — *everything* was false. According to him we'd lost 300 planes in Greece to the Italian fifty, the Albanians resent the Greeks coming through their country, Great Britain is in dire straits for fresh fruit, milk and eggs! The d∗∗∗ swine! I really delight in swearing at this traitor and his lies. There is a lot of sabotage going on in Norway and in Paris hundreds of students have been imprisoned by the Germans. The Germans tried to alienate the Parisians from Britain recently by showing the 'cruelty of the RAF'. When the pictures showing damage to Germany appeared the audience got up and cheered and cheered! In England there is a growing feeling of confidence spreading. Food *is* plentiful on the whole — certainly eggs *are* scarce (Mollie gave us seventeen on Sunday which was lovely) but no-one need go hungry. Black out lasts from 5.30 to 8.20 am now owing to daylight saving still being in force — it's to enable Londoners to get home before the blitz starts.

December 2nd Had an excellent carol practice — thirty-seven there! The Italians are still retreating and there is *much* trouble in all the countries 'protected' by Germany — Quisling has been shot at in Norway. He became leader of the Norwegian Fascist Party in 1933 and aided the Nazi invasion this year by delaying mobilisation and urging non-resistance. Rumania is in a *terrible* state. Over here Southampton and Bristol have been very badly raided. Lord Woolton says we shall have to alter our diets — less food is to come by ships as the ships are needed for war material. The U-boat campaign is proving very virulent — sometimes we lose over twenty ships in a week. The sailor's life is very hazardous. I gave a talk at the Women's Luncheon Club on 'London under Fire'. I tried to point out how much we owed to the East-enders for sticking Hitler's savage onslaughts.

December 7th There was a terrific explosion about eight o'clock last night. Apparently it landed in the sea near Ham Rd. It blasted to death many very choice bass which were thrown up on to the beach and collected and eaten by the soldiers! How amazed Hitler would be!

December 10th Owing to the blackout continuing till after eight in the morning we have to get up with curtains still drawn but on the other hand we can still have tea in the day light. Marvellous news from the Middle East — 4,000 Italian prisoners taken and our troops were on the *offensive*. This is the *first* time this has happened during this rotten old war! Mussolini must be feeling distracted as *everything* is going wrong *everywhere!* The Greeks are still pursuing fleeing Italians in Albania and we are doing the same in the African campaign — gorgeous!

December 11th A quiet night so we got good sleep at the Report Centre apart from snoring etc! Hitler has made a speech. He does not seem quite so confident! The PM spoke cheerfully of the African campaign — he is usually very guarded so we take this as a very good sign.

December 12th Uncle Bert, my godfather and formerly Father's business partner, got knocked down by an army lorry and is pretty extensively hurt — the young lorry drivers are *very* reckless. In December 1939 alone there were nearly 1,200 road deaths. I saw a very unusual looking lorry today, labelled up BDS I realised it was a Bomb Disposal Squad.

56

December 15th I went to the eight o'clock service this morning — I had to put my cycle lamps on as it was almost pitch dark. The church looked very eerie as it's not blacked out so very little light must be used.

December 21st Our Carol Party in aid of the ex-Service men at Gifford House has got going in spite of blackout, sirens and all the difficulties. We've been out three times this week and so far have raised over £12. At some houses we've been invited in but that takes so much longer and several times we've lost half the party in the blackout! Unfortunately the moon does not rise till too late to be any use. The war in the East has progressed remarkably well and Mr Churchill has spoken most confidently about it. Christmas shopping is going on apace but some articles are very scarce. Mother bought six oranges today — the first for ages.

December 29th The Carols did awfully well despite rain and biting wind and intense darkness which necessitated very dim torches. We went out six nights in all, including singing to the soldiers at the YMCA canteen and ARP and FAP (First Aid Post) at the Town Hall. Whether it was due to the weather or to a truce England had no raids for three days and nights over Christmas (nor had Germany). Food has been fairly plentiful — we had an extra 2 oz of tea last week but there were no dates and no white icing on cakes. The turkeys were the best anyone had ever had — much more tender than ever before. We ended up the Christmas festivities by giving a party to the nine Hoxton old-age pensioners now living in Worthing. Their combined ages came to 703! We had crackers, a Christmas tree and carols. Each went off with a parcel of ¼ lb of tea, nine lumps of sugar, a tin of jam, a tin of soup and a jar of potted meat. Lord Halifax was appointed our new Ambassador to the USA and Mr Eden again became Foreign Secretary.

December 30th For the first time for ages the London papers were late. London had an awful raid last night — the raiders tried to set the whole city on fire. About five hours of continuous fire bombing and many famous buildings are completely destroyed, including the Guildhall and many churches. President Roosevelt made a most important speech last night urging far more aid for Britain.

This is my house in Shakespeare Rd which was a Czech hostel. I'm glad it's going to be used.

1941

January 1st Major Cave said that Lloyds in London are laying five to two that peace (and victory of course) will be here by June *this year!* Hitler's plans are going more and more awry — the occupied countries are more and more restive under German domination. Italy is going downhill fast. We are mastering the U-boat menace and our morale is good! Meat is scarce in Worthing this week — in fact it's almost non-existent! But I was able to buy 1 lb of oranges and 1 lb of lemons today!

January 3rd I had to rush down to Mrs Wetherston about old Mrs 'All (one of the Hoxtonites — the only undesirable one). The old girl has taken a great dislike to Worthing and all pertaining to Worthing and has wired to Hoxton saying she's returning. They've wired begging me to try and induce her to remain but there's no luck and she's off this afternoon. The poor old girl is not wanted anywhere — she's seventy-seven, half blind, very quarrelsome and . . . drinks!

January 5th ARP service at Holy Trinity. Hundreds of ARP workers gathered outside the Town Hall at two o'clock and we 'processed' to the church! There were the firemen of AFS, police and war emergency police, wardens, FAP people, Red Cross nurses, WVS, Report and Control Centre members (our people), Observer Corps, Rescue workers, Demolition squads, mortuary squad, the band of the Royal Scots Fusiliers and the Mayor and Corporation. Mr Wilkinson took the service awfully nicely.

Bardia has fallen to General Wavell's forces. This is the first and best military victory of the war and may be the forerunner of all sorts of events.

January 14th I went along to see my house in Shakespeare Rd opened by the Mayor as a rest home for city workers.

January 18th The net seems to be closing round Mussolini! He is being beaten all over Africa and in Albania and all danger of Egypt being invaded is over. The Abyssinians are being helped by the British — a colonel and a party of his men having got into Abyssinia very secretly. The Worthing Old Girls party was quite good fun — it started at 3.45 and owing to there being no blackout in the hall it stopped soon after six

o'clock. Miss Reid, who took over as head mistress from Miss Kate Coast in 1938, made a very good speech reviewing the school's activities during the past very trying war year. She said how comparatively calmly the girls reacted to shelter life and other wartime restrictions. Like everyone else they are to be thoroughly trained in fire fighting. A very vile wet-snowy day.

January 20th Everyone is awaiting tidings of the struggle raging around Tobruk. It will be a great blow to Italy when it falls. Mussolini and Hitler met yesterday 'in an atmosphere of cordiality' (as usual) and discussed plans of closer co-operation, ie complete German domination! President Roosevelt was sworn in on Monday as President for his third term.

January 23rd Tobruk is ours! The Australians and the British tank corps were the first to enter. It is a wonderful victory and on the nine o'clock news it is reported we are pressing on further. The three services worked together awfully well and General Wavell is a magnificent leader. 20,000 prisoners have been taken and we've had less than 500 casualties.

January 25th The Fleischmanns came over and we went to see Charlie Chaplin in *The Great Dictator* at the Odeon. I thought it excellent.
Lord Halifax is safely in Washington having sailed in a new warship the *George V*.

January 26th Private Weingarten of the Pioneer Corps came at about 7.30 for his forty-eight hours leave. He is stationed at Newbury in the stables there! He is awfully bucked to be in the British Army and his one desire is to march into Prague in a victory march at the end of the war and then come back to be naturalised! All goes well on the four African fronts. Mussolini must be tremendously fed up.

January 29th General Metaxus, the Greek PM, has died, which is a great blow. President Roosevelt is pushing on with his 'lease and lend' bill. Mr Wendell Wilkie, his defeated opponent in the last presidential election, is here in Britain as a private citizen; he's very impressed with the British morale. He was mobbed by cheering crowds in Lancashire and is reported to have declared: 'I don't believe any nation in the history of the world was ever more united in a cause than the people of the British Isles are now.'

January 31st Anyone could make up one of Hitler's speeches for him. They are all modelled on the same style — boasts and promises, jibes and sneers. He threatens to torpedo US ships now, to launch his U-boats in dead earnest and to invade us — we shall see. There is talk of the use of poison gas by the

Germans. This is certainly alarming some people but on the coast this horror is not so possible although the invasion threat is extra horrid here. Wardens are going around telling everybody to have a bag ready for a sudden departure.

NAZI AIRMEN BURIED IN SUSSEX CHURCHYARD

Protests by residents of Steyning, Sussex, against the burial of five German airmen in the village churchyard did not prevent the funeral there yesterday. Above, military Guard of Honour presents arms as the coffins pass. The Nazis were fatally burned when their Heinkel bomber crashed on the outskirts of the village on Sunday night.

February 1st Mr Churchill has visited Portsmouth and he made a most cheery and hopeful speech. He actually said: 'We shall pull through, we cannot tell when or how, but we shall come through. None of us has any doubts whatever.' This is the first time he has been so optimistic. He usually warns us of a dire time ahead of us. Our carol party gave its party to the ex-Service men at Gifford House. The war has upset many of these men and matron said several had died without putting up much of a struggle in consequence. They'd imagined they'd fought in 1914–18 to prevent this sort of thing happening again in a lifetime.

February 9th It's been a very full life domestically this week as we are still maidless. A lot of the young girls are munition making.

Benghazi was captured two days ago. This is *terrifically important*. Here invasion threats are still very much to the fore. The greengrocers are a very sorry sight — very little fruit and no onions. Leeks 4d or 5d each. Plenty of potatoes and carrots though. Sweet shops are shut for days at a time and one

t, Thursday, Jan. 23, 1941 5

From All Quarters

PROTEST ON NAZI AIRMEN'S BURIAL

A number of residents in the Sussex village of Steyning are opposed to the burial of five German airmen in the churchyard. The Nazis were fatally burned when their Heinkel bomber crashed in flames on the outskirts of the village on Sunday night. Mr. H. F. Holland, a member of the British Legion, said yesterday: "Why should they lie among our loved ones? They came over here to wreck our homes and murder our kith and kin." The vicar of Steyning, Rev. E. W. Cox, stated that there could be no question that the men should be buried in the churchyard. He declined to give the time of the funeral and added, "We do not want a crowd."

January 23rd

jeweller only opens for the mornings — no Swiss stuff, I suppose. But very few air-raids over England these days — apparently the weather accounts for the lack, bad visibility and bogged aerodromes.

February 13th   Mother's seventy-third birthday! We all gave her an electric coffee percolator and it works beautifully. The Balkan situation looks very bad. Germany has a terrific number of troops in Rumania, some even in Bulgaria. Jugoslavia and Bulgaria are in a quandary, Turkey is definitely ready to resist. Japan is not behaving amicably either and the papers suggest Hitler is wanting to spread the war. Mussolini has met Pétain and Franco but the outcome of the meeting is not clear.

February 16th   Worked hard on the allotment in the afternoon and on to the canteen at 4.30.

February 22nd   Up to London to a Massage meeting. The bomb damage is very extensive but the surprising thing is how used one gets to the sight of it. St Paul's has escaped in a most remarkable manner as *all around* there is much desolation. Met Copper for lunch and afterwards we went to the British Museum. There is very little left to see as all the most precious things have been stored in safer places. I caught the 6.28 back and as there was no 'alert' the train had its lights on. There were several men in the carriage who'd been to a football match and their conversation was a great relief and contrast to the confounded old war! They'd got a huge packet of real *ham* sandwiches and I was offered one — you can't get ham these days. In fact things really are a bit difficult. Seville oranges are supposed to be in but no extra sugar is allowed. Marmalade is unobtainable at the moment. The fruit and sweet shops are the most desolate.

February 23rd   Worthing made £590,000 during its War Weapons Week! Barbed wire is springing up all over the place in the town. It must be very difficult for all the blind people here. The front is absolutely blocked by terrific quantities of it.

March 4th   Ken, Helen and I offered to be 'blood donors' when there was an appeal just before the war in August 1939 and we were placed in 'A' group; as this is not the 'universal' group 'O' we shall not be called on so frequently apparently. There were many donors and four doctors were extracting the stuff. Most of the Worthing blood goes up in refrigerators to London but there is sometimes an emergency call from a nearer city — Portsmouth and Southampton for instance. I had no bad after effects although several people nearly fainted. We had a hot drink and rested for fifteen minutes. We were told not to work again that day but as I'd not made suitable arrangements, I did, and all was well. To the Report Centre at

"All I can say is, it's either Grace going upstairs or the barrage, NOT Daphne coming downstairs or H.E."

"That will be all, Watkins, and if you hear the church bells, let me know."

These two jokes from the current number of Punch will probably be difficult to understand in the future. The church bells refer to the fact that we never hear them now as they are to be pulled only if there are airborne enemy troops landed on British soil.

5.30. I'd just got to bed at 9.30 when the siren sounded and I had to arise until 3 am! No other excitement though.

March 8th I heard that Worthing produced five and a half gallons of blood last Tuesday! The doctors were very pleased with the result.

I took an electric carpet sweeper and 'did' all the carpets at Shakespeare Rd hostel. It may have to close if the ban on movement around the coast is very strict.

CAR WHICH CRASHED INTO BRISTOL CRATER

This unusual accident occurred in Bristol when a motorist could not stop in time to avoid diving into a bomb crater in the middle of the road.

March 9th A great blow today. Following on the proposed ban on Worthing, it is now official that there is to be a 'voluntary' evacuation of school children. Ken and family will be going to a 'north midland' locality. What to do about his allotment!

March 12th The evacuation of the schools is causing a great stir naturally in the town. Ken came in to tea and seems fairly reconciled to it all. Some parents are very up in arms. President Roosevelt signed the famous 'Lease and Lend' Bill today.

March 19th Help! I've not written this old diary for nearly a week. It's the allotment's fault! The weather has been so good that I've gone up most evenings and got too tired digging to write the diary. The two oldish men on the next plot have helped me a bit as they are taking over a bit of Ken's plot which is already dry. There is a very friendly spirit up there and I hope to learn a lot. One of the men on the allotment wrote a 'poem' and dedicated it to me! Here are some extracts:

> I'm sure twill interest you all to know it,
> I've blossomed out into a full blown Poet:
> And though it sound ambitious, well, it may be
> My resting place might be Westminster Abbey:
> Packed midst the noble dead in Poet's Corner
> With all good diggers as a mighty mourner
> And graceful Latin 'neath my noble bust (shall say)
> 'Here lieth an illustrious Briton's dust' (some day),
> And should the sad event occur in summer
> Place on my grave a wreath of Scarlet Runner.
>
> And now, this year, I have such paltry onions,
> It pains me more than my two vicious bunions.
> (Forgive me please for using this last line
> But I can get no other word to rhyme.)
> Lord Woolton to my mind is quite a hero,
> Contrasted with that other German Nero:
> But he would be a conqueror it seems,
> Who could present Black Fly to our Broad Beans.
> We're living now on coupons and on points,
> And not on gory steak, or greasy joints:
> I know a lady now whose figure
> Proves that the Milo de Venus was a digger,
> So take to digging, not as a source of wealth,
> But England, home and beauty and for health.
> Though meatless meals may lack your special gravy,
> Just think of how you spare our matchless Navy.
> And when you hanker for a plate of veal:
> Think of the waste that finds you such a meal —
> A calf is after all a future cow
> So to the vegetarian I'll bow . . .

Roosevelt has made a magnificent speech, pledging fullest help for Britain and Allies — 'planes, ships, food, tanks'. The public is being warned still again about what to do if invasion does take place. A pamphlet is to be delivered to every householder with full details. The capital of British Somaliland, Berbera, has been recaptured and all goes well for us on all Africa fronts especially in Abyssinia. Nightly bombings both over England and over Germany are taking place with almost monotonous regularity. Last week we brought down over forty Nazi bombers at night! The moon was full and bright, which helped enormously. Merseyside, Clydeside and Hull have been badly bombed with over 1,000 deaths in Scotland. The 'Battle of the Atlantic' is being waged remorselessly — our losses are heavy every week from U-boats, surface raiders and bombers — *terrible* for our sailors. Women of twenty-one and twenty-two are to register now. Kit phoned to say she's been appointed to the managership of the Chelsea Housing Department. London had its worst raid last night.

April 1st The talk and newspapers are jubilant over the bloodless revolution in Belgrade which has blotted out Jugo-slavia's agreement with Germany. Prince Paul, the Regent, resigned and the young King Peter assumed full regal responsibility — the ministers who signed the Axis pact have been arrested. People even say quite seriously it may be in answer to the National Day of Prayer last Sunday — a difficult problem. I've started planting my early potatoes in the allotment. There were bombs at 2 pm and later we heard five had landed on the golf course!

Miss Kathleen Strange, daughter of Mrs M. Strange, of 13 Langton-road, an old girl of Worthing Girls' High School, has just been appointed Housing Manager to the Chelsea Borough Council (See next column).

Worthing Woman's Important Post

CONGRATULATIONS to Miss Kathleen Strange on her appointment as Housing Manager to Chelsea Borough Council.

Miss Strange comes from a very well known Worthing family and was once a student at the High School. She continued her studies at London University, and by a coincidence her first five years' work connected with housing management was at Chelsea, so she now returns to the district where she had most of her training.

The post is an important one, particularly at the present time, when the area includes the re-housing of many bombed-out tenants. There is, of course, an increasing demand for intelligent and well trained women in this occupation, as it certainly comes under the heading of practical social welfare work.

April 5th Lyons have ½ lb packets of pastry and unless you get there at 8 am you can't get any! A man had even cycled in from Rustington to get some. The famous home-made sweet shop at Broadwater 'Luffs' was open when I passed this morning so I went in and got a whole pound — still only 2/4d. Miss Luff is said to make all the sweets herself. Two hours later it was shut — the whole month's supply sold out. Went to the Wooltons' Cafe in Lyndhurst Rd and had a wonderful 'communal meal'. Soup 1d, choice of meat (I had liver and sausage) and two vegetables 5d, choice of pudding (rice or sultana batter) 2d and cup of tea 1d. The public is being encouraged to eat there but one feels one should leave it to the needy. Unobtainable at the moment are onions, oranges, lemons, grapefruit and marmalade. Rare commodities are bird seed, cheese, chocs, sweets, biscuits, tomato soup, eggs, meat and dried fruit.

April 6th Germany has invaded Jugoslavia and Greece but both countries are standing firm. Sir Kingsley Wood, the Chancellor of the Exchequer, has brought in the budget and income tax has gone up to 10/– in the pound — terrific. He looks so benign too! Mother's made a sweet little smock to be raffled in aid of funds for Mrs Sangster's 'Bombed-out Working Party'.

May 3rd For four weeks I have had acute neuritis in my right arm thanks to 'digging for victory' in the north-east

64

GAS WITHOUT TEARS

PICTURE that points a moral, taken during Kingston's tear-gas test. How people not so prepared were affected is told, right...

WARNING
TEAR GAS
IS BEING
DISCHARGED

wind in the evening! — so the news has had to be put down in tabloid form.

Bad Items first. After a heroic struggle Jugoslavia has collapsed and the young King Peter and ministers have managed a dangerous escape. We have suffered a setback in Libya owing to our forces being needed so badly in Greece. Germany is threatening to overrun Spain to attack the west end of the Mediterranean.

Better News USA help becoming more and more a reality. Abyssinia all but wrested from the Italians. Terrific RAF raids on German naval bases, especially on Brest where the two powerful raiders, the *Scharnhorst* and the *Gneisenau* are being forced to keep in dock. A most remarkable evacuation of our forces from Greece.

Personal and Local News The Battersby's only son has been killed fire watching in Coventry where there was another terrible raid just before Easter. Ken writes very happily from his evacuation centre in Newark. Mr Frampton has sown my second early potatoes and main crop, etc for me in the allotment. Milk has been rationed. Paper has been further reduced — the *Telegraph* is down to a double sheet on some days and is now 1½d.

May 4th   Mother and I ate one *small* orange between us today! Lovely! They were thirty-six for 1/– before the war. We decided the skin must not be wasted so it's to be grated and used in a baked pudding! Cooking is very difficult and monotonous these days.

May 6th   The defence of Tobruk continues. The Emperor Haile Selassie re-enters his capital, Addis Ababa, in triumph, exactly five years after his exile from his country. There was an interesting by-election at a Birmingham constituency today. There were three candidates: a government man, a Peace Pledge Unionite and an Independent Reprisal Candidate. Both the latter only polled 1,000-odd votes and the government man had a majority of 19,000. It's good that the reprisal man had so little support.

May 8th   There was a big debate in the House of Commons yesterday and a vote of confidence taken: 447 for and three against! Mr Churchill summed up most confidently. Mr Wendell Wilkie has made a wonderful speech in New York urging Roosevelt to *convoy* the USA munitions to us.

May 10th   Did two hours digging up of the lawn for extra root crops. It's still very cold and there was a severe frost last night — I do hope my new potatoes haven't suffered. Today is the first anniversary of the Nazi aggression on Holland. Queen Wilhelmina broadcast a very good message (in English) on the nine o'clock news. Now that Haile Selassie is back in his capital hopes are high for the others.

May 12th The House of Commons, British Museum and Westminster Abbey were hit last night, two mayors were killed while fire fighting and two women ambulance drivers were also killed. There was a big casualty roll. No news from Kit yet. Hitler's deputy — Hess — is reported missing from an aeroplane. Cause?

May 13th *Most extraordinary news.* Hess has landed in Scotland! Everyone is talking about it and the most wild surmises are being put forward. Nazis say he has been suffering from a progressive disease for some time and for this reason he was forbidden ever to fly a plane. Mr Fadden, the New Zealand premier, remarks that Hess *has been* suffering, but is now cured! The disease being Nazism! Anyhow the whole world is agog and we listen in to every bulletin. He's at present in Glasgow with a broken ankle — the result of landing by parachute for the first time in his life!

May 14th Most of the news is still about Hess! Some people feel it's too good to be true — others say he's 'the first rat to leave the ship'! It looks as if he really has fled from Nazism which denotes a split in the Nazi party. Mother and I went to see a picture at the Odeon called *Escape* which is about two people escaping from Germany by plane — a curious coincidence in the circumstances. Apparently Hess had never flown a Messerschmitt before and had never 'baled out' previously. Our doctors are very insistent that he is sane — Nazi radio reverses the diagnosis!

May 16th We were just going to sleep when we heard a terrific amount of gunfire. We looked out of the window and saw a Nazi bomber crash in flames on the Downs — a terrifying sight with terrific explosions as the bombs went off. We heard later that all four crew were killed and burned. A terrible death but very quick.

May 18th This looks a nice peaceful picture to start off this new book — the sixth. Who knows but that peace may have been proclaimed before I've finished writing it. From the headlines, however, the world seems to be in a most ghastly state. Here are the *Sunday Times* headlines: 'Britain takes off the gloves — Vichy now an open accomplice of Axis Powers', 'Nazis bombed in Iraq', '500 Germans captured in desert thrust: counter-attack at Tobruk', 'The Premier and Hess — Keeping Nazis guessing', '6,065 killed in April air-raids, including 680 children'.

Radio Times

. HALF THE BATTLE of the Atlantic will be won by the farm workers in the fields of Britain, on whose skill depends so much of our food supply. The programme tonight at 10.30 tells the story of the work of farmers of this country from the harvest of last year to the spring of 1941.

May 22nd I thought I would mention food today. It is the most talked about subject now that Hess is stale! I actually brought Mother some salt-cod from Godalming but she wasn't very keen! I was lucky today and bought ½ lb of currants quite by chance. I had posted a parcel of flowers to one of Kit's bombed tenants and the man who also has a grocer's shop asked if I'd care to have some! I was lucky last Sunday too as Frammie, the nurseryman, gave me six ripe tomatoes and they are about 5/– a lb in the shops.

May 23rd A terrible battle is being fought in and for Crete. We have command of the sea and the Nazis have command of the air. Dive bombing and other ghastly actions are taking place day and night. Our relations with the Vichy government are becoming increasingly strained — the Navy has seized a large French tanker.
 I went to the YMCA where we were fairly busy.

May 24th Hess is in the news again! He says he wants better food and to be treated as befits his high rank! General Smuts has been made a Field Marshal on his seventy-first birthday. He is a very outstanding figure of this war. On the nine o'clock news we heard the sad news of the sinking of HMS *Hood*, the biggest warship in the world. A freak shot burst in the magazine and the boat blew up with 1,300 men on board. Few are expected to survive. I called on an ex-patient who I seemed to remember had her husband on the *Hood*. The husband had previously been torpedoed on the *Ark Royal* and survived. He leaves two small boys.

May 25th Mother remarked as she set out for church: 'Now which shall I take this morning — my gas mask or my umbrella?' Here are two poems. The first from today's *Sunday Times* and the second from this week's *Punch*:

POSTSCRIPT

The bright green leaves, this May, dance on.
Though homes and monuments have gone:
And hideous, gaping wounds hard by
Are vaulted by an azure sky.
Concealing heartbreak, there's a smile
Among the patient, homeless file
Who, knowing not, reveal a soul
Of which no foe can take its toll.
In death is life, immortal, strong
This travail will not last o'erlong
And something, finest, greatest yet,
Will come through blood and tears and sweat.

W. Spenser Lemming

1941

AFTER HESS

Nothing I think about this war
Can surprise me any more —
Sit down, dear Lindbergh, over there —
Let Mussolini have a chair —
Are there enough sardines today
For Quisling — if he comes to stay?
You heard no doubt that Darlan fell
Down from the skies at Camberwell
And Pétain in a tiny boat
Came up the Thames and left a note
And schoolboys on the village green
Reported they had found Stalin —
The air is full of flying sheikhs —
Laval has landed near the Lakes —
But I'm engaged. Don't bother me
When Matsuoka comes to tea
So that is Goering, is he dead?
Then leave him in the potting shed.
I think the small spare room should do
For Himmler and for Goebbels too.
I have to be on watch tonight
For louts who set the roof alight.

Evoe

May 26th Lord Kindersley announced the
London War Weapons Week total tonight
£125,000,000! Not bad! The *Hood* which sank
on Saturday (there were only three survivors)
cost £6,000,000 and the Americans are hoping
their government will give us their new battleship in its place. There's another fright over
possible invasion again. The Worthing Mayor
invited all his 'Mayor's Canteen' workers to
tea at the Town Hall today. Quite fun and a
good tea!

May 27th I was up at Mrs Wenban-Smith's at one o'clock and heard the news — 'The *Bismark* has been sunk'. This is the Nazis' new 35,000-ton warship which sank the *Hood* three days ago and has been chased ever since. It was claimed to be unsinkable. There were 100 survivors out of a probable 1,500. The hunting down of the *Bismark* was a wonderful feat by the RAF and Navy — the *Hood* hit her, planes crippled her and a cruiser finally sank her.

The Queuesling

AN old lady out shopping with her basket saw a queue and from force of habit attached herself to it. After a quarter of an hour, having made very little progress, she asked her neighbour what they were queueing up for.

"Blood transfusion," was the reply.

PETERBOROUGH.

I was discussing this with Dorothy Macpherson who capped it with her own experiences in Woolworth's one day this week. She saw a queue and asked the woman at the end of it what it was for. 'I don't know' was the reply. 'Well,' said Dorothy, 'if you'll keep my place I'll go and enquire.' She asked the assistant what the queue was for and the girl said 'It's for biscuits — but they've not arrived here yet'!

June 4th Reports are coming in about the pathetic evacuation of our troops from Crete. The trouble was lack of air support but even so 15,000 got safely away. The Vichy government are becoming more and more pro-Nazi and allowing the Germans entry into Syria. This is bad. The Americans are becoming more and more pro-British! Everyone's talking about the clothing ration and congratulating themselves if they've just bought some clothes.

June 8th Mollie's garden looks wonderful and there seem to be hundreds of birds and rabbits. On the drive back from her house we gave lifts to two soldiers — a private and an officer. They had to sit carefully as we brought back over 100 eggs and flowers and some soot for my allotment! The officer was returning from seven days' leave in Scotland.

June 12th A terrifically noisy night, ending up with bed shaking by bombs dropped at Goring about daybreak. The Allies progressing well in Syria. Nazis are reported massing 130 divisions on the *Russian* border . . .? The Free French have reached Damascus. In a German air-raid over England last night leaflets were dropped telling us we should starve next winter.

June 21st At 4.30 am the Germans attacked the Russians — there had been no ultimatum, no demands even! The fighting front is over 2,000 miles long, from Finland to the extreme south. Unfortunately Finland feels bound once again to fight Russia. The USA has frozen all German and Italian moneys and announced the closing of all German consulates — a drastic step.

June 28th   Now the evenings are so light (blackout is after 11 pm) I either work on the allotment or in the garden. The allotment is looking wonderful and I cut 2 lb of spinach today — the first fruits! King Peter of Jugoslavia has arrived safely in England. He was at school here for a short time just before his father was killed. There are now the governments of six foreign countries established here — Norway, Holland, Free France, Czechoslovakia, Belgium and Jugoslavia. In Britain a wonderful new invention has been made known to the public as 'radio location'. The Women's Auxiliary Air Force girls are used for it and do it well.

June 30th   Glorious weather. The Russian and German reports are conflicting and it is doubtful which side is doing what! Anyhow terrible battles are raging all along the front and losses on both sides must be tremendous. I dug my first early potatoes but they are small and need rain — only 1¼ lb on two roots.

July 5th   I went up to London for a Chartered Society of Massage and Medical Gymnastics meeting and a lecture. Kit met me for lunch and afterwards we cycled miles through London streets. A glorious day and the population looked much better than three months ago. In Hyde Park there is a central dump for rubble, etc — it's a young mountain with a road over it. I wonder how many houses have helped make it — thousands? Next to the mountain were the bowlers playing hard! Hundreds were bathing in the Serpentine and allotments abound everywhere! I bought some tennis balls (they are *very* scarce) at 19/6d a dozen! We called on Aunt Dot, Mother's younger sister — she is a doctor and going to the big RAF hospital at East Grinstead working on burns. I forgot to take my gas mask and identity card and two policemen were on the barrier at Worthing station when I got back but they let me through when I showed them my National Savings card which had my address on it.

July 10th   The Syrian war front is showing signs of coming to an end. The RAF is continuing its powerful offensives against the German industries — few Nazi raids over this country are being experienced. We've had two alerts this week but they were the first for twelve days. The USA is taking over Iceland — this is a most important feature, as it will aid us in the Battle of the Atlantic and free our men from Iceland. The Russians appear to be holding the German onslaught but the two communiqués are very conflicting. Driving back from Mollie's I picked up various people en route including three very nice school children — London Docks' evacuees. They spoke very nicely and had good billets. They've been away from their homes since September 1939. The RAF have made 128 raids on Germany and enemy occupied countries in seventeen days.

July 13th   We were told on the nine o'clock and one o'clock news that a most important item of news would be announced. Some people thought it might be the announcement of America's entry into the war. Actually it was a treaty made between Russia and Britain announcing a definite alliance.

Rain at last! Lovely.

July 17th   Mollie went back after tea, the car laden with rabbit food (oddments from the allotment and garden) and such things as tomatoes — 6 lb at 1/– a lb. She has to queue just to get a lb at Godalming. She also took a chocolate cake for the boys, lime juice, etc. My allotment peas are finished — I've picked over 20 lb from 6d of seed! It's very annoying for Ken and Helen who are having to pay 12/– a week for vegetables at Southwell.

July 19th   I went up to London for a CSMMG meeting. Met Kit in the lunch hour and we went to her allotment in Battersea Park where I planted her leeks and thinned out her carrots. London looked much tidier and I was surprised so much building repair is going on. I went into the undamaged part of Westminster Abbey — the east end is all scaffolding. Kit and I returned by the 7.25 and there was a bobby on the barrier! But Kit got through!

July 20th   This is V Sunday for Churchill's victory salute! A big campaign is afoot on the continent. Even we put Vs on our windows and Kit wore one on her bike! Childish? Well the whole war is founded on the weak. Verses of childhood — 'you've got something I want'. 'Oh, have I?' — result, blows.

July 28th   Attacks and counter-attacks continue on the Russian front. Where the Russians have to give up ground Stalin has ordered everything to be destroyed rather than let anything fall into German hands — machinery, oil, harvests. It's called the 'scorched-earth policy'. Japan continues to make ugly faces and the USA is doing the same back. The Japanese have landed in Indo-China. Will there be another declaration of war? A Nazi bomber was brought down at Partridge Green last night, after lightening its load of bombs in a field luckily.

July 31st   The Russo–Polish agreement has been signed and 200,000 Poles set free to fight against the Nazis and so this confusing war goes on. The RAF are now using the famous American 'flying fortresses'. They fly over seven miles up — terrible — deadly. The Duke of Kent has flown to Canada — it took him only nine hours. The Worthing Home Guard had a big practice today, co-operating with the military here. There was much amusement in Chapel Rd where the Home Guard men were aiming bags of soot at some target or other.

August 6th   Japan's attitude still ugly — she's probably being prodded by the Nazis. The Russians are resisting the strong Nazi efforts in the Ukraine. Harvesting is proceeding at great pace and what can't be stored in safe places is burnt. Britain and USA have both warned Japan not to invade Thailand.

August 9th   Roger is seven today and Mother has found about ½ lb of *icing* sugar in the back of the cupboard! Lovely. We shall take the cake to him on Sunday. I saw thirty-six fighters in formation setting forth for a raid this morning. They join other fighters over Kent and the bombers too join them there. Mussolini's youngest son has been killed flying in Italy. There has been a consignment of oranges in Worthing! I got two = 1 lb = 9d. We've not had any for eight months.

August 10th   Mother and I and Kit drove up to Mollie's to celebrate Roger's seventh birthday. We had a lovely dinner of duck and green peas! Called in at the Mills' on the way back for coffee. Gladys is home — she's a State Registered nurse in the Navy and has been on a troopship taking men and munitions to the Middle East. Coming back she helped bring evacuees from Syria, Greece and Malta — all sorts of nationalities. The boat also brought a cargo of oranges and she was allowed a crate! She gave us twelve — six are for the sale next Thursday — we retaliated and gave her three eggs! Mollie had given us twelve to bring back — everyone is resorting to the old fashioned system of bartering.

Issued on behalf of the   *Ministry of Transport*

IMMOBILISATION OF VEHICLES IN THE EVENT OF INVASION

EVERY OWNER of a motor vehicle should be ready, in the event of invasion, to immobilise his car, cycle or lorry the moment the order is given.   Failure to act promptly would give the enemy the chance to provide himself with transport.

It is important that owners of vehicles should understand now what they have to do, and satisfy themselves that they can carry out the order at any time without delay.

With a view to helping them, the Ministry of Transport gives the following information and advice on what they must do when informed by the Police or through the Civil Defence services that immobilisation of vehicles has been ordered in their area :

PETROL VEHICLES

Remove distributor head and leads and empty the tank or remove the carburettor.

DIESEL-ENGINED VEHICLES

Remove the injection pump and connection.

Hide the parts removed well away from the vehicle.

[P.T.O.

August 14th I got up early and cycled to the allotment to get some vegetables for our 'Bring and Buy' Sale in aid of the Mayor's Rest Centre. I brought some lovely carrots, lettuces, beetroots and marrows. The sale was a wonderful success — we got over £42! Harold Frampton brought us tomatoes, onions, beans and grapes from his greenhouses — grapes are fetching 12/6d a lb nowadays! Mrs Claff sent us two chickens and we got over £4 for them at an auction and weight guessing. The Mills' oranges brought in 10/6d. Rationed foods — clothes and foodstuffs — are not allowed to be sold at sales like this but a few things turned up! Unfortunately the police have been casting doubts on Londoners entering a banned area. Patients are allowed to come to a *convalescent* home but this is only a *rest* centre! All England was excited at a very important announcement which was advertised for 3 pm. Mr Attlee, the deputy PM, was to make it. Why not Mr Churchill? Because he and Mr Roosevelt are meeting in person somewhere! To discuss peace aims.

Drawn by a Czech cartoonist a month ago.

Drawn by a Czech cartoonist a month ago.

August 16th Britain and US have made an offer to Stalin. There is to be a three-power conference in Moscow. In the meantime, aid of all sorts is to be sent to Russia. Hitler has ordered: 'Moscow at any price.' The British and US co-operation discussed by Roosevelt and Churchill on board HMS *Prince of Wales* is a declaration of war by the USA in all but the actual deed.

August 18th The Russians are retreating in the Ukraine but at the same time are preparing for a winter campaign — just what the Nazis want to avoid. President Roosevelt is asking Congress for an extra £2,500,000,000 for 'Lease and Lend' to Britain. Mr Churchill is back in Britain having visited Iceland en route home! Milk is to be rationed very heavily — adults are to have only two-and-a-half pints a *week*. I queued in Marks and Spencers and got 1 lb of sultanas today!

August 22nd Iran has admitted thousands of Nazi agents into her territory and is being truculent in her attitude towards a British protest. I drove the mobile YMCA canteen to Shoreham beach this evening. I felt a bit scared as it is all heavily landmined these days and there have been a few fatal accidents. However all went well and we did brisk trade for about an hour. Bungalow Town in Shoreham, mostly holiday homes, is no more — the bungalow and houses proved troublesome to the gunners who fire into the sea from the Downs and so they have all had to be demolished.

August 25th On the one o'clock news it was reported that British and Russian troops had entered Iran. The population welcomes the entry.
 Dorothy went blackberrying today and brought back 6 lb of

good fruit. Prices of wild blackberries, which are plentiful, will be controlled from Friday at 5½d a pound retail and 4d wholesale. Pickers will be paid £28 per ton. The *Daily Telegraph* reports that school children are to be encouraged to gather the wild fruit and housewives will be asked by the Ministry of Food to make the fullest use of them. Reservations with retailers for the season's supply of onions — 2 lb a head — must be made during the week September 1st to 6th. Those failing to register with their greengrocer will not get any. Laval, the Vichy France politician, is reported to have been shot and badly wounded along with several other 'Quislings'.

August 28th RAF raided Cologne on Tuesday night with terrific damage. Let's hope the cathedral is unscathed but it's very near the station. Mother and I went to a garden party in aid of Mrs Sangster's Working Party for bombed cities. It brought in about £40. Since February 21st the party has actually made over 1,500 garments and twenty big parcels have been sent off. We called on the Fleischmanns in the evening. Mrs Fleischmann told us that this time last year, fearing invasion, she'd burnt many letters, papers etc which she was now regretting. She told us that when the Nazis were threatening Czechoslovakia she cooked for two weeks on books, beautiful books, which would have told against them when the Nazis arrived.

September 3rd Today marks the second anniversary of the outbreak of war and roughly the present position is that Russia, although gradually losing ground, is putting up such terrific resistance as to throw the Nazi timetable out. The Battle of the Atlantic is being won. The RAF continues its offensive. The Nazi air war has been in a quiescent state for some months over here — only occasional night raids have taken place throughout the summer. The Italians have lost pretty well all their African empire. The Nazi 'infiltration' into the Middle East has been checked decisively — Syria, Iran and Iraq being under our control. All enemy occupied nations are seething with revolt against the Nazi 'new order'.

September 14th Ken and family arrived back from the evacuation in Newark and today they all came to lunch — quite like old times! I've been busy on the allotment — digging up the rest of the main crop potatoes and onions. Sacks are unprocurable now so I bought some hessian yesterday and Mother's made three good sacks. So far over 30 lbs of ripe tomatoes from the garden.

September 15th A large RAF 'wing' has arrived in Russia. Machines have already been sent but now some of our men are there too. A 'wing' is an indefinite term and was used to keep the Nazis guessing. The Nazis are doing everything they can to break the Russians before the winter arrives — already bad weather is hampering them. Kit sent a lovely food parcel containing chocolate, suet, sultanas, corn flakes, salad dressing — all of which are difficult down here. The Shah of Iran has abdicated — he was pro-Axis and was not fulfilling our terms.

September 18th US Navy is now definitely convoying their goods to us and will 'shoot first' if necessary. The new Shah of Iran, Mohammed Riza Shah Pahlavi, son of the old Shah, promises to co-operate with us and to see that all Nazis are removed.

September 21st Today is a Sunday devoted to thanksgiving and intercession for the RAF. It's about a year ago that they were fighting in, and winning, the Battle of Britain. The fate of Kiev is still in the balance — fighting is assuming ghastly proportions. Mother and I to tea at Hilda's — wartime teas are very plain now. Yesterday no butter at all at the Moores' and today no cake at Hilda's!

September 27th I went up to London to attend the Annual Massage Conference and bought a *Times* for the journey. It's 3d now! But it has eight pages against the Saturday four of the *Telegraph*. Specially interesting articles were accounts of the 'Contribution of Science to World Order', 'The Soviet and the churches' reporting Mr Maisky's claim that religion is very much alive in Russia and another article reporting the growing resistance of the Czechs against the Nazis, organising 'go-slows' and acts of sabotage.

September 29th Visited the Wartime Allotment Show at the Town Hall today — *wonderful*. The heaviest marrow weighed 57 lb!

October 3rd Lying in bed this morning I was thinking of all the places I'd visited on the continent and I remembered my holiday in Stuttgart when I visited the Moses family in Esslingen. I was hoping it hadn't been bombed and to my surprise I read in this morning's paper that it had.

October 5th Some 1,500 sick and wounded German prisoners of war are on board two white hospital ships at Newhaven and negotiations are going on to form a neutral corridor across the Channel for twenty-four hours and exchange them at a German-occupied port in Northern France for 1,500 British prisoners in similar case. There is some hold-up. It seems the Germans want some civilian internees returned. Some people wonder if the demand is for Hess!

October 8th The *Daily Telegraph* reported another hitch to the exchange of prisoners and in the Stop Press a definite

Worthing Gazette, September 17th

Can The Church Help The Germans?

The important part the Church must play in reconstruction after the war was a topic of keen discussion at two conferences on the "Church and Reconstruction" arranged by Shelley-road Congregational Church, Worthing.

Among the opinions expressed were:
That the Church of Jesus Christ should be the first to enter both the occupied and enemy countries immediately on the cessation of hostilities.

That the British Christian Council, which comprises all the non-Roman churches in the country, should take the initiative in co-operation, if possible, with the Roman Catholic Church, in convening through the World Council of Churches a conference of all the Christian Churches in the world in order to focus the best Christian thought upon the issues which will be at stake.

That there should be an immediate rapprochement between the Christian Churches in this country and allied countries so that representatives of the Church should be the first to enter Germany and Italy to relieve famine, disease and general after-war distress.

It was also stated that the Shelley-road Congregational Church should give more active support to social and civic authorities in the town. This was agreed and arrangements were made accordingly.

Another suggestion was that individual Churches in this country should, as soon as conditions allowed, "adopt" individual churches in Germany and Italy and arrange for personal meetings between members, personal help and exchange of letters.

r. and Mrs. Churchill with French boys whom they ceived at 10, Downing-street yesterday. The boys caped from France by canoe and reached England last hursday after spending two nights and a day in the hannel. The Prime Minister's toast was "Free France."

e French lads who had ed the Channel from Occu- France in flimsy canoes, g out water with a sauce- evading German E-boats 'planes, met Mr. Churchill wning-street yesterday.

was the culminating aph of their adventure, and were flushed and excited they left No. 10.

s is what the 17-year-old navi- said :

'e did not want to stay and be itioned by the Germans, as id once before, when they made iblic schoolboys carry sand for heer pleasure of annoying us, ot for any practical purpose, so paired two Canadian canoes aited for favourable weather. hen our chance came we stole coupons from a shop and gave back in exchange for 20lb of . We put 30 pints of water d the canoes in a petrol can and ties, and 75 army biscuits.

30-HOUR VOYAGE

"We had a compass in each boat, and, helped by the polar star, we landed in England at the point we intended 30 hours after leaving France at midnight. We saw E-boats and a German 'plane, but they did not spot us. We paddled most of the way."

The youth added that German soldiers in occupied France listen-in each night to the B.B.C. They force the French families on whom they are billeted to switch in to London so that they themselves may listen. The German soldiers get drunk fre- quently. Invasion of England is now "out of fashion."

The boys thought that Mr. Churchill was splendid, even though he talked to them in English, which they did not understand. They said that he was shy—"like Gen. de Gaulle." But Mrs. Churchill spoke to them in French and they were charmed.

Before they left No. 10 Mr. Churchill, smoking a cigar, called a butler and a bottle of champagne was brought. Glasses were filled and in the garden of No. 10 the Prime Minister gave the toast "Vive la France!" Raising their glasses the young Frenchmen responded.

Telegraph and Morning Post, September 23rd

cancellation. One feels like weeping. Such high hopes last week and now despair of any exchange during the war.

October 10th To the Town Hall to hear a most interesting and inspiring speech given by Mr A V Alexander, the First Lord of the Admiralty. The First Lord takes such an interest in his sailors and his speech was devoid of any bitterness and revenge. He said he *could* tell us a lot of very encouraging facts but he wasn't going to! In the meantime the Nazis are hurrying up their offensive, this time with Moscow as their prize. The Russians are defending and contesting every inch of the soil. Mr Alexander says we are getting a great deal of war material over to Russia.

October 11th Uncle Bert took Dorothy and me to the Brigh- ton Symphony Concert. It seemed quite like old times. Quite a number of the forces both in the audience and in the orchestra itself. The concert ended up with Beethoven's V Symphony — the 'Victory' one!

Note the V... — postmark on this letter from Janet, Mr Ritter's fiancée, in Australia.

October 13th I've taken on my new allotment today! As I drove past Walton's fruit shop lo and behold a pile of oranges! I enquired if they were for sale for children only and they were, for children under six, so I cycled up to Ken's after tea and told him he could get some for John and Richard as long as he took the children's ration books. The fruit shops look very nice now — plenty of apples at 9d a lb, Cox's Orange Pippins are 1/3d a lb — all controlled prices. Our RAF made its most extensive raid on Germany last night — over 300 bombers being used. Targets as far south as Nuremberg were attacked.

October 15th A Nazi radio voice has been butting in to the news for the last three days. It's absolutely *childish*. He is not nearly quick enough and is devoid of all wit. Tonight all he could think to say was 'That's a lie' and 'of course' and then 'That's a lie' again — it's too feeble to do any good for the enemy. Dora and I had a good hour's tennis in the Denton Gardens. The courts are near the sea and are surrounded by barbed wire and notices saying 'Danger Mines'.

October 17th The Moscow situation is very critical. The Soviet government has removed to some other destination. Japan's cabinet has resigned and an uglier one has been formed.

October 31st I listened to 'Colonel Britton' giving his weekly talk to his 'V Army' in occupied countries. He urged them to continue with their 'go-slow' movement and also implored them not to give up any blankets or rugs to the Nazis. Today at four o'clock for five minutes, French people everywhere stood in silence in remembrance of the hundred hostages shot dead by the Nazis as a reprisal for the shooting of two Nazi officers.

November 1st To London for a CSMMG meeting in the morning. Kit and I gave our tea party to all the Chelsea people who've spent holidays in Worthing after being bombed, thirty-six of them. It was great fun and most entertaining. We went to supper with Miss Rattenbury who won the George Medal for driving injured people to safety in a bad blitz. Kit pointed out how improved many places in London are after the removal of the railings for armament production.

November 2nd To church at eleven o'clock. Congregations in London are naturally very depleted and of course many churches are completely destroyed. I came back to Worthing in the evening armed with a few wartime trophies: two oranges and the skin of another, chocolate for Ken's boys, porridge,

and my one and only extravagance for the whole winter! A new hat costing 49/6d — awful! When I got home Mother told me of a horrid raid in Haynes Rd — seven people killed (including two children), thirty-six injured and over 700 houses and shops damaged by just two bombs but of very huge dimensions.

November 11th Today is Remembrance Day but the two minute silence is not being observed nowadays. Yesterday was Lord Mayor's Day in London and one of my patients saw the wartime procession of civil defence workers, contingents of British Dominion troops, as well as contingents of Free French, Polish, Norwegian, Dutch, Belgian and Czechoslovakians. Very impressive. I met a man with a dog this morning — the dog dashed up to me and wanted to be stroked. The man said he was one of the animals rescued from the latest air-raid; he was buried under débris for many hours and his mistress was killed. He rushes up to any woman to see if it's his old mistress.

November 12th Two crews of RAF bombers have been rescued in their rubber dinghies after being on the sea for over twenty-four hours. HMS *Cossack* has been sunk — it attained fame when it rescued our sailors from the *Altmark* in 1939. Mother finds it difficult thinking out meals — our meat ration is still 1/2d worth each per week (we're sure we had horse meat last week!) and it's difficult to get any offal. We did have half a calf's head last week which made some excellent brawn. Milk is rationed now and we get one pint a day. Sugar is 6 oz a week, butter 2 oz and margarine 4 oz, cheese 4 oz and 3 eggs a *month*! It's very difficult thinking out puddings and having visitors to meals. Other things which are difficult are all things to do with hairdressing — setting lotion, hair nets, hair pins, kirby grips, permanent waving appurtenances etc. Tinned fish and meats will be obtainable next week when the 'points' rationing comes into force. Dog meat is very erratic — Mike goes off every day somewhere (probably to the soldiers' billets) and comes back licking his chops! Jewellers are finding stock difficult, so are ironmongers. There is a great shortage of paper. We are urged to use as little fuel as possible. Chocolates and sweets are scarce but tobacco is more plentiful.

November 15th HMS *Ark Royal*, the aircraft carrier, has been sunk. The torpedoes from her aircraft's planes fatally slowed down the fugitive *Bismark*. She also shadowed the *Graf Spee*, gave brilliant service in the Norwegian campaign and fought the Italians on sea and shore. Only one man out of 1,600 was lost. Important news from the USA — by a majority of only sixteen it has been decided that US merchant ships shall be fully armed and will be allowed to enter belligerent waters. Many of the grocers' shops here are proudly displaying food that we haven't seen for a long time — tinned salmon, herrings, etc.

Daily Telegraph, August 27th

THE PRINCESSES IN THEIR GARDEN

A new photograph of Princess Elizabeth and Princess Margaret watching their pet chameleon. The Princesses have been taking a great interest in their vegetable plots in their garden where this photograph was taken. *Studio Lisa*

November 16th I took the car to forage for some cakes in West Worthing as Mrs Frampton had exhausted the East Worthing shops. Mother had a lovely Christmas parcel from Canada today — tinned cheese, butter, fruit juice, Callard and Bowser's fruit drops and tea. Ken and Helen to tea — they have given up a maid and find a little respite very pleasant occasionally! They've also given up telephone and smoking! Their boys, John and Richard, are very amusing — they don't like me to let the car's engine tick over if I stand still as it's 'wasting petrol'! They gave a 'concert' in aid of Mrs Churchill's Russian Red Cross Fund. It was awfully amusing — ½d and 1d seats and a collection which amounted to 3/10½d. There was a programme. Sen I — Tin Soldiers. Sen II — Elves. Sen III — Merry Wido Bally!

November 23rd Today the milk rationing came into force — each adult will get *two pints per week*. Now if there are tea parties, visitors will be asked to bring their milk as well as their saccharine! Not to mention their butter.

November 27th Terrific battles are being fought in Libya with big tank losses on both sides. Moscow is being threatened severely again, bloodshed and more bloodshed is the order of the day. The cut in our milk ration assumes paltry dimensions when viewed in the light of the sacrifices being made on the two chief battlefields.

December 6th The Finns have rejected our note to them asking where they stand and no answer has been received from Hungary and Rumania. We are now officially at war with these three countries. How difficult the history of this war will be for the children of the future. Britain nearly went to Finland's aid early in 1940 when Russia attacked her — now we are allied to Russia and fighting Finland. Today I drove the YMCA canteen to Shoreham and getting back earlier than usual Miss Thompson asked if I'd go to the Connaught Theatre to collect some books. She and I had to meet Cicely Courtneidge in person! It *was* a thrill. All this week Miss Courtneidge has been appealing for games, books, musical instruments etc for the AA and BB crews — our men who are in isolated spots. The YMCA was asked to collect the thousands of really good things that had been given. It took us one and a half hours loading and unloading. When I got home Mother had had a thrill too — Uncle Herbert had sent a cheque for £25 for us to use at Christmas time for needy cases! Lovely.

December 7th On the nine o'clock news — Japan has attacked US bases in Manila and the Hawaii Islands. So the war spreads. Mother told Mrs Wenban-Smith that our meat this week was half a leg of mutton, mostly bone. Mrs Wenban-

Smith told Mother: 'We had beef — hard as a rock!'

December 10th   Bad news from the Far East. One of our latest and most powerful battleships, the *Prince of Wales* (the one Mr Churchill sailed in to meet President Roosevelt two months ago) and an older ship, the *Repulse*, have both been sunk. Casualties are expected to be heavy. Nazis *withdraw on all Russian fronts*. Axis position in Libya is worsening. We had our usual carol practice tonight — eleven came and it went well.

SANTA CLAUS
_ a la mode !

Daily Mail

MANNEQUIN TRICKS NAZIS

CHEATED GESTAPO

By Daily Mail Reporter

ENGLISH internees in the German prison camps of France still talk of how 23-years-old June Bowman and her mother " gave the Gestapo the slip."

They still tell the story of their breakaway from an internment camp, and of their audacious drive through Occupied France.

The two women, first British civilians to escape from a Nazi camp, arrived in England recently.

Miss Bowman, a tall blonde, told me: " We lived in Paris for eight years before the war. I was a model at a gown shop. When war broke out I took up canteen work at the British Army social centre in the Champs Elysée.

" We got out of Paris when the Germans came in, but returned to our old apartment later. We lived in Paris under German rule for two months.

" Then one day the police called to arrest us. We were driven off to Besançon Camp, with 6,000 other women.

" Only the day before we arrived the camp had been occupied by thousands of soldiers. There was no proper accommodation for women.

Wore Army Boots

" Sanitary arrangements were dreadful. We had to sleep on straw —the same straw that the soldiers had slept on the previous night. It was a job to prevent ourselves becoming verminous.

" Fourteen of us lived and slept in a small, cold room. We lay on straw and were soon bitten all over.

" We had no proper clothes. We wore soldiers' overcoats and heavy Army boots to try to keep warm.

" If you had money you could buy food from the canteen. If not, you had to try to exist on the awful stuff they served up.

" We made plans to escape. After 11 weeks in the camp, the great day came. Everything went smoothly.

" We decided to go to Cannes. We were stopped several times, but managed to reach Cannes.

" I was hungry practically the whole of the time I was in France. There is very little to eat; the Germans seem to have taken it all."

JUNE BOWMAN.

June Bowman is my patient's (Mrs Chalkely's) grand-daughter. She and her mother had a hair-raising time coming home from France. They spent five months in Lisbon.

December 23rd   Startling news! Mr Churchill *is in the United States*. He is there to confer with the President on war strategy, etc. The Japs are bringing terrific pressure to bear on many British and US possessions in the Far East. 100,000 are attacking the Philippines. Hong Kong holds but it will have to fall eventually (and temporarily!). Sir Mark Young, the Governor, cables: 'I resist till I am captured.'

December 27th   We've had a really lovely Christmas. Moll and her two boys, Michael and Roger, arrived on Christmas morning — she'd already sent a turkey and Uncle Ted sent three pheasants! Food was good thanks to the Canadian and Australian parcels and my allotment! — 4 lbs of Brussels sprouts from it. Ken and family and Mrs Wenban-Smith and a Canadian soldier came too. Our carols brought in over £22. We all went to the *Forty Thieves* pantomime on Boxing Day and the boys *loved* it and made gorgeous remarks. There was quite a topical flavour to the jokes of course. The King broadcast on Christmas Day and Mr Churchill on Boxing Day. The war will be over in 1943 — according to Mr Churchill. A Canadian soldier has been shot and killed here over the holiday. They get rather fed up and have a drink and get out of hand. A sentry challenged and got a wrong answer or something and shot. The Worthing shops have suffered from much broken glass over the weekends — Hubbards have hastily rigged up a wooden contraption for protection. The men I've spoken to at the two canteens have been awfully decent — it's just a few who spoil it and give them a bad name.

LONDONER'S DIARY

VIGOROUS YOUNGSTER

1942

January 1st The year begins with success in Russia, Libya, on the Atlantic, in the air, but with withdrawals by the US and Britain and much bombing by the Japs in the Far East. All speeches speak of the increased chance of the Allies' victory within the next eighteen months. Very different from a year ago.

January 2nd The paper reported that Mr Churchill and the President attended a national day of prayer service. They went to Alexandria, a few miles from Washington and knelt together in a pew once used by George Washington. In his address the youthful rector of Alexandria's Christ Church, the Rev Edward R. Welles, criticised the United States and praised the British people for having displayed qualities on a national scale which were almost unique in history, and also for their genuine humility for past imperfections. Rev Welles declared: 'We have wanted other nations to pay the supreme price for human liberty while we gave them dollar credits. That is not the way of Jesus Christ. He endured the Cross and we as a nation must accept the cross. By far our greatest sin as a nation is the sin of international irresponsibility. We want our country and our people to have power and prestige and the pleasure of possessions, but we balk at the international responsibility those privileges impose.' The rector based his sermon on the President's proclamation asking the country to seek forgiveness of their shortcomings in the past. In the same paper was an article reporting a broadcast made over the German radio yesterday by Captain Wolfmittler, a spokesman of the Luftwaffe, who said: 'As after the last world war, the cry "Never again" will be heard after this war, but this time it will not be forgotten so easily. Behind it will stand many a man, woman and child. Behind it will stand the people who have looked total war in the face, people who know what it is all about. Those who know how near death can sometimes be, know what it means to live. Let us in the midst of the smoke of battle not forget this call for which all of us must be striving. Peace on earth and goodwill towards men. May this wish for the New Year be granted to all of us.'

January 3rd   Went to the canteen in the evening and had most interesting conversation with a Canadian from Edmonton. He thinks it a pity that we British do not make more efforts to harvest the untold natural wealth of Western Canada. We usually are not bold enough to take a risk but the Americans are and so are benefiting.

January 4th   In today's *Sunday Times* is a report of a speech Lady Astor made in London yesterday: 'Unless after the war Europe hands over some of its tasks to women, it will go from mess to mess. Hitler and Mussolini are going to see that their vision of what women are good for is all wrong. Women have a bigger task than to give birth to children to fight — they are here to give birth to the spiritual idea of the membership of God and brotherhood of man.'

January 7th   Spent evening at Ken's to let him and Helen go out to the pictures. Very black out and Helen tried to post a letter mistaking a man for a pillar box!

January 8th   There has been another 'commando' raid on a Norwegian base. I went to a party at the Mayor's Rest Home — quite good fun and a wonderful spread including dates and ginger! The ban on movement is coming into force again on February 15th and after that date no Londoner can come to Worthing. We think the hostel can be used for Sussex people in need of a rest.

January 11th   To the allotment — severe frost but managed quite a bit of digging. Came home to a lovely Sunday dinner of roast beef, Yorkshire pudding (made from a packet of 'batter flour' and some condensed milk), two veg (my own potatoes and cauliflower) and Christmas pudding. Then read in the *Sunday Times* about starvation in Greece where the sea route is closed to merchant ships. The Greek merchant fleet is bringing food to Britain. In Greece thousands of half-starved people are lying in the streets, too weak to move and many children who have lost their parents are dying of cold and hunger. With Uncle Herbert's fund's help Mother and I sent a sum of £3 3s 0d to the International Red Cross which is helping to distribute food sent to Greece for the Greeks.

January 13th   Weather turned *very* cold and snowy. One begins to realise how ghastly the conditions are on the Russian front. Many people say they *are* sorry for the German soldiers. To the Report Centre as usual — the central heating was very welcome!

January 14th   I went to Mr Loader's shop to collect some snaps; he was explaining to a Canadian soldier the difficulties he was working under. He'd sent a letter to the Ministry of

Supply urging that more photograph stuff should be released.
To make photography difficult is lowering to the morale and
he stated cases of soldiers' wives not being able to send snaps
of the babies and children to their husbands. Wars seem to be
made up of gigantic problems and trifles. The British withdrawal in Malaya continues and the Japs claim to be 130
miles from Singapore. There is much 'armchair' criticism of
our lack of success in the Far East. The fact is that it's not
possible for us to defend the whole world! There are many
schemes for saving paper, rubber, metal. Nothing is to be
wrapped in paper at the shops except a few commodities. I
bought six yards of pink flannel from Walter Bros today for

*Daily Telegraph,
January 13th*

ESCUING SURVIVORS OF A MERCHANT SHIP TORPEDOED IN MID-ATLANTIC

GRIPS ON KEELS
OF LIFEBOATS
TUES. *Jan 13*
NEW SAFETY DEVICE

Daily Telegraph Reporter

Official advice was issued by the
Ministry of War Transport yesterday
that lifeboats on all sea-going ships
should be equipped with under-water
grab-lines to serve as hand-holds for
men in the water should the boats
be overturned.

The fitting of such hand-holds was
advocated in THE DAILY TELEGRAPH
yesterday in a letter from a reader
after seeing the picture in Friday's
issue of three men clinging pre-
cariously to a capsized boat.

The Ministry advises that lifeboats
should be fitted with ropes passed
under the boats from gunwale to gunwale and knotted at intervals to
form grips. The lines should be
looped at the keels, to support the
arms of men who have clambered out
of the water. These lines could also
be used to right an overturned boat.

A dramatic photograph of three survivors of a merchant
ship, torpedoed in the Atlantic, as they were rescued by a
patrolling British warship. Utterly exhausted by their
ordeal, they still clung to the upturned lifeboat on which
they were found. Only one of them had enough strength
to grasp the line which was thrown to them. Another
picture on the Back Page.

84

Mother's working party and Sid (Sidney Walter) did it up in a piece of string! I had to give up twelve coupons.

On the wireless we heard Captain Balfour, Parliamentary Under-Secretary for Air, urge constant ruthlessness against the Germans: 'Let there be justice to the Germans,' he said, 'but let it be tempered with memory — and let there be a devil of a lot of memory about it too.' Ken and Helen heard it too and are very distressed and can already see the *next* war looming up ready for their two boys, John and Richard. This attitude of mind breeds war but it *is* difficult to know how to overcome the warlike mentality. It is said that *because* we did not realise the German outlook and that we disarmed so drastically that we *encouraged* the Nazi onslaught. But many of us know that hate and revenge are the real breeders of war and therefore we've got to aim at international goodwill.

January 19th All newspapers are full of the exciting details of Mr Churchill's return from Canada and his meeting with President Roosevelt in Washington. Everything was kept exceedingly secret — other fellow passengers on board the 37 ton Berwick Boeing flying boat were kept in ignorance of his presence. The PM had spent a week's holiday in Bermuda and the flight home was 3,287 miles and took eighteen hours. Mr Churchill actually took over at the controls for a time; seventy-four people can travel in these aircraft. Scenes of great relief and joy were witnessed at Paddington on his arrival from Plymouth.

January 20th Seventy-nine British prisoners have been recaptured in Libya. The garrison was in charge of a German major who was formerly a Lutheran pastor. He allowed our men to use petrol tins placed in position P O W so that our bombers could avoid them.

Terrific cold spell still on! To Report Centre; we were paid our 'subsistence grant' for the last four weeks — 18/- or 4/6d a night. Rather too heavy many of us think, as supper and breakfast only cost about 2/-. Today loudspeaker vans were patrolling the streets reminding us to have our salvage paper and cardboard ready. The King has turned out a lot including old menu cards of Queen Victoria's dinners! Fancy her lending a hand!

January 22nd The Archbishop of Canterbury has decided to resign his Archbishopric next year as he feels at the age of seventy-seven he should give way to a younger man.

January 24th Japs are landing in New Guinea and Australia's plight is serious. There is a suggestion that a Canadian division be sent from England. The Canadians are aching to be more active but whether the wives and families left behind in Canada are in the same state of mind is another matter. All the men produce photos of their families, having been separated

RETRIBUTION

To the Editor of The Daily Telegraph

Sir—May I suggest that you publish no further letters on the question of retribution and revenge? Most of them are nauseating to Christians. If the peoples of the earth must inflict every known horror upon their fellow beings; if, indeed, we must face recurring warfare between nations, then let us get on with this phase of the turmoil, and at the conclusion of it pray to God that we might be given strength to tackle the problems of reconstruction.

If some of your contributors even now begin thinking on these lines, they would be giving far greater service to mankind. Yours, &c., Prestwich. R. E. COLLIS.

Daily Telegraph, January 21st

from them for two years. But many feel better bored than blitzed. The tank corps here in Worthing are moving today and unfortunately used our road. The result is two big holes at the corner where they swivelled round and a very rough surface. Thousands of American troops have landed in Northern Ireland. They form the vanguard of a huge force.

January 30th   Bad news from the Far East — the Japs are within fourteen miles of Singapore. In the Middle East Rommel has recaptured Benghazi (the fourth time this place has changed hands).

January 31st   I went to Betty Patching's wedding and to her war-time reception at Cranleigh Court afterwards. Really quite a 'do'! The 'iced' cake was very cleverly camouflaged — the white icing being some rice paper neatly placed on top and around. The inside was quite good. Almond icing is still allowed if you can get the almonds, which are usually peanuts!

February 2nd   A most interesting talk at the Luncheon Club by a Free French woman, on 'The Resistance of France' — stories of escapes to General de Gaulle and over to England. It seems that France on the whole is tremendously pro-British. General Wavell says big reinforcements are en route for Singapore. It's a race against time.

February 9th   The Japs have started their full-scale attack on Singapore. Sir Archibald Clark Kerr, the British Ambassador-designate to Russia on his way to Moscow from China, in an interview in Calcutta, said: 'I do not believe the Japanese will get as far as India. They will be held in Burma. The present success of Japan in the Far East was like the sting on the rump of an elephant. It makes the elephant uncomfortable, but when its tail and trunk get working there is not much left of the wasp.' Because of the ghastly battle for Singapore some of the Report Centre people are very depressed and depressing. Luckily one other is very optimistic and I think she and I did some propaganda work and helped them to 'take a long view'. People are either extremely depressed (especially readers of the *Daily Mail* and *Express*) or confident of final victory and so, though temporarily worried, these try to convert the others! Rather uphill work. My patients are fifty-fifty.

February 15th   On the six o'clock news the Jap communiqué reported their capture of Singapore. On the nine o'clock news Mr Churchill was grave but confident, ending up: 'So far we have not failed. We shall not fail now. Move forward steadfastly together *into the storm and through the storm*.'

February 16th   Expected a bad day after last night's bad news about Singapore, but strangely enough all the patients

BADGE TO CHECK WHITE FEATHERS

M.P. URGES ISSUE

The suggestion is again to be made in Parliament that a badge should be issued to men discharged from the Services as unfit to protect them from being given white feathers.

Mr. F. J. Bellenger (Soc.) will raise the matter in a question to the Secretary for War, Capt. Margesson.

He will mention the case of A. V. Burtenshaw, late of the R.A.S.C., who was discharged for heart trouble after Dunkirk and had since received a number of white feathers.

Correspondence on this subject has appeared in THE DAILY TELEGRAPH recently.

WHITE FEATHERS

To the Editor of The Daily Telegraph

Sir—During the last war an R.N.V.R. commander with the D.S. in "civies," was given a white feather in Regent-street. He promptly called a police officer and charged the young woman with "accosting."

They proceeded to Vine-street, and when the lady's father arrived the commander agreed to withdraw the charge on condition that she was put to some war work, and that her father gave a certain sum to the Red Cross as an apology. Yours faithfully,
London, W.2.　　　　N. S. EVANS

---

were pretty calm and confident. Mr Churchill's broadcast has had a steadying effect. Japan says we have lost 60,000 men in Singapore (prisoners and casualties). It seems that munitions, food, water, petrol etc were all giving out. 'Warship Week' has started in Worthing. The target is £500,000.

February 17th　In today's paper, Mr Curtin, the Commonwealth Prime Minister of Australia, has stated in Canberra: 'It is apparent that a Japanese attack on Australia is inevitable. Dunkirk began the Battle of Britain and Singapore begins the Battle of Australia. Our honeymoon is finished. It is now work or fight — and work or fight as we have never worked or fought before. No man or woman must go to bed tonight without having related his or her job to the war effort. Such a race as ours must put playtime aside; the hours previously devoted to sport and leisure must now be given to the duties of war. All of us are called by fate to take up a more salutary way of life. Whatever criticism that may evoke, I must tell the nation that today Australian brains and brawn are worth more than bets and beer.'

In the same paper Reuter reports that Lt General Yamashita peremptorily accepted from Lt General Percival, the British GOC, full responsibility for the lives of the British and Australian troops and British women and children remaining in Singapore. He declared: 'Rely on Japanese Bushido'. Bushido is the ancient Japanese code inculcating courage, loyalty, courtesy and self-control. A despatch to the Domei News Agency states that there are 15,000 British forces, 13,000 Australians and 32,000 Indians with 120 British women and children, and 1,000,000 civilians in Singapore.

February 18th I had a Canadian soldier as a patient today and he gave me three lemons! We gave away one and swapped another for an orange and Mother made 2 lb of marmalade! The Dutch are putting up a magnificent fight in their Far East possessions. In Sumatra they have destroyed their oil refineries etc rather than let them fall into Japanese hands. They've been the pride of the Dutch Empire and their destruction is comparable to the Russian destruction of their Dnieper dam last autumn. Millions of pounds have gone west overnight.

February 23rd Dr Temple is to be the new Archbishop of Canterbury. Russia is celebrating the twenty-fourth anniversary of its 'Red Army'. A Turkish steamer loaded with peas, lentils, beans, salted fish and many other foodstuffs has sailed for Athens to ameliorate the mass starvation in Greece. It is estimated that 900 people are dying every day. Every morning lorries patrol Athens and take away the bodies of those who died in the streets; they are buried in common graves without coffins. Whooping cough and diphtheria are wreaking havoc among Greek children. There is urgent need for serum against these diseases and of anti-typhus injections.

Sold Ritter's typewriter (Remington portable but with German keys) for £12. This is £4 more than I was originally offered when he was interned. No typewriters are being made now, hence a good second-hand price.

March 1st We heard a tremendous number of bombers going over us on Friday night and learned today that they were British on a 'paratroop' raid on Bruneval in occupied France. It was highly successful — we brought back prisoners and information and our casualties were light — and it goes to prove we can *do something* sometimes. The RAF, army and navy all took part and the co-operation between them was perfect.

March 9th The nine o'clock news was awful. Mr Eden has made a statement in Parliament describing the most ghastly atrocities by the Japs to our prisoner soldiers in Hong Kong — fifty were bayonetted to death after being tied hand and foot. Other ghastly things — too ugly to commit to writing.

'Black market' offenders are to be very harshly punished and a good job too. The war reserve policeman on duty tonight won the King's Police Medal last September and received it at Buckingham Palace last month. He prevented a jilted soldier from committing suicide on the railway. Basic petrol ration is to disappear from July onwards. That will mean no private cars will be on the road after that date — and quite right too. No white bread will be made after April 6th, but the government wholemeal is excellent.

March 12th Conversations with patients this morning were most varied. Mr R made me very angry and were it not that he was such an invalid I should have crossed swords with him. He is everything an Englishman should not be in wartime. In fact today's leader in the *Telegraph* about 'Croakers' seems to recognise people of his kidney. I hope he reads it but he enjoys his *Daily Mail* too much I'm afraid. Luckily Lady Hope Simpson was my next patient and the conversation was exactly the opposite. She and her husband have led such interesting lives abroad and are so sane and reasonable. Sir Hope Simpson re-established 700,000 Greek refugees back in Greece from Asia Minor in 1922.

March 13th Miss Goldsmith demonstrated the treatment by splints and strapping of children's foot deformities. She says she gets many more children with deformed toes since shoes were rationed. The kids wear their shoes too long (or rather too short!). I'm reading W. Shirer's *Berlin Diary*. In September 1940 he writes: 'The subjected peoples of Europe will be saved of course, if Britain holds out and ultimately wins this. But even if Germany should win the war it will lose its struggle to organise Europe. The German, I am profoundly convinced after mingling with him for many years, is incapable of organising Europe. His lack of balance, his bullying sadism when he is on top, his constitutional inability to grasp even faintly what is in the minds and hearts of other peoples, his instinctive feeling that relations between two peoples can only be on the basis of master and slave and never on the basis of let-live equality — these characteristics of the German make him and his nation unfit for the leadership in Europe they have always sought and make it certain that, however he may try, he will in the long run fail.' And in November 1940 he recounts a few German jokes which are rather significant — here is one. *Question*. An aeroplane carrying Hitler, Goering and Goebbels crashes. All three are killed. Who is saved? *Answer*. The German people. And this from Germany! On December 4th he writes: 'My last night in a blackout. After tonight the lights . . . and civilisation.' He is now lecturing in the USA. He has explained something that has always worried me — the fact that our fighter aircraft did so comparatively little at Dunkirk. Our fighter strength was not great and the greater part had to be kept for the 'Battle of Britain'. The decision proved to be a great one.

March 19th The Home Secretary said in the House today that he had warned the editors of the *Daily Mirror* to 'refrain from further publication of matter calculated to foment opposition to the successful prosecution of the war'. The government had decided, Mr Morrison said, that in the case of persistent disregard of such a warning the right method would be to apply Defence Regulation 2D, which authorised suppression of the paper.

March 22nd   It was announced in the *Sunday Times* today that by the King's wish Palm Sunday (next week) will be observed as a National Day of Prayer. The announcement from Buckingham Palace stated: 'His Majesty hopes that on this day his people will, wherever possible, unite in giving thanks to Almighty God for past blessings and in humble prayer for strength and guidance in facing the tasks that lie ahead.' This will be the sixth Day of Prayer since the war began. The following prayer has been issued by the Archbishop of Canterbury, Dr Lang, and the Archbishop of York, Dr Temple, for use on the day: 'Oh Lord, the only wise God and Father of us all, Whose judgments are far above out of our sight, Who yet withholdest not the Presence of Thy strength and of thy mercy: Hear in this hour of need our prayer for the Allied nations; for their cause, for their operations, and their common spirit; for all who command, who serve, who suffer, who lay down their lives: And, through the courage and sacrifice of all, reveal and bring to pass, O Lord, that new heaven and new earth wherein dwelleth righteousness, and the Prince of Peace ruleth, Thy Son our Saviour Jesus Christ: To Whom with Thee and the Holy Ghost be the victory and dominion for ever and ever. Amen.'

March 23rd   Mother and I went to a lecture, 'The Voice of Canada', at the Town Hall by Major Coulter — most interesting, especially as we've thousands here in Worthing. The major put in a plea for the 'black sheep'. Every week there are several in the courts. Drink is responsible for most of their escapades. There are very few private cars on the road now and people have cancelled their licences as the 'basic' ration of petrol has been so drastically cut. I get two gallons of basic until the end of July and then none. I do get 'supplementary' but that has been reduced too.

March 28th   On the allotment all afternoon. Mrs Wenban-Smith to tea. She is *furious*. In Beach House Park, Worthing Corporation are remaking the *fourth* bowling green. It was damaged by bombs last year. Ken, Mother, Mrs Wenban-Smith and I have all written letters to the local paper deploring this unpatriotic action. I'll paste in the winning letter at the end of next week! I saw in a fish shop this morning a board saying '3 pm fresh herrings. Bring your own paper.' Often one sees 'Sorry — no sweets or cigarettes', 'Sorry — no onions, no oranges, no saccharines'. Other things which are very scarce are cosmetics, especially face powder, hair nets and pins, camera films, etc. Newspapers are very reduced in size. On the eleven o'clock news came reports of a successful commando raid on St Nazaire. It was led by Lt Colonel Newman, who did not return with the rest of the forces. He is the son of Mrs Alice Newman, former headmistress of Holy Trinity Church School in Worthing.

INVASION

NOTICE TO HOUSEHOLDERS

The Government has decided that if the danger of invasion grows everyone who is not needed to man certain essential services may have to leave this town. Plans are being made for the evacuation on threat of invasion of all civilians other than those who will receive a notice on the authority of the Regional Commissioner, requiring them to remain at their posts.

If circumstances permit, the first to be evacuated will be children and their mothers. Arrangements are accordingly being made to enable children and their mothers (or other women undertaking to look after them) to leave in advance of the evacuation of other people. All parents are urged to register their children for this purpose now; children over 14 years who are still attending school may be included. Children cannot be registered unless they will be accompanied by a woman who will be responsible for looking after them. School children whose parents cannot arrange for someone to accompany them when the time comes should be sent away now to join the school parties already in the reception areas—the Council will arrange for this on being requested by the parents.

April 4th At the canteen tonight the Canadian soldiers were in great excitement. Reports had come through that Nazi paratroopers were massing in big numbers on the French coast. Will there be a Nazi commando raid now? To even things up with ours on St Nazaire?

April 6th A big Jap raid on Colombo, capital of Ceylon. But twenty-seven out of seventy-five raiders were brought down. The RAF raided Germany last night with over 300 bombers and only five are missing. Today is the first day of the 'national loaf' — a wholemeal one. I like it, Mother does not. No white flour will be seen till the end of the war now. Jap aircraft have bombed the Madras district in India from an aircraft carrier. All clergy in Norway have resigned as a protest to the Quisling government; Hitler made him premier. Reprisals are expected.

April 9th In bed this morning I saw a plane circling round. Good, I thought, one of our RAF back from its night work. Not a bit of it — a horrid whistle and then a plonk and Mother called out she could see flames at once. A nasty lot of machine gunning and then silence. Ken came in soon after and told us it was the gas works and there was a lot of damage to property and the hospital had been hit. The mortuary received substantial damage. Two workmen were killed. Sir Stafford Cripps' mission to India, with a proposal of full independence after the war, failed through the attitude of the All-India Congress headed by Gandhi and Nehru. Gandhi's policy was total pacifism, but Nehru promised no surrender to the Japanese and no embarrassment of the British war effort.

April 12th The news is so bad. We have lost several more big ships in the Far East, including the aircraft carrier *Hermes*. In the Far East, the Allies are retreating on all fronts. Malta is being bombed incessantly but is showing amazing defence and spirit. And also on the other side of the picture is Russia's terrific resistance, the RAF continues on the offensive against Germany and nearer home my beans and peas are showing on the allotment. I went to a Home Guard service at Goring on Sunday; it is a jolly fine body of men of all ages, shapes and sizes.

April 14th There was such sad news when we got to the Report Centre tonight. Marjorie Carter is one of the volunteers and her fiancé was killed whilst on manoeuvres on Salisbury Plain. A brigadier and twenty-three soldiers were killed when a Spitfire opened fire when carrying out a power dive. There are two theories about the accident: the pilot either mistook his target while diving at 450 miles an hour or live ammunition was loaded by mistake. It's especially sad as Marjorie's father died suddenly last Christmas and her fiancé's brother was killed at sea six weeks ago.

'Our workers in the shipyards are soldiers too, and in the most vulnerable of all our fronts'

92

April 17th The King has presented Malta with the George Cross in recognition of its remarkable defence and fortitude. It has been bombed over 2,000 times. In a recent broadcast the Governor, Sir William Dobbie, said: 'We have been sorely tried, but are not crushed nor one whit less fit to face whatever lies in front of us — rather the reverse.' At the canteen on the nine o'clock news we heard of the day attack of twelve new bombers (Lancasters) on a German diesel engine factory at Augsburg. They flew thirty feet above housetops all the way. Only five returned but it is considered a wonderful feat. USA announces that American aircraft and airmen will be installed all over England soon and will help in the raiding. Everyone senses a subtle change-over in the Allies' war effort. Many still think it will end this year — October is the month! Also on the nine o'clock news, *Tokyo* and other Jap cities have been raided. Apparently seven areas were attacked and the Japs say it was an 'inhuman attack'. And after Pearl Harbour too. These Axis countries are very difficult to understand. Laval has now taken over France as virtual Dictator and a pro-Nazi one at that.

April 25th The RAF have raided Rostock, the Heinkel works, with a heavy force two nights running. Corned beef is banned from today. We've been having 2d worth each for the last few weeks. Now the meat ration is 1/– a week. Luckily sausages and various other meat concoctions are unrationed. Worthing has had an 'Aid for Russia' week, ending up with a flag day. The Canadians have had a seven-day manoeuvre and were all back, full of it, at the canteen tonight. The weather's been lovely for it and they all look well but tired. Everyone feels there's something big afoot.

May 5th There was a lot of gunfire and vibration from bombs in the night and we had two sirens. During the day all sorts of rumours got about. The Isle of Wight was the target. We had a postcard from Uncle Alfred saying they were all safe and it transpired that Eastbourne had a daylight raid at midday — six bombers suddenly appeared out of the mist, dropped their loads and rushed off. St John's Church is a complete ruin, the station and gas works were hit and the Cavendish Hotel in which RAF men are billeted.

May 8th There's been a big naval battle in the Coral Sea. It seems as if Japan was about to invade Australia, and the US and Britain engaged a large force. Two Jap aircraft carriers have been sunk. The US are 'elated' at the news — the best they've had since entering the war.

May 9th The Japs are being held in Burma. Mother and I gave a bridge drive today for the Worthing Council for Social Service and raised £7 7s 0d. Eight tables and tea and raffles. For raffles we had strawberries, a terrific treat given by Mrs

Claff from her father's nurseries, two lots of eggs and a *rubber* hot-water bottle! For tea we had *white* bread and *butter* (Mother had saved white flour) and the butter came from Canada last Christmas. Tea from Australia and we saved milk from yesterday.

May 14th   Mr Noel Baker, the MP, wrote a very interesting article in *The Listener* about transport. He said that transport is vital to victory. New means of transport and shorter routes had to be found — air routes across jungles, lorry services even through country where the local population object to motors because they are not mentioned in the Koran, barges along rivers. We have to increase our means of transport: every day in the shipyards is vital. We have to plan the loads so that 'priorities', essential goods and passengers, get transported first which means no trains for summer holidays this year. We have to save shipping space which is every bit as urgent as making tanks and guns. So beef is deboned before importing and ground nuts are brought in without their shells. 'Cross hauls' have to be cut out; there must be the shortest route from the nearest sources of supply and transport has to be turned around in the shortest possible time. The MP called on the public to help with salvage of rubber and paper, to kill rats which destroy £70 million of imported food a year and not to travel. He mentioned a little boy saying goodbye at the station as he went to school may have had his special reasons but he was sound in spirit when he asked the question: 'Is this journey really essential, mother?'

May 21st   We picked up an Austrian refugee near Godalming — at least we hope he was! Jack said he might have been an escaped prisoner! Anyhow we only took him a couple of miles. Brighton station was bombed. I have started to give a course of hygiene lectures to the newly formed Girls Training Corps (GTC) up at the High School. Girls of sixteen and seventeen have to register now and are advised to join either the Air Cadets or the GTC. They are quite keen. It is 'pre-service' training but also the training is given with a view to post-war reconstruction plans. Sir Stafford Cripps has announced in parliament the Allied intention of invading Europe later on. It is thought that many small 'commando' raids are already taking place. New ration books are out this week. I've seen tremendous queues but we've decided to wait till next week when we hope they'll be less. The Admiralty have asked every-one to look through their holiday snaps and send any likely to be of use (in our invasion?). I've looked through mine but none are suitable. At the YMCA tonight we were allowed a *ham* sandwich each. Lovely!

May 25th   Mother and I went to hear Sir John Hope Simpson lead the Goring study group on the International New Order.

94

I registered on Saturday! Not a forty! Only thirty-nine! The stirrup pump practice was very well done. The wardens made us form up into teams and we put out incendiary bombs and burning shavings.

WOMEN OF 40 REGISTER
About 250,000 women of 39 and 40 registered for National Service yesterday, bringing the total to well over 6,000,000.
Most of the married women have young families, and come under the "Married Women's Reserve." Unmarried women with no domestic ties and not doing work of national importance may be drafted to factories away from home.

It was most interesting. He had to assume that the Allied nations would win so that at the end of the war there would be: (a) victors, (b) vanquished and (c) neutrals. Of the neutrals most are Moslems. There must be a time of convalescence after the war and *before* the peace is finally arranged. A new League of Nations must be brought into being but there must be an *international* force to safeguard nations against aggressors, and also nations must not be allowed to secede. He also said that 'wisdom' is far more important than retribution or even justice. Steps must be taken to re-educate the German nation. This might be done through their own *burgomasters* (professional mayors) or through their civil service. He can foresee great difficulty in occupying enemy countries at the end, as there is so much justifiable hate between say the Poles and the Nazis, the Chinese and Japs and so on. On the whole his tone was hopeful and optimistic but he showed how immeasurably vast the whole affair is. Study groups are running throughout Worthing in preparation for the Christian New Order Week next week.

June 2nd Canterbury was bombed last night as a reprisal for Cologne where terrifying damage was done. The German Cathedral was untouched but the casualties are said to be over 20,000 killed. No-one gloats but the feeling is that it may help to bring the end nearer. Essen was bombed by over 1,000 bombers of the RAF last night.

June 7th All the Canadians in the town have taken part in a ten-day 'super austerity' endurance test planned by the GOC South-Eastern Commander, Lt General Bernard Montgomery, the keenest physical fitness chief of the Army. To harden his men he arranged a great battle in which a whole Canadian corps and an English division took part. An English Tank Corps (or whatever it's called) which is now in Worthing took part. At the canteen the English tank boys don't like the Canadians — a lot of jealousy between them — pity. I had a lovely game of tennis in the afternoon. Balls are not being made now and everyone has very old ones — 'austerity tennis' as Kit calls it.

June 14th Rommel is trying to break through the right wing of our Eighth Army at Tobruk and cut its coast line of communication. In the paper it was announced that the Victoria Cross has been awarded to Major Geoffrey Keyes, only son of Admiral of the Fleet Sir Roger Keyes, for his valour in leading a commando raid last November to attack Rommel's headquarters in Libya, 250 miles behind the enemy's lines. He was shot in Rommel's house and died within a few minutes. I went to the war casualty hospital at East Grinstead where very important work is being done in connection with burns and facial injuries, chiefly airmen. Aunt Dora is working there now but I didn't see her.

SMILING THROUGH . . . *By LEE*

[No. 2,405]   OPERATIONS ORDERS

"... and if you *should* happen to pass that little shop just off the Rue de la Paix ..."

DESPATCHES FROM THE HOME FRONT

June 21st   A perfect longest day for weather but all spoilt by the news from Libya. Tobruk has been captured by the Germans. Now that the coast here is being fortified so much more and slipways made for embarcation of troops etc, we feel we're more of a military target. 'Allied Youth Week' has started in Worthing and our Luncheon Club entertained about fifteen young women from Russia, Poland, France, Holland, Czechoslovakia and Belgium. The Tobruk news hangs over everyone like a dark threatening cloud. Mr Churchill is in the USA again — one wonders if he would have gone had he known about the quick fall of Tobruk. It was all quiet at the Report Centre but it is expected that Worthing is in for it soon. We have hundreds of tanks here; the beach is being cleared, boats are camouflaged overnight, slipways are being made all along the coast, the Americans are nearby on the hills. A US Tank General (Eisenhower) has come over to Britain — he is to command the US troops in *Europe*. Everyone wonders — when? Sebastopol still resists terrific Nazi attacks.

June 28th After an early breakfast I set forth to queue up for fruit — gooseberries and strawberries if possible! I managed a lb of cherries at 1/6d a pound. Fruit is very difficult to come by but our loganberries are ready for the weekend and we'll pick peas too. In today's paper is a report of three Bretons who escaped by boat from France and have been presented to General de Gaulle in London. None of them had ever seen a photo of the general and when asked what their impressions were after meeting him said they were surprised he was so young and so tall. 'We expected to find a little old man with a white moustache,' they said.

In Holland all Jews have to wear a yellow star to distinguish them by order of the Gestapo. Result — everyone wears one!

July 2nd Still glorious summer weather but the news is still bad. Rommel is only eighty miles from Alexandria and the battle for Egypt has begun. The Nazis claim the fall of Sebastopol. There was a vote of censure in the Commons. Mr Churchill wound up the debate and he won the day for the government. The vote was 450 to 25! Hore Belisha never ceases to criticise the PM ever since he was ejected from the War Office.

July 6th News from Egypt is better. General Auchinleck is counter-attacking. Went to see a US film on 'Unexploded Bombs' (UXB) at the Boys' High School — a grim subject but we should know something about it as a bomb exploded in London the other day which had been dropped last year. It killed many people.

July 8th Mother and I went to see *Next of Kin*, an excellent film warning of the danger of careless talk. It showed how quite trivial items may be just the bits of information fifth columnists and Nazi agents are needing. It should help in stemming the numerous rumours that are continually flying about.

July 14th The Nazis continue to force the Russians back but with terrific losses. A big battle in Egypt appears to be imminent. General de Gaulle broadcast to the French people as today is Bastille Day. There is much sabotage in France. There is much talk of the big camps being built around here in the country north of the coast. Theories are either that coast inhabitants will live there or French refugees when the second front is finally established in Europe.

July 16th Our ARP sector had a fire-fighting practice tonight. We lent our garage for the fire and we all had to crawl round the garage to get used to the smoke. I bought 100 lovely leek plants for 2/6d and planted them.

August 3rd Bank Holiday Monday and as usual a showery

one. Everyone has been asked to make it a stay-at-home holiday. As there is no private petrol the roads are very quiet. Buses are very full, trains are restricted. Yesterday Ken and Helen and I went to Glyndebourne to hear Leon Goossens and the London Philharmonic Trio play at Mr Christie's famous private musical hall. His large country house is now taken over and is an LCC Nursery School. After the concert we walked around the lovely gardens — it is an ideal spot for the London children. Gandhi is about to cause an upheaval in India. I can never make out whether he is a saint or sinner!

August 10th We went to bed earlier yesterday to save fuel but just before 11 pm we had an 'alert' and then firing and other ominous sounds. Two hit-and-run planes came over. It turned out that Dr Marjorie Davies' house in Homefield Rd, half a mile away, was hit but she was away at the time. Also some newly arrived Canadian soldiers lost their lives. The new phosphorous bombs were used and they burn the flesh badly. In Littlehampton a bomb hit the minister's manse and the Rev Hailstone and his wife and two friends who were staying with them died. The Rev Hailstone had been in the town a little more than a year having lost his church in the raids on Southampton.

August 12th American forces have effected a landing in the Japanese-occupied Solomon Islands but there is very stiff resistance. Harold Frampton brought me two gorgeous bunches of grapes for my birthday — muscats. They are 15/– a pound in the shops! Mother gave me two pairs of gloves — *four coupons!* I saw Dr Marjorie Davies outside her house that had been bombed — she was salvaging her things.
   Things in India are far from happy, troops are standing by in many towns, but Gandhi's followers have failed to start big mill and shop strikes. In south Russia the oilfields have been set on fire and are 'an inferno of flames'.

August 14th A big Allied convoy has got through to Malta although it was subjected to a three-day terrible attack from the sea and air. We lost an aircraft carrier though — HMS *Eagle* but over 900 men were saved. Everyone is saying: 'Where is Mr Churchill?' No reference has been made of him in the papers for over two weeks. The most popular guess is Russia. The entire stock of iron railings and gates in Worthing is being removed. We shall soon become accustomed to the sight. Apparently the whole of Britain is being de-ironed!

August 19th Tremendous air activity all day. On the news there are reports of big commando raids on Dieppe. The 1st Division of Canadians were used and they were on French soil for nine hours but there were heavy casualties on both sides. Despite this it is claimed a success. The Canadians, the British

MR. CHURCHILL MEETS GENERAL SMUTS

MR. CHURCHILL conferring with Gen. Smuts in the garden of the British Embassy, Cairo, during his recent visit to Egypt.

*Daily Telegraph,
August 19th*

and the Free French combined in a most meticulous way. Three landings were made, some even with tanks. Air fights were numerous with almost 200 Nazi aircraft shot down — we lost ninety-five. No wonder we had hundreds of aircraft over Worthing as some pilots flew over to France and back to refuel three or four times. We destroyed an ammunition dump, a radio-location station, a six-gun battery. The returning Canadians are very battle scarred and dirty — a terrible ordeal in every way.

I took Mike to the vet to be put to sleep — heart and kidneys very bad.

August 21st Mother and I started our holiday. Mother trained and I cycled up to Mollie's. At Dunsfold I could scarcely recognise the scene as there is a tremendous bomber aerodrome in process of being built. My cyclometer went wrong and only registered twenty miles instead of thirty-three. I had a fright as I thought it was old age creeping on rapidly — each mile seemed so long! Brazil has declared war on Germany and Italy after Nazi submarines had sunk several Brazilian vessels. It was a great effort getting ready for a wartime holiday. In addition to the usual arrangements to be made about patients etc I had to fix up a deputy at the Report Centre, two canteens and firewatchers. Then we had to tell the warden we should be away and tell him our key was at Mr Tyler's. We turned off water, gas and electricity and only half-drew the curtains to enable ARP wardens to look inside in case of incendiary bomb trouble. I got 'emergency' food cards for two weeks and arranged for our paper the *Telegraph* to be delivered to our neighbours, the Shepherds at 25 Langton Rd — if you cancel the delivery altogether it's impossible to get it again when you return. We brought our soap ration with us. We've left Worthing just when there's more talk about evacuation because of commando raids and possible invasion. Our road is lined with troop carrying lorries and all roads with trees have numerous camouflaged tanks hiding beneath them. Lord Haw Haw has mentioned this fact more than once! I took out the rotor arm in the car and rendered it immobilised!

August 26th On holiday at Mollie's at Godalming. Having bought a mac cycling cape (six coupons) I set off for Oxford at about ten o'clock and arrived there at five o'clock. The weather cleared! The roads are very clear except for army, air force and navy lorries. The harvest looks very good and there is a lot of cutting going on — the rain of yesterday does not appear to have damaged it at all. The Duke of Kent has been killed in an air crash in Scotland.

Daily Telegraph, September 7th

September 1st I cycled eighty miles to Winchester, arriving at 7.30 in the rain! I was glad of my six-coupon mac cape. It was a lovely ride; I used an AA map and did not miss my way at all. I stopped at Swindon and asked if there was a 'British Restaurant' there and was surprised not to find one. I had difficulty in finding anywhere for a cup of tea, rather different from peace days when you see 'Teas' up everywhere! I eventually got a cup at a 'Pull-in' for lorry drivers! A rabbit sandwich, cake and tea all for 6d! The only travellers are lorry drivers.

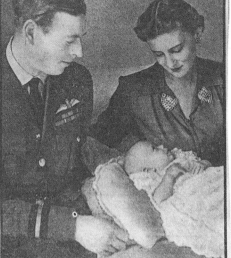

PRINCE MICHAEL AND HIS PARENTS

This charming study of Prince Michael of Kent with his parents was taken 10 days before the Duke of Kent's death. It is one of the last photographs to be taken of the Duke. (Photo by Cecil Beaton.)

September 2nd Winchester is very full — so many South-ampton people are living there. I could see the barrage balloons both at Portsmouth and at Southampton. I stayed with Mr Rowland, the vicar of Christ Church; I'm godmother to his daughter Beryl. The vicarage is rather big but a bombed-out lady from Hull has a wing of it. Mrs Rowland and I had tea at the nicest tea shop in Winchester but they only supply jam on Saturdays and there's a ration of one cake per person!

September 13th The most gruesome battles of the war are going on near Stalingrad. Can it hold? Snow has already fallen in the Caucasus; this is a deadly enemy to the Nazis. In France Laval has conducted some ghastly anti-semitic measures, removing thousands, including young children, to Germany. Dorothy, our maid, has left to do war work in Coventry. Dr McCall has joined up and Worthing has to relin-quish six more doctors! Uncle Bert brought a pamphlet that had been dropped by the Nazis showing what a failure the Dieppe raid had been! I did wish he would give it me for this diary! It was officially announced in Ottawa that the Canadian casualties in Dieppe totalled 3,350, including 130 officers and 2,417 other ranks missing.

September 22nd Mrs Corbett Ashby told a League of Nations Union meeting at the town hall that after the war the world must be regarded as a single unit, and the old contro-versies about Free Trade and Protection will have to be resolved in the common interests. The mayor of Worthing, Dr Annis, said he thought it would be a good thing if some of our bishops and clergymen and ministers played a part in the peace conference. Mrs Corbett Ashby stayed with us for the night. She was awfully nice; she'd recently visited Sweden — by aeroplane — travelling in the stratosphere! The Swedes were awfully interested in having a real sincere Englishwoman to talk to them as they are sick of Nazi propaganda.

September 24th A very big convoy of British, American and Russian ships has arrived in a north Russian port after being subjected to a powerful four-day attack by Nazi bombers and U-boats. It must have been a terrible ordeal. Over forty Nazi bombers were shot down and several U-boats sunk. All our escort ships arrived but some merchant ships were sunk. However the supplies landed in Russia were the biggest yet.

September 27th Kit went to the big meeting at the Albert Hall addressed by the two Archbishops and Sir Stafford Cripps, the Lord Privy Seal. They urged all church people to call for a new social order. Dr Temple said: 'The profit motive can have its own right place, but it must not be allowed to predominate over the general interest.' The Archbishop of York, Dr Garbett, said: 'I should place a comprehensive housing policy first among social reforms after the war' and Sir Stafford Cripps: 'We might well adopt the five simple desires of the American people as expressed by President Roosevelt — equality of opportunity, jobs for those who can work, security, ending of privilege and civil liberty.' There is a growing feeling throughout Britain that Christian principles must be adhered to in all spheres of life.

September 29th There was a terrible raid in Petworth. Two bombs hit a school and the headmaster and twenty-eight boys were killed. Several of the boys were evacuated from London where their parents still live. It was Petworth's first raid and helpers were called from Worthing and Horsham under the 'mutual aid' arrangement.

FUNERAL OF BOMBED SCHOOL VICTIMS

SOLDIER'S TRIBUTE.—After the coffins had been lowered into the single grave and the mourners had moved away a soldier walked the length of the grave, scattering flowers

A SUSSEX VILLAGE, Saturday.
WAR has struck a bitter blow at this peaceful little village nestling on the slopes of a fertile hill in Sussex. To-day I watched the villagers bury their dead —the village Head Master and 28 of his boys who were killed with him when their school was bombed in daylight by a lone raider.

October 6th Hitler is ready to take over Denmark with Gestapo-rule threat to King Christian. Diplomatic relations have been ruptured. The Germans say the King insulted the Führer! Hitler sent a fulsome telegram to the King congratulating him on his seventy-second birthday and the King replied by telegram 'Thanks. Christian X'.

Ken and the two boys came here as Helen has had to go to a nursing home.

October 8th We have conducted a small 'commando' raid on Sark and found out that some of the islanders have been deported to work in Germany. The Nazis are so furious we have found out that they've raked up an old grievance and said we maltreated Nazi prisoners at Dieppe — consequently they are threatening to put some of our men in irons. The British government has threatened to do the same to German prisoners in return! And so the wretched affair goes on. In Norway the Nazis have shot another nine patriots and arrested seventy more. Stalingrad continues to hold but two-thirds of the city is in ruins.

October 11th Helen has been ill and today has decided that she will not have her baby in April. The doctors put it down to the bombing in Worthing last Wednesday week. Her boys and I went up to the allotment this morning and dug up carrots and potatoes. They loved doing it and we got a good crop. We only have a three-hour daily maid now. Resident maids are almost non-existent — many people have daily women plus babies! Mrs Haigh looks after her maid's baby while the maid does the house work!

October 23rd Boys of eighteen are to join the services this year. Eighteen and a half was the previous age. We need all the available men and women for the promised 'offensive'.

Mrs Roosevelt has arrived in Britain by air. She is staying with the King and Queen at Buckingham Palace for a week and then having a ten-day tour around Britain. She toured the bombed parts of London today.

October 26th The British offensive in Egypt is on a very big scale and General Montgomery is confident but it will mean bitter fighting. Our RAF is keeping up tremendous attacks on Rommel's supply lines. Here we've had three alerts and our new barrage opened up fire for the first time. Mrs Wenban-Smith lay down flat in the road and got very muddy. Bombs were dropped in Storrington and two raiders were brought down. We learned later that the Worthing AA gunners got so excited that they fired at one of our own Beauforts!

October 31st The ban on central heating has ended. We had our first coal fire two days ago. All car owners with cars laid up are to fill up a form giving details of their tyres. There will be a big round up of rubber soon we imagine. Worthing has had a 'non-ferrous' metal drive for a week. I took some decrepit coffee pots to the centre. We have a lot of collecting receptacles in the scullery now: one for waste paper and cardboard, one for pig food, one for compost, a jar of milk tops metal, bones, a jar of cheese rind etc for Ken's hens and so on! Our egg ration is down to one a month. As we are registered with Mollie we do get more if her hens do their job well! They are mostly given to

Issued by the Ministry of Fuel & Power

invalids who find the restriction very hard. *Fuel* is a great topic — the BBC give 'fuel flashes' — ways of economising. Everyone is asked to have no more than five inches of hot water in the bath. Bread is a grey colour, because of the flour. We are advised not to make Christmas puddings till much nearer to Christmas as they get mouldy quickly. The few advertisements on hoardings advise us to 'Save more and lend it to the Government' and 'Less shopping means more shipping for vital supplies'.

November 2nd   The switch over to the offensive is seen on all fronts — from the short rather reticent communiqués from Cairo it seems that the Eighth Army is doing very well indeed against Rommel. We have been reinforced tremendously and more rapidly owing to the opening up of communications *across* Africa instead of the stuff having to go all the way around by the Cape. Stalingrad holds firm and the Russians are gaining some ground. The Australians are doing well in New Guinea and the Americans in the Solomons. Over fifty Nazi raiders bombed Canterbury yesterday — they came in covered by low cloud. We destroyed nine and two of ours are missing. Mrs Roosevelt only visited Canterbury the day before. Cold has really set in and we are enjoying coal fires though no one is having big ones. I see fire bricks everywhere and many people are living partly in their kitchens. We have breakfast and supper out there — so do Sir John and Lady Hope Simpson.

November 5th   Firework Day and great news from Egypt. I came downstairs at 7.15 and the paper arrived soon after. The headlines: 'Axis Forces In Full Retreat' — *official*! I dashed upstairs and Mother and I both read the details. Already over 9,000 prisoners have been taken; half Rommel's tanks have been destroyed.

It's been a real wet November day — raining the whole time but no one has minded! One of my patients coming off night duty as an ambulance driver dropped into her butcher's and he was so excited 'he even offered me a marrow bone if I'd anything I could take it home in'. She said she'd got her tin hat! We can't help feeling this is the beginning of big things.

November 6th   I went to the YMCA canteen this evening as usual and coming home saw a lovely searchlight display. It quite lit up the blackout which this week is *very* black. I lost my way last night after leaving the Girls' High School!

November 8th   *Tremendous news.* The Americans have landed in several places on the north coast of French Africa. There is news of success everywhere. Between 30,000 and 40,000 prisoners have already been taken in Egypt and we are now into Libya again. Algiers has capitulated to the US troops. Oran is surrounded. The Axis' desert army is described as a 'broken remnant'. We feel it really is the turning point of the war.

November 10th The Prime Minister's speech at the Mansion House was re-broadcast at nine o'clock. He is delighted obviously but says we must not think this is the beginning of the end 'but the end of the beginning'! The PM announced that church bells are to be rung next Sunday to celebrate the Egyptian victory. They have not been rung since the fall of France in June 1940 and were to be rung only when an invasion by the enemy had taken place.

At the Report Centre I heard that a girl of fifteen had been accidentally killed this afternoon when an anti-aircraft shell from the hills dropped short in Pavilion Rd. She worked in the bakery in Westcourt Rd and had served me this morning. She was killed outright. I heard on the wireless that at last a Lutheran Service is being broadcast from the BBC in German for the benefit of Christians in Germany. I had a most glorious bunch of chrysanthemums given me by Miss Piper. Her brother cannot sell them as transport for flowers is not allowed. Growers were allowed to grow only a limited quantity but they were not aware that they could not get them to London.

This news is bad. We knew it was happening from what our ex-Worthing refugees have said in their letters that their people in Europe have 'disappeared'.

EUROPEAN JEWRY IS BEING EXTERMINATED

MASS BUTCHERY BY GESTAPO

FROM OUR OWN CORRESPONDENT
JERUSALEM, Monday.

A special message from Geneva to the Palestine Post this morning suggests that it is time to drop speaking of the persecution of the Jews of Europe, since what is happening is systematic extermination.

"The simple fact is," it says, "that Hitler is making good his promise to destroy European Jewry."

Germany, Austria and Czechoslovakia have been cleared almost of the whole Jewish populations, numbering over 1,000,000 before the war, and the survivors are being rapidly liquidated. A similar process is being applied to the Jews in France, Belgium and Holland.

Only Switzerland, Sweden, Italy and Hungary are still free from the plague. "In Eastern and Central Europe, with the exception of Hungary, the mass of Jewry, numbering several millions, is in process of annihilation."

Citing instances, the Geneva correspondent reports recently that about 24,000 Jewish men, women and children inhabiting the Riga ghetto were taken out of their hovels, stripped naked and mowed down with machine-guns by the Gestapo and the Latvian police after being forced to dig their own graves.

The Geneva account is supported by reports reaching the Jewish Agency executive here. These reports are appearing to-morrow morning in the entire Hebrew Press in black-bordered columns.

The Jewish Agency's information concerned mainly the systematic extermination of the Jewish inhabitants of Polish towns after Himmler's visit to Warsaw last spring. He established a commission, which visits all parts of Poland and directs the wholesale wiping out of the surviving Jews. This commission is under the leadership of a commissar named Feu.

SLAUGHTER OF INNOCENTS

Among the unbelievable atrocities reported, Jewish children, including many below the age of 12, have been executed in their thousands, and elderly people murdered wholesale.

An eye-witness report said that 27,000 of the 30,000 Jews in the town of Kielce were ordered for deportation, but 1,500 were killed on the spot. The remainder disappeared on the journey.

In Bialystok the authorities herded 1,500 Jews in the great synagogue, where they were burnt alive. Most of the Jews of the hamlet of Tiktin were buried alive.

Basing itself on the official Polish Black Book that 200,000 Jews have been wiped out in Poland during the three years of war, the Palestine Post said editorially: "This matter goes to the very core of the moral position of the United Nations. An answer must be found if we are not to be accused of complacency."

November 13th Almost the whole of north Africa is in US and British hands. The Germans say the whole of Europe is impregnable and can be defended from any attack. We shall see.

DESPATCHES
FROM THE
HOME
FRONT

1942

105

November 23rd   Developed a horrid cold and it's not possible to get quinine or vapex now! I caught it at a meeting on 'Common Wealth' — very poor. On Friday I went to another meeting on 'Federal Union' — I was not impressed either. I feel neither of these parties has the prize of lasting peace and an improved social and economic order in their programme. I still favour the League of Nations.

November 27th   A staggering piece of news on the six o'clock — the French fleet in Toulon harbour has scuttled itself. The Nazis marched into Toulon (although Hitler promised he would not) early this morning and this is the result. It must come as a relief to France in a sense. It's one way of showing how they will not collaborate with Hitler's new European order. Hitler sent Pétain a most fulsome letter explaining why he had to break his promise. It was 'to forestall Anglo–American aggression'!

November 30th   It is 'Prisoners of War Week' and it started today with a 'Bring and Buy' sale in the Assembly Hall. Mother found it impossible even to force a way in. It raised over £2,300. The target is £5,000.

December 5th   It's the 170th week of the war. The Beveridge Plan for Social Security has been published. The papers report the only really basic innovation among the multitude of changes is the establishment of a national minimum level of subsistence below which no one may be allowed to fall. This is achieved by doubling or trebling all existing benefits and adding new ones, and including everybody in compulsory national insurance. The plan brings every citizen, irrespective of occupation or class, into a comprehensive scheme of insurance covering every risk of loss of income from the cradle to the grave, whether through unemployment, sickness, accident, maternity, widowhood, retirement. In addition it proposes free medical treatment for everybody and introduces children's allowances into the country for the first time. His plan 'treats man and wife as a team'. It was announced last week that Sir William Beveridge, the Master of University College, Oxford, is soon marrying his secretary.

December 10th   At 4 am this morning we nearly shot out of bed as a mine exploded on the beach during a gale. Our 'Prisoners of War Week' realised £8,500. Nazi prisoners of war are to be unshackled, it was announced today.

December 23rd   Everyone is talking of food this Christmas. Mother was lucky in swopping with Miss Duncan ½ lb of suet plus two preserved eggs for 1 lb of currants. Now she can make some mincemeat and Miss Duncan can make a Christmas pudding!

December 25th Heard on the 7 am news bulletin that Admiral Darlan has been assassinated in North Africa. He has been a great problem to the Allies. Violently anti-British at the time of the fall of France he recently came over to our side. The Americans especially found his co-operation 'useful'. But no-one found it easy to trust him. It has solved a big problem. Now General Giraud has taken his place.

The Russians are doing *remarkably* well in their offensives. Here in Worthing a quietish Christmas. Mrs Wenban-Smith brought her eighty-eight-year-old mother and her two Australian airmen on Christmas evening and we had a jolly evening. Supper was quite a spread. I'd managed to queue up and get a few apples on Christmas Eve and I swopped three preserved eggs for three oranges with a patient! A lovely box of chocolates arrived from Mr Durst in America (he is one of the Jewish refugees who was here in 1939) on Christmas morning. We've made £32 singing carols and we only went out twice. Luckily there was a moon. We visited Mr Wheatland on the front — although the sentry had been told to expect us he wanted to see identity cards and we were all counted through the barrier. There was an awful lot of barbed wire so it was good that there was a moon. Our red rear lights on our bikes looked rather effective.

December 31st Eastbourne had another daylight raid yesterday and Marks and Spencer was hit. We're being urged to be very careful with fuel. In the hotels people are asked to make do with one bath a week! The year ends on a very optimistic note.

' 1942—THE END OF THE BEGINNING '

January 1st   In *The Listener* an editorial quoted the Prime Minister: 'The dawn of 1943 will soon loom red before us and we must brace ourselves to cope with the trials and problems of what must be a stern and terrible year. We do so as a nation with a strong will, a bold heart and a good conscience. Be it good cheer or be it bad cheer will make no difference to us; we shall drive on to the end, and do our duty, win or die. God helping us, we can do no other.'

January 3rd   There has been much air activity today. American heavy bombers escorted by our fighters have attacked the U-boat base at St Nazaire. Lord Hankey writing in the *Sunday Times* says: 'Apart from U-boat warfare — the gravity of which is not yet realised by the general public, the United Nations enter the New Year on comparatively favourable circumstances. They have passed to the offensive.'
   Today the bus restrictions come into force in Worthing — no buses run on Sundays until 1 pm and all buses stop at 9 pm in the future. This will make a lot of difference to cinemas, church etc.

January 9th   Mother and I took the boys to the pantomime this afternoon. It was quite good. The funny man made some remark about the war being on this time next year. In Roger's prayers tonight he made up an impromptu one: 'Please God, let the war stop earlier than the man said in the show, or if not earlier, only a bit later'! Mollie says he often makes up one about the war according to the latest news!
   In the Atlantic the dreadful U-boat war goes on. Today comes news of a convoy that fought its way through to Murmansk. It beat off thirty-five attacks by packs of U-boats in a continuous battle off North Cape which lasted four days and nights.

January 18th   Excellent news from everywhere. Our Eighth Army is doing well in Libya; the Russians have relieved Leningrad. Berlin was raided last night but we lost twenty-two planes. The Nazis lost ten planes over Britain last night. Mrs Wenban-Smith got caught in the raid on London; she said the barrage was terrific and she was scared stiff.

DON'T WASTE FUEL

Keep warmer on BOVRIL

January 23rd Tripoli is ours! Rommel's forces are retreating with all speed to Tunisia! In another daylight raid a London elementary school was hit at lunchtime and forty-one children, aged between five and seven, and five teachers were killed.

January 25th I've just read a 3d pamphlet called 'Let My People Go' by V. Gollancz — a most stirring appeal to the government to grant visas and other help to Jews on the continent now under Hitler's awful laws. In yesterday's *Sunday Times*, a statement issued in the name of the Anglican Episcopate, urges the British government to give a lead in finding an immediate refuge for all Jewish refugees from Axis lands.

January 27th Mother was right! Mr Churchill is in North Africa — he's met Mr Roosevelt in Casablanca! They spent ten days there each accompanied by Service Chiefs of Staff and expert advisers and decided on future offensive campaigns. This is their fourth wartime meeting. Premier Stalin was invited but was unable to leave Russia on account of the great offensive he is directing. Generalissimo Chiang Kai-Shek has been kept informed of the steps proposed for the assistance of China. General Giraud, High Commissioner for French North Africa, was invited to confer with the combined chiefs of staff and to meet General de Gaulle, leader of the Fighting French. The French leaders are reported to be 'in entire agreement on the end to be achieved'.

January 29th Mr Churchill must be out of the country still. Some say he's seeing 'Joe' (Stalin). Still who knows where he is? This war is more and more involved and deceit is certainly one of war's allies. Anyhow Mr Eden says a statement will be made at the earliest opportunity on the Casablanca meeting, now known as the 'unconditional surrender' meeting. The RAF raided the U-boat base at Copenhagen yesterday — luckily the works are on a small island apart from the city itself.

February 1st Mr Churchill is still away although Mr Roosevelt has returned to the USA via Liberia and Brazil. General Paulus (made a Field Marshal last Saturday) has surrendered in Stalingrad, together with sixteen other generals. The Nazis are going from bad to worse everywhere. Everyone wonders about the invasion of Europe and speculation is varied. Anyhow Worthing is preparing for it as I counted ten new landing boats all finished and ready outside Wenban-Smith's wood yard today. Dr Hunter has died as the result of an accident in India.

February 7th We heard at one o'clock that Mr Churchill is safely back in England after twenty-four days away and having covered 10,000 miles with almost all of his travelling done in a Liberator bomber. He visited Tripoli two days ago and congratulated General Montgomery and the Eighth Army on a victory that had 'altered the whole character of the war'. Mussolini is reshuffling his cabinet. There is a rumour that Hitler is dead! In both Axis countries troubles are mounting up and no amount of reshuffling and speeches and threats will help now. It is impossible not to feel the end is in sight.

February 9th There was a lot of damage done in Worthing yesterday by Nazi raiders. Mrs MacRae, eighty-eight years old and her invalid daughter were killed when a bomb flattened their house in Homefield Rd. Dorothy Macpherson was helping at the Woolton Restaurant in Lyndhurst Rd when it was hit; she cut her leg and was thoroughly frightened. It was extremely lucky that I changed a patient's appointment as otherwise I should have been exactly where a bomb fell at 2 pm. Children at St Mary's Catholic School were machine gunned but only a few were injured. The Americans have reported that no Japs remain in Guadalcanal and that the Japs have lost 50,000 men and 800 planes. We had an alert at 4.20 pm followed by very loud gunfire and other sounds. Mother was at a Whist Drive and owing to the noise there did not hear the battle!

This was the spot I should have been passing had I not changed a patient's appointment.

RESIDENTIAL AREA suffered damage during a Nazi raid on a south coast town.

February 18th Kharkov has been recaptured by the Russians and the Nazis are being pushed back. The French battleship *Richelieu*, 35,000 tons, has reached the USA from Dakar; it will be repaired and refitted for the coming operations. This is symbolic of France's return to the fight against the Axis. Florists are protesting against the ban on sending flowers by rail or post which came into force yesterday. A florist said

FREAK DAMAGE to a house after a Nazi raid on a south coast town. The top room was demolished, but the roof remained in position.

that he had been receiving many cables from the USA and Canada ordering flowers to be sent to Canadians wounded at Dieppe and now in hospital. They will have to stop. The papers reported there were no flower-sellers outside hospitals yesterday and no 'lovely violets' at Piccadilly Circus. Mother and I

The Crazy Cartoon is a result of the advertisement. All private cars are banned now and one often sees them in their garages, jacked up and covered over. I get eight gallons of petrol a month for my work so I'm still on the road. I have a note pasted on: 'Registered Medical Auxiliary' to show I am genuine.

went to see Noel Coward's wonderful naval film *In Which We Serve* this evening. It is amazing that so many men have such courage. The film brings home to us landlubbers the hazards — mines, torpedoes but worst of all dive bombing — each sailor has to steel himself to face for Britain.

February 22nd Mr Churchill does not seem to be at all well — possible pneumonia. Dr Spellman, the Roman Catholic bishop of New York, had a three-hour conference with President Roosevelt before leaving America for a private audience with the Pope. Can Italy be about to make some peace overtures?

There was a mine explosion again today. Later we heard a dog was the cause of it. The dog and mine are no more.

CRAZY CARTOON

" We've furnished this little spare room with bits of the car."

February 27th Mr Churchill has had pneumonia but is on the mend. Hurray! Interest and excitement grows, the town is packed with troops. The flat-bottomed boats to be seen are pontoons for bridge building. Very busy at the YMCA canteen but the men say there may not be a single customer tomorrow! We had to do up large parcels of cakes and sandwiches for men travelling through in convoy. Ken and I gave a pint of blood which was used on a special case at Southlands Hospital, Shoreham — there are a lot of tip and run raid victims there.

March 1st A terrific exodus of most of the soldiers, Canadians and British, from Worthing today. The pontoons have also gone. Traffic was diverted as the roads have been blocked by tanks. It seems the men have gone on three weeks of man-

oeuvres. A terrible tube shelter disaster in London — a woman stumbled and fell on the entrance stairs during an air-raid and 178 people were crushed and suffocated. But where were the wardens and police? London has opened its 'Wings For Victory Campaign' and over £30 million has been subscribed today already. Worthing holds its week in April and the target is £500,000. Eric Davis came for the weekend — his last probably as he is now an officer and will be posted somewhere soon. He looks very different now that he's in a decent uniform. I got his weekend rations just before the shops shut (still 5.30 pm): 2 oz tea, 1 oz lard (3/4d!), 1 oz butter, 2 oz marg, 2 oz rashers and 2 oz sugar. It's a great help to have them; we especially wanted the bacon as there were no sausages in the town today.

March 7th A typical wartime Sunday: 7.45 got up to do housework; 8.45 breakfast; nine o'clock wireless news; ten o'clock went to church to a united youth service, most of the children were in uniform, 500 of them; eleven o'clock worked on the allotment; one o'clock news and dinner in the kitchen; two o'clock to the canteen; 6.30 free for the rest of the evening!

March 9th Very nasty tea-time raid. Twelve raiders flew in towards the coast at 'zero feet', just above sea level and so were not located by radio-location. Six attacked Worthing and the others flew over towards Brighton. Three people were killed, literally 'blown to bits', three are missing and twenty-five injured. There's masses of glass and débris and corporation workmen everywhere.

March 18th We gave a concert at Gifford House — the ex-Servicemen there are facing a boring time as all the things they need for their handicrafts are unobtainable — pewter, wood, beads, material for soft toys. Hitler has made a broadcast speech but there was no fire or ranting, just a read affair. Peterborough remarked in yesterday's *Daily Telegraph* that the ban on flower transport had been partially lifted as Mr Churchill had derived so much pleasure from flowers during his illness. Even bunches of flowers, taken in the hand by train, have been prohibited until now. Kit asked a bobby if she could take a few daffodils back with her to London today!

Mr Churchill broadcast an outline of a Four Year Plan for social reconstruction and progress at home. National compulsory insurance for all classes from the cradle to the grave and the elimination of want are the main objectives and will be implemented after the final defeat of Nazism.

March 27th We had an excitement here today. The 'alert' sounded at about two o'clock and as I was cycling along to the canteen terrific anti-aircraft gunfire sounded. As we are told to seek cover at once I hopped off my bike and was about to drop ignominiously down behind the wall of a previously bombed house in Lyndhurst Rd when a warden called to me to rush over to the shelter. It was all over soon and later the soldiers in the canteen told us a Nazi raider had been brought down in the sea at West Worthing before it even reached the coast.

April 3rd   I went to London for a CSMMG meeting. I had lunch with Fritz Kransz and then called on the Steinharts and the Morgensterns. All are working now and Fritz is earning over £6 a week, most of which he is saving against his future emigration to the USA. These Jewish refugees from Europe are an extremely good type of human being — thank goodness some have been saved from Hitler's clutches. Often there is news of the ghastly persecutions continually going on in Nazi occupied countries. One of my patients told me he's connected with a big Blind Institution in London which has a factory doing war work. One of their orders is to make 200,000 enormous wicker baskets capable of holding a half ton of foodstuffs which will be dropped on the occupied countries immediately hostilities cease.

April 10th   Worthing has over-reached its target of £500,000 for the 'Wings For Victory' week. We've had a remarkable meeting today arranged by the Worthing Council of Christian Congregations. Dr Bell, the Bishop of Chichester and Victor Gollancz, the publisher, spoke on the urgent question of aiding persecuted Jews on the continent. Both speakers pointed out how dilatory the government has been and still is. 'Jews are being tortured and taken off in trucks. 6,000,000 are affected of whom 1,500,000 had already been destroyed and 4,500,000 were crying out with a most piercing and anguished cry,' said the Bishop. The speakers called on Britain to give a lead by taking in 2,000 or 3,000 Jewish children with their adults and other nations — America, the Dominions, Russia and Turkey — would follow suit.

April 12th   Sir Kingsley Wood brought in his budget yesterday. There are higher taxes on beer, tobacco, wines, entertainments and non-essential goods such as jewellery. Mrs Wenban-Smith is feeling very sad as her Australian airman Arthur is missing after a big raid on the Ruhr.

April 20th   Hitler is fifty-four today. The RAF visited Berlin as did the Russian Air Force. A street newsvendor in London displayed in place of the usual home-made contents bill: HITLER IS 54 TODAY — OUR WISHES ARE CENSORED. The ban on bell ringing in church is to be lifted from Easter Sunday. They may be rung on special occasions and every Sunday to summon worshippers to church. But there is a shortage of skilled bell ringers.

April 26th   Kit cycled down from London for the Easter week-end. The public is asked not to use the railways if possible. She stopped at Lou's on the way to collect a *lemon!* A soldier bought Lou six and as they are absolutely unobtainable she thought we might like to raffle one for some cause. A lovely Easter day — sunny and warm.

News is of continuing fierce battles in Tunisia and of a gradual advance all along the front.

We had two visitors to supper and we opened a tin of salmon — twenty-four points gone west! The *Telegraph*'s Moscow correspondent reported that the Commandant of Moscow City had lifted the curfew for one night and 50,000 people attended the Easter Midnight Service, the most important in the calendar of the Orthodox Church. The thirty Moscow churches that are still open could hold only about a third of the 50,000 worshippers. The rest stood, tightly packed, in the pitch darkness outside the open portals. The correspondent, A. T. Cholerton, says he was struck by the number of young people at church.

We had a 'raiders passed' signal this morning without a previous 'alert'. Everyone wondered why and later at the Report Centre we heard that someone dusted the switch too thoroughly!

April 27th   The breaking-off of relations between Poland and Russia has come as a shock to all of us. The immediate cause of the quarrel is the Polish government's demand, considered by Moscow as an insult, for an inquiry into the massacre of the 10,000 Polish officers whose bodies the Germans claim to have discovered in a wood near Smolensk. Also there is developing irritation over the question of future frontiers which involves many and delicate problems. As the editorial in the paper said: 'What all of us must never lose sight of is that without victory it will not be the United Nations but Hitler who will solve all frontier and all other problems. Let both sides recall Mr Churchill's remark at the signing of the Soviet–Polish pact in July 1941 that it was "sign and proof of the fact that hundreds of millions of men all over the world are coming together on the march against the filthy gangster Power which must be effectively and finally destroyed".' The issue is very complicated and gives one an idea as to the settling up after the war. A wartime advertisement states that a million and a half pounds of rubber go on every 1,000 bomber raid, 176 lb go into a tank and 6 lb are needed to equip a commando. Rubber is vitally important for our offensive this year; but the enemy holds 90% of the world's natural rubber resources . . . more rubber must be salvaged!

April 30th   We had our annual meeting of the Worthing Branch of the League of Nations Union with an excellent speech by Miss Freda White on 'Winning the Peace'. After I had supper with her and the Framptons and we had a most interesting talk on current events. Miss White said relief would have

1943—HOME GUARD
On the way to the range, complete with gas-mask and Lewis gun.
106

to be on a terrific scale and probably carried out by the army, properly trained women would be able to do this work well. We should not allow one country more than it could consume while another starved.

May 1st   Every first of the month we wonder: 'will this be the one?' The one in which the Axis will suddenly crumple up and give in. We hear little of the Channel Islands. Red Cross letters come occasionally to relatives. Mr R. W. Hathaway, Seigneur of Sark, has been deported to Germany. The Dame, Mrs Sybil Mary Hathaway, is still in the island and is well. The Seigneur, an American who became a British subject, married the Dame, then Mrs Dudley Beaumont in November 1929.

May 8th   The papers headline the capture of Tunis and Bizerta by the Allies — the inhabitants enthusiastically greeted our soldiers with hugs and threw flowers in front of our tanks. In Poland patriots have executed the German head of the Gestapo. I went to a meeting addressed by a former German clergyman, Reverend Oelsner, who knew the famous Pastor Niemöller. As the speaker is half Jew he is over here as a refugee but the Bishop of Chichester has got him a curacy in Brighton.

May 10th   The Bishop of Chichester addressed a meeting of Worthing Christian Council on the plight of Europe's starving millions particularly those in Belgium. He urged us to write to Lord Selborne, the Minister of Economic Welfare and the PM.

May 16th   Over 225,000 prisoners have been captured in North Africa. Admiral Kimmins praised the wonderful co-operation between all three services in the campaign and said how important was the work of the 'factory front'. In Holland all wireless sets have been confiscated by the Nazis.

I saw *The Silver Fleet* yesterday in which Ralph Richardson plays a Dutch ship builder; he poses as a quisling in order to carry on his sabotage. Also in the film are Esmond Knight, who was blinded in the *Bismark* fight, and Googie Withers. It was excellent.

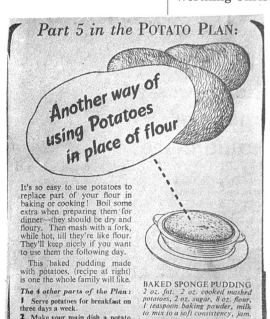

General von Arnim, Commander-in-Chief of the Axis armies in Tunisia, was brought to England yesterday as a prisoner of war. He will be treated in accordance with his rank. His pay, which he will now receive from Britain, will remain the same as if he were still with the German army. One article in the Geneva Convention states that the pay of prisoners of war should be the equivalent of their rank in the army of the detaining power.

Three of the German generals captured in Tunisia, photographed as they walked in to surrender. Left to right are, Gen. von Vaerst, Commander of the 5th Panzer Army, Maj.-Gen. Bassenge, commanding the 19th Flak Division, and Lt.-Gen. Karl Bolowius, commanding the Manteuffel Division. Since the beginning of the war 19 German generals have been taken by the British and United States forces. (Picture by radio.)

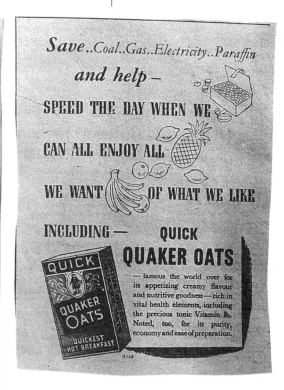

May 18th The RAF blew up three enormous dams in the Rhine and Ruhr last night. The floods are spreading in a terrible manner. Everyone I've spoken to feels that as it is bound to shorten the war it is a good thing, but for the terrible misery it is causing it is a bad thing to have to resort to. It seems thousands must have drowned. Reconnaissance photos already show much damage to war industries. The PM has said that it's a question of speed now — the Axis need time to recover from recent blows. We can't afford to let them have it. I believe it'll be peace this year!

Other things which are not available: tennis balls, salad cream, dairy cream, ice cream, watering cans, small garden forks, face flannels, loofahs and rubber-soled shoes. **Very difficult to get:** elastic, films, rhubarb, bed linen, flower seeds and custard powder.

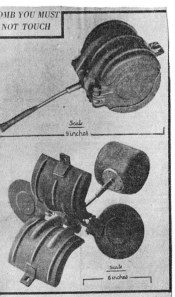

MB YOU MUST
NOT TOUCH

Scale
9 inches

Scale
6 inches

Two views of the new German anti-personnel bomb, a
number of which have been dropped in the last few days,
as reported in THE DAILY TELEGRAPH on Saturday. Usually
painted greyish-green or yellow, the slightest touch
may explode it. Above: The bomb with its outer
casing shut and a thick wire protruding. The casing,
when open, expands into four hinged portions at the end
of the wire, as seen in the lower picture.

May 24th The RAF bombed Dortmund very heavily last
night — thirty-eight planes are missing. This intensified air
war is awful. Yesterday Hastings and Bournemouth were
bombed in daylight using hit-and-run tactics. Uncle Will's
house in Bournemouth had a direct hit; luckily he was out and
Aunt Hilda saved herself by going into a cupboard. There
were many casualties including children.

We've had most welcome rain today, especially as I planted
nine rows of greens in the allotment yesterday. Everything is
growing well.

May 26th Mrs Wenban-Smith's Australian airman Max is
here on four days' leave; he took part in the awful Dortmund
raid two days ago. Dusseldorf and three Italian islands were
bombed last night — over 1,000 Allied planes took part. I
cycled to a CEMA concert in Goring Church this evening. It
stands for the Council for Encouragement of Music and the
Arts and is sponsored by the government. Musicians go around
to factories, hostels, camps etc, and give good music to the
people.

June 1st Italian naval bases and airfields are being relent-
lessly pounded by allied aircraft. When will the invasion take
place? And where? Perhaps not in Italy after all? The lull in
Russia continues. Torquay was bombed on Sunday. Ten boys
and ten girls and three teachers were killed when their Sunday
school was hit. The children were buried in a common grave.

June 3rd A British air liner has been shot down in the Bay
of Biscay with Leslie Howard the film actor who starred in
Pygmalion and *Gone With The Wind* on board and several
children returning from Canada. It is thought the Nazis were
hoping to 'get' Mr Churchill on his way back home from where?
He left the USA some days ago.

June 9th The Premier's speech to the House stressed 'the
hazards of our invasion' and 'amphibious actions of great com-
plexity'. He mentioned the *great* improvement in our fight
against the U-boats. Mrs Mitchell at the Report Centre told us
her seventeen-year-old second son came safely through with a
convoy across the North Atlantic recently. But it was a terrible
experience — fourteen out of forty merchant vessels were sunk
— five being meat ships. No wonder our meat ration remains
at 1/2d per week! It only costs 3d to send an airgraph to the
forces.

Mother and I went to a most enjoyable Canadian Legion
Concert Party in the Pier Pavilion tonight. All the artists
were soldiers and were really gifted. The audience of about
1,000 men were most appreciative.

June 13th Whit Sunday. Mr and Mrs Ward (Weingarten) are staying here for their seven days' leave. Aliens in the Pioneer Corps are able to change their names for English ones now. A nice and sunny day — I picked my first peas — 2¼ lb. They are still 1/– a lb in the shops.

June 20th The King is still away visiting the troops in North Africa and calling in on Malta. I had a game of tennis up at the club. It's the first time I've played there for three years. The place looked awful — only two courts are usable, weeds are everywhere, the ARP have two huts there, allotments have been dug on the car park. The Working Men's Club, which was bombed, now uses the pavilion. The balls were awful and the net very bad — tennis under wartime conditions!

June 25th Worthing is to have 500 'commandos' billeted in Broadwater! It is now known that the Lancaster bombers which bombed Friedrichshafen recently flew on to North Africa, re-fuelled and re-loaded and returned to England, bombing Spezia en route! 'Shuttle service!'

June 29th At the Report Centre I heard some Canadians enticed the commandos to 'do their stuff' with the result that two Canadians are in hospital! The PM has said that no German arms town will escape the RAF and that Italy has only felt preliminaries. The British public feels strongly and differently about this large scale bombing. Some people fatheadedly say 'they've asked for it and they are getting all that they deserve' (who are 'they'?). Others do not wish the civilians to have to suffer so much, admitting that it's part of the 'insane logic of war'. If only there were some less wicked way of ending the whole affair.

July 1st Underground resistance in Europe keeps many Axis divisions away from the front line, slows down Axis production and transport, and saps morale. In *The Listener*, this week, there are reports by Russian guerrillas behind the German lines being helped by collective farmers, the underground press in Holland and Belgium, the stubborn resistance of the Greeks, a picture of a gas works blown up in Marseilles for which the Vichy government blamed de Gaullist and Communist elements, 'go slows' in Czechoslovakia and the refusal of the church, teachers and trade unionists in Norway to assist the Nazis.

July 4th I took Kit some tomatoes as they get very few in London. There are lots of advertisements urging people to 'stay put' for their holidays this year in view of the coming 'liberation of Europe' offensive. There are bands etc in the parks to entice Londoners to stay!

July 5th On the one o'clock news we heard of the death of General Sikorski, the Polish PM and Commander-in-Chief, a great patriot and democrat, in a mysterious plane crash. It is a great loss. Colonel Cazalet also died in the crash in Gibraltar — only the Czech pilot survived.

I went to a meeting at the Town Hall tonight on the Beveridge Report. It was arranged by the trade union people and urged us to support a proposition asking the government to put the proposals into action with little delay. I've dusted my greens well to prevent the ravages of the flea beetle.

July 8th Today the papers are printing photos of Cologne, showing the only damage done to the beautiful Cathedral is some to the roof. The Nazis have been proclaiming our wickedness and saying it's a heap of rubble and so on. We've been warned about further reductions in clothes coupons. Everyone has to be awfully careful with their old ones now. Mollie has sent an old silk dress today in the bag containing six eggs, along with socks and stockings that Mother mends weekly for her. Mol hopes Mother can remake the dress into a pair of pyjamas for Michael.

July 10th General Eisenhower and the Allied forces have invaded Sicily. Early this morning I heard a buzz and looked out and counted 205 four-engine bombers flying out to sea. Occupied French air bases were the target and I heard a few explosions.

July 12th Alas! A bobby knocked us up at 1.45 am as I'd forgotten to switch off the kitchen light! It will be a £2 fine I'm afraid. Blow.

July 13th To the Report Centre as usual — it is my third anniversary there today. Nothing happened except at 7 am there was a noise of aircraft and a policeman told us it was a sight worth seeing so we went outside and saw a lot of 'forts' flying out to sea. It was 'Bastille Day' by that time and we gathered this was a celebration. Later we heard that French pilots had taken part. In *The Listener* this week, J. B. Priestley wrote a piece: 'Let Us Salute . . .', in which he quietly saluted the people who will never be decorated with medals and cheered but are making tremendous self-sacrifices. Like all people who have been brought out of retirement because of the war — doctors, waiters, civil servants, old actors and actresses. Also girls working switchboards, understaffed shop keepers, men in lighthouses, grey-haired ticket collectors, BBC engineers, postmen, those in charge of the mentally deficient. He ends by saying: 'And let us remember — for otherwise all this saluting and tribute-paying is so much eyewash and bunkum — that we are in truth one people, completely dependent on each other, a community in which each must serve according to his

DESPATCHES
FROM THE
HOME
FRONT

1943

119

The Premier, arriving with his daughter Mary at the Mansion House, after receiving the Freedom of the City of London, acknowledges the cheering crowds by waving his hat on his stick. Other pictures on Pages 3 and 5.

capacity. We recognise all this in the hour of danger. What we must remember from now on is that the hour of danger never really ends.'

July 16th On the three o'clock 'overseas' BBC broadcast came the news that Mr Roosevelt and Mr Churchill had broadcast an ultimatum to the Italian people: 'The time has come for you to decide whether Italians shall die for Mussolini and Hitler — or live for Italy and for civilisation.' Malta's long siege has happily ended — we all knew they had had a thin time of it but no-one knew how thin. Victory Kitchens provided one cooked meal a day to be collected at noon or 5 pm. There was a long line of pots outside the kitchen by 9 am. These pots formed the queue and no-one disputed their position. All the island's goats were eaten; there was only tin and powdered milk for the babies. Eggs, if there were any, were 15s a dozen. One lady bought a rabbit for 17/6d and then couldn't get rid of the idea that it was the shopkeeper's cat. A tin bath of water was put on the roof in the early morning and by the afternoon it was warm enough to bathe in. A bootlace stuck into a potted meat jar with a little paraffin provided light in the evening.

July 19th We had an amusing letter from Mollie today describing the boys' sports day. Commander Kimmins made a speech and gave the prizes. He was in the Sicilian landing just a week ago. He told the boys how important sports are and how when one ship arrived on the Sicilian beaches one important piece of equipment had been left behind. A volunteer rushed back for it — a football!

Aunt Alice spent the day with us and told us news of cousin Nevill that was relayed by a repatriated British prisoner. Nevill has made four attempts to escape from a prisoner-of-war camp. Once he was free for two months in Holland and then a wretched Dutchman gave him up to the Nazi police. He's in Poland now but writes fairly cheerfully.

On the news came the report of the bombing of Rome. The 'soft under-belly of the Axis', as Mr Churchill calls it, is in for an extremely bad time in the very near future.

July 25th I'm writing this at eleven o'clock in the evening and the news has just been broadcast that *Mussolini has resigned!* If only it weren't so late I'd phone up someone!

July 26th The whole world is agog with the news from Italy. Has Mussolini been dismissed, arrested or resigned? Marshal Badoglio is taking over and has already declared martial law throughout Italy. The papers remind us he used poison gas against the Abyssinians in 1935. He is apparently anti-German and anti-Fascist. The King has become Commander-in-Chief — rather pathetic. Both are over seventy.

July 28th Confusion reigns in Italy. Mr Churchill yesterday praised the Italian people but warned them that unless they surrender we shall have to intensify our efforts against them. Mr Roosevelt broadcast last night and started by saying: 'Over a year and a half ago I said to Congress that "the militarists in Berlin, Rome and Tokyo started this war, but the massed angered forces of common humanity will finish it". That prophecy is in the process of being fulfilled.' Fighting continues in the north-east tip of Sicily; the Nazis have flown over strong reinforcements.

TUESDAY, AUGUST 3, 1943

HOW THE CROWDS GREETED THE NEWS OF MUSSOLINI'S DOWNFALL

August 1st Bank Holiday weekend. Despite newspaper and radio warnings against travelling, thousands have tried to get away for a bit of a break, some standing in railway queues all night long. On arrival at coastal districts accommodation and food have not been sufficient. Moral 'Stay at Home'.

August 4th We had a 'Bring and Buy' sale for the Rest Home today. I had an excellent 'produce' stall and made £12. The sale raised £74 in total – a record. In the evening I played a tennis match against an RAF team at the radio-location place stationed in the Manor Club buildings at Goring. We won although we only had one man to their three. Marjorie Carter and I won all three matches. Wonderful news – the Russians have recaptured Orel after two and a half years' occupation by the Nazis and the Eighth Army has captured Catania and the inhabitants are jubilant.

August 7th Nazis continue to retreat in north-east Sicily and so far over 125,000 prisoners have been taken. Leaflets are reported to have been dropped on Berlin telling the people to expect the same fate as Hamburg. It is hoped the German

122

people will learn a lesson from the Italians and oust their government and demand peace. David Scott, the diplomatic correspondent of the *Daily Telegraph* shows very clearly the predicament Badoglio is in as the successor to the Duce in Italy: 'On the one hand he has the demand of the Allies for "unconditional surrender", to be followed by an Allied occupation of vital strategic areas which the Germans, heedless of Italian interests, will try to defend. On the other hand he must face the increasing pressure of the Italian people themselves for peace at any price. Over all hovers the threat of German reprisals if Rome breaks its word to Berlin.' Today's article concludes: 'Marshal Badoglio had better give up his attempt to steer in mid-stream and make for an Allied harbour while there is time.'

August 9th I was asked to give a talk to the Junior Red Cross on 'Rehabilitation and Occupational Therapy' – learnt a lot getting it ready! A Rehabilitation Centre is to be opened at the Royal Sussex County Hospital soon. We heard today that parts of the South Coast are to be banned again from next Saturday. It is to extend from Newhaven to Lancing and people travelling from Worthing into the banned area are to have permits. Cycling along to Lancing to the cinema will be prohibited. There are thousands of troops all along the coast – Canadian tank troops and British commandos. The continent is seething everywhere and occupied Europe awaits the call of liberation.

August 17th Important talks are going on in Quebec between Mr Churchill and Allied leaders. Norway is declared to be in a state of siege – all sorts of ugly happenings are going on between Nazis, Quislings and loyal Norwegians. It's been such a rush this week getting ready for my holiday on the land. The government calls them Volunteer Agricultural Camps and the type of work includes hoeing, planting, weeding, harvesting and picking vegetables. Volunteers are accommodated at the camp but their engagements are with the farmers who accept their services and pay them the agreed rate at the end of the day: all males 1/- per hour; all females 10d. The cost of living at the camp is 4/- per day or 28/- per week and the minimum period for a worker is four days. A farmer cannot employ

people in wet weather. Volunteers take a mug, plates, cutlery, tea towel, towel, soap and a pillow slip. Bedding is supplied. Volunteers should wear their oldest clothes and thickest footwear. Volunteers of sixteen and over will be welcome. According to their information leaflet 'there are no irksome regulations and volunteers will have every evening entirely free to do exactly as they like. Avoid all forms of waste. Every hour that you give to the land brings us nearer to the day of Victory.'

August 22nd   I went to Victoria by train and met Kit. We tidied up her allotment at Battersea and on our way home we looked in at the Chelsea Police Pig Club. A block of flats were demolished and on the site allotments and pigs are being kept. Vegetables appear to grow out of a concrete bed quite well! The pigs look in excellent condition. Crowds everywhere in London – people are having 'staying at home holidays'. We went on the river for two hours (12/6d); you can't go for less time and you pay a 7/6d deposit as soldiers have been leaving the boats anywhere.

August 23rd   Kit and I cycled from London to the Agricultural Workers Camp at Ampthill – a lovely easy ride of fifty to sixty miles. We arrived at 7 pm and discovered it is a real camp of tents! I'd hoped it might be a building. We had an evening meal straight away and were given a ground sheet and blankets and a straw mattress! The camp is in a lovely situation and there are between 250 and 300 people.

August 24th   Up at 6 am and queued for breakfast at 7 am and then queued again for work. There seems some difficulty about work. The farmers send in lorries for so many people but usually there are more people than the farmers need. We were not lucky so took to our bicycles.

August 25th   We were lucky today. Eleven of us went by lorry to Stanghams Farm where we were met by a very nice foreman, Mr Wilmot, a schoolmaster in ordinary times. He showed us how to shock wheat – stand twelve corn-sheaves close together in the field. We had a meal at twelve o'clock provided by the camp: bread and margarine, meat (de-hydrated) pies and tea made at a neighbouring cottage. Mr Wilmot said we did very well having shocked a nine-acre field and started on another one. We all earned 5/10d and arrived back in the lorry at 7.30 pm. Most of the people are from London and the North and there are a few foreigners. Something is organised in the camp most evenings but Kit and I go to our hard and boney bed early. News is that Berlin was very heavily raided last night – fifty-eight bombers are missing.

August 26th   A terrible morning – drenching rain – the camp a quagmire. Kit and I discussed the situation and in view of the fact that there is not enough work to go round we decided to cycle back to London.

Dominating the news is the mystery surrounding the death of King Boris of Bulgaria. He was only forty-nine. He 'fell ill' after meeting Hitler a few days ago – I don't wonder. But although some say it's his heart, others say he was shot by a Bulgarian policeman with Russian sympathies. He was the only king who was a member of a trade union; the Bulgarian Railwaymen's Union made him a life member as a wedding present. Denmark has so hated being called the 'perfect occupied country – the Nazis' showpiece' that she's flared up and the Nazis have had to declare martial law throughout the whole land – ugly scenes and happenings have taken place. Mr Churchill has made an excellent speech from Quebec but was very vague about the 'invasion of Europe' and the possible end of the war. But you feel he is more than satisfied with the way things are going.

September 3rd The fourth anniversary of the outbreak of the war. Mother and I and the two boys to church at ten o'clock as the King has asked for it to be a National Day of Prayer. It was a children's service and it was absolutely full. One small boy opposite me had an enormous half-eaten apple crammed into his pocket!

The BBC news announced a British landing on the toe of Italy. Hitler's fortress is attacked! General Montgomery is proving a wonderful leader. It was reported some time ago that he says he is never anxious about a battle – if he feels anxious he does not fight it! Certainly he's been victorious in everything he's set out to do so far.

September 8th *The greatest news of the war*. Italy has capitulated! Not only that, Badoglio has called on the Italian armed forces to help the Allies to eject the Germans from their soil! From Russia comes news that the whole of the Donets basin has been recaptured. Mother thinks Hitler must be chewing his carpet pretty hard tonight!

September 11th Hitler really did speak last night. He says he was tricked: Badoglio and King Victor Emmanuel both said that Italy would never capitulate – on the very day the armistice with us was signed. He praised Mussolini in fulsome terms. He conveniently forgot what he had said on September 30th, 1942: 'We have extended our alliances with our oldest ally – Italy. Enemy hopes of splitting us are sheer lunacy.' The Allies have captured Taranto and Salerno but the Nazis appear to be in control in North Italy. Most of the Italian fleet has escaped to Malta. In Rome there was violent street fighting – Italians trying to prevent the Nazis from establishing themselves in key positions. It is said that the German retreat in Russia is the biggest retreat in history. On the sea it is reported that more U-boats were sunk than merchant ships last month.

September 12th   A special victory peal was rung from St Paul's Cathedral today to celebrate the surrender of Italy but a shortage of trained bellringers prevented peals from being rung in many places. Today is the third day of National Thanksgiving held in Britain since the war started. The first was Sunday November 15th 1942 for the victory of El Alamein and the second was Sunday May 16th this year for the North African campaign. The editorial of the *Sunday Times* called on Rumania, Bulgaria and Hungary to follow Italy: 'Leave the sinking German ship before you drown, and don't be afraid of the pirates calling you rats.'

September 13th   The Nazis claim to have freed Mussolini! Nazi paratroopers are supposed to have landed in the Abruzzi Mountains north of Rome and released him from the hotel where he was being held. The Metropolitan Patriarch Sergei has been officially installed in Moscow Cathedral as the head of the Russian Orthodox Church. Stalin has recognised the new Patriarch. One of the troubles with the 'men in the street' is that they've had the idea that Russia was completely Godless. This has never been so; what took place was that the *government* dissociated itself with anything to do with religion.

September 14th   Chiang Kai-Shek has been elected to the presidency of China. Today's *Telegraph* says that at no time since the fall of the monarchy over thirty years ago has China been so united as she is today thanks to Chiang organising resistance to the Japanese and creating a national spirit. Under his guidance China will emerge from this war with a status and a prestige such as she has not enjoyed for centuries; that he possesses the enthusiastic allegiance of an overwhelming majority of his countrymen is not in doubt.

Blackpool Queueitis
A HOLIDAYMAKER back from Blackpool tells me he was waiting for his wife outside a greengrocer's when the greengrocer came out and said, "Would you mind not hanging about outside the shop, sir, or they'll form a queue on you. They always do."

September 19th   Today 'milk zoning' started in Worthing. We now have Edwards' milk, having had to give up Leeds. Only two milk firms are allowed in each road now – a private firm and the co-operative. Mr Churchill and his wife and daughter are safely back from Canada today. People are always anxious while he's away. The *Telegraph* says no man could more truly interpret or attract deep and reciprocal feelings between the two great Western democracies. Perhaps not the least cause of Mr Churchill's success in this matter is the knowledge that however much he may be at home across the Atlantic, here is his home.

September 21st   Marshal Badoglio has called on the Italian people: 'Today to resist is to exist. It is the only way. Italians, you have powerful means in your hands, especially guerrilla war, of which you have an example on the other side of the

126

Adriatic. The Germans want to harm us. It is your absolute duty to fight on at the side of the British and Americans.' The PM says the Italian front is not the promised invasion of Hitler's fortress of Europe. This 'second front' is still to come.

September 25th I went up to the annual congress of the CSMMG in London. Later I met Fritz Krausz. He says all the refugees are feeling very apprehensive about their future after the war. They wonder if they will be deprived of work again and even ordered to leave Britain. They realise there will be difficult times here – even now the miners are frequently striking.

September 26th It is 'Battle of Britain' Sunday today – to commemorate the RAF's decisive victory over the Luftwaffe in September 1940. Hitler thought he could finish the war in a matter of weeks. We saw the procession of Worthing's armed forces and Civil Defence people – thousands. After tea we saw a great force of bombers flying due south, making white vapour trails in the sky.

September 28th I attended a small committee about the local Anglo–Soviet Friendship Committee at the Town Hall tonight. It would seem that a feeling of friendship for us does not exist very strongly in Russia — these committees are hoping to produce mutual understanding and sympathy. Lord Woolton, Minister of Food, hopes that within the next few months we will 'taste some of the fruits of victory in the shape of a few oranges and lemons and onions which I have already bought in considerable quantities from the Mediterranean'. This news is welcome. One of my old lady patients stuck me out by saying we're half-starved! I said I'd not lost an ounce during the war and that my teeth had not decayed so much during these four years! The wartime diet is excellent from a health point of view. It's very plain, certainly, and at the end of the week housekeepers do find difficulty in finding the meat course.

October 1st Our troops are in Naples. The Germans have carried out very widespread demolitions in this beautiful city. Three British war correspondents with the Fifth Army have been killed on the Naples front. Their deaths bring the total war casualties among correspondents to eight; twelve are wounded, four are missing and eight are prisoners of war or interned. Among Empire and American correspondents: twenty-seven killed, thirty-three wounded, seven missing and forty-five prisoners of war or interned. Three American correspondents and Noel Monks, a British correspondent representing the Combined British Press, report that they were the first to 'take' Naples. 'We drove in ahead of the British and American patrols and as we reached the centre thousands of yelling, hysterical people rushed up to us, tore us bodily from the jeep

Worthing Herald, September 25th

Czech Refugee Boy's Brilliant Examination Success

When Martin Fleischmann came to England in 1939 he was twelve years of age, and knew no English. He and his sister were refugees from Czechoslovakia.

Fleischmann entered Worthing High School for Boys in the autumn of 1939. Now, at 16 years of age, he is in the lower-sixth, and of the school's recent successes in the Cambridge School Certificate examination his is most remarkable.

The boy who four years ago knew no English took nine subjects in this English examination, and in seven subjects out of the nine he was marked (a) which stands for "very good," the highest marking possible. One of these subjects was English literature. In his other two subjects English language and Art, he was marked (c) which stands for "credit," and is the second marking possible.

Mrs Fleischmann, who makes a home at Allangate, Station-road, Rustington, for her son and her twenty year old daughter, who is working locally in the Land Army while modestly deprecating "fuss" about her son's success, admitted to a "Herald" reporter that she was very pleased he had done so well.

and smothered us in embraces.' Dr Garbett, the Archbishop of York, has returned from Moscow via Cairo. He says: 'The future of religion in Russia is assured' and has given an enthusiastic account of two services there each attended by 10,000 persons.

October 3rd   Richard is five today. It seems much longer than five years since Mr Chamberlain flew to Munich to 'appease' Hitler. Helen made quite a decent looking wartime birthday cake with some chocolate icing. We found difficulty in finding birthday presents as toys are almost impossible to procure. The policeman at the Report Centre is making a wooden train set for me but it is not quite finished. Ken bought a second-hand clockwork train from one of his pupils – a great triumph! Civilian casualties due to air raids in the UK in September were the lowest since May 1940 when only three were injured and none killed. Since the beginning of the war 48,282 civilians have been killed and 62,192 have been injured. A new conference dealing with inter-Allied relief and rehabilitation is to begin in the USA on November 9th – the United Nations Relief and Rehabilitation Administration. UNRRA will be notable as the first time that the four major powers – Britain, the US, Russia and China – have collaborated in setting up definite machinery by which they can work together to attain their common objectives. According to the newspapers over 1,000 Jewish refugees fleeing Nazism have reached Sweden safely having paid Danish fishermen between £100 and £200 to cross the stormy Oeresund which separates the two countries.

October 10th   I travelled to Epsom to see Mrs Albrecht, one of the Austrian refugees we had in Worthing from 1939 to 1940. She's found life very hard being separated from her husband who has been on a tanker in the Mediterranean for the last five years.

The 'domestic' problem really is a problem. We are lucky to have a morning woman from 9.30 to 12.30 not Sundays (£1 a week). Many people have no help at all. Mr Ernest Bevin, the Labour Minister, has said that he wants to make domestic service a craft, akin in its organisation and work to nursing. He wants domestic service to be available to all classes by the day, week or month according to need – as, for instance, a confinement – or permanently. He wants the status of domestic service to be raised so that it will be much more attractive and offer regular and congenial employment to thousands of women after the war.

October 12th   A most courageous attack has taken place by 'midget' British submarines on Nazi battleships in strongly defended Norwegian fiords. Three submarines are lost but the *Tirpitz* has been hit as reconnaissance photos show oil all around the ship. The Germans may try to get the ship back to Germany. Other news is that Britain and other Allied nations have been granted the use of the Portuguese Azores Islands in the Atlantic by Dr Salazar. The mid-Atlantic 'gap' can now be covered by land-based planes.

October 13th More outstanding news is that Italy has now declared war on Germany! She now ranks as a co-belligerent but not as an ally. Allied forces of all services have already landed in the Azores.

HE SUNDAY TIMES, OCTOBER 17, 1943

TO FIGHT FORMER ALLIES

Sunday Times, October 17th

Picture by radio from Algiers showing Marshal Badoglio reading Italy's declaration of war on Germany on Thursday afternoon

October 17th Ken's boys and I collected up fallen leaves for the allotment compost heap! They loved doing it. Marjorie Carter and I cycled to Steyning and back in the afternoon. Hardly a car on the roads. We called on Mrs Ing – her nephew John Stevens is in command of a submarine in the Mediterranean. He's got the DSO and bar and the DSC already! Eisenhower says he's the most daring of all our sub men. He is twenty-seven.

An article in the paper said that the introduction of the Lend-Lease foods – canned luncheon meat, ham loaves, dried egg and more cheese – has provided more variety to the national diet. Scientists discovered that a monotonous diet leads to a decline in the people's weight even when sufficient food is available – in 1940 and 1941 people were not eating enough for their physiological needs.

General MacArthur has carried out a surprise bomber attack on Rabaul in New Britain; this is the principal advanced base and depot of the Japanese forces operating in New Guinea and the Solomons. The exchange of prisoners between Germany and Britain is really going to take place in the neutral Swedish port of Gothenburg. It was over two years ago that the plans all went wrong. In the First World War, the Swedish Red

Cross carried through the exchange of no fewer than 73,000 Russian and German war prisoners. Correspondents in Sweden report that the ex-prisoners want to know the latest racing and football news, what had happened in their favourite strip cartoons in the English newspapers, was Portugal really in the war, what was the truth about Hess and how about the beer at home.

October 24th It was disclosed by Mr Hudson, Minister of Agriculture, in a broadcast last night that 1,000,000 tons more bread-corn and more than 250,000 tons more potatoes have been grown in Britain this year than in last year's record breaking effort. Enough shipping space has been saved to transport overseas vehicles, guns, ammunitions, supplies and equipment for eight or ten divisions. The fields of Britain had had much to do with the collapse of Italy.

In *The Listener*, Professor Salisbury, the new director of Kew Gardens, drew attention to the rosebay willowherb growing right in the middle of our cities on the debris left behind by air raids. It never used to be a common plant but with up to half a million seeds released from a single plant rosebay gets about now as it is tolerant of ground recently heated and the nitrates associated with ash. In America it's called 'fireweed'.

The former prime minister Mr Lloyd George has married his secretary Miss Frances Stevenson whose parents live in Worthing. He married his first wife Margaret in 1888 and she died in 1941.

October 27th To the WEA monthly 'Current Affairs' talk. It was on Jugoslavia and showed how extremely complicated all the Balkan problems are – geographical, religious and political differences and much hatred between small groups. The news today is excellent with headlines like: 'Russians cut German front to pieces', 'Bombs sapping Nazi will to fight', 'Germans talk of beginning of the end' – it really looks as if we may have a peaceful Christmas. British prisoners who returned recently say food is so bad in Germany that without Red Cross parcels many of them would not have survived. Private Rowan of Hull is quoted in the paper: 'The Germans are browned off. They know they are licked. They live practically on potatoes. The guards of late were either boys, wounded men back from the Russian front – some without an eye or an arm – or men over 50.' Lord Wavell has taken up his appointment of Viceroy of India and has quickly used the army to help feed the famine-stricken areas.

November 3rd I went to London for the day and took Kit some blackout curtains for her new flat. Mother made them but now there is such a feeling that we are very near the end of the war she wishes she'd used an inferior quality! There was an 'alert' as we got to Croydon and the train continued in

130

complete darkness for about an hour. Voices out of the blackness recounted earlier blitz experiences and a good time was had by all! The papers report the successful Moscow Conference and steady progress in Italy and Russia. The only trouble is strikes – both here and in the USA. The fighting men can't understand it. Uncle Ted wrote saying Hector, who is forty-three, has 'got' his second Nazi plane. He is in coastal command. He says the Home Guard love having a crack at Jerry with the anti-aircraft batteries which they man one night in eight; it is a bit of a tonic as most gunners are civilians in factories and offices all day. One of my former patients, Captain Dilloway MC, was interviewed by the *Worthing Gazette* about his prisoner-of-war experiences. He says: 'Perhaps it may ease the minds of many who have close ties with British prisoners in Germany when I say that I did not see any active ill-treatment throughout my period of captivity.'

November 7th This is Soviet Day. Marshal Stalin broadcast last night on the eve of the twenty-sixth anniversary of their revolution. He paid tribute to the Allied efforts and declared that the war was 'nearing final victory'. The editorial in *The Listener* said: 'Today the Russians and ourselves are comrades in arms. Tomorrow we shall be sitting side by side at the conference table to map out the peace. The degree of harmony we can achieve in that process will depend on the ability of each to understand the other's point of view. The task of all men of goodwill in both our countries is to face the differences fairly and squarely and starting from the feeling of confidence that the war has fostered between us, to forge a friendship based on respect – a relationship such as befits two great peoples inhabiting the same world.' Worthing had a 'Salute to Russia' meeting. A Russian woman born in Kiev spoke and Russian songs were sung (in English) by the Boys' Choir.

Radio Times

BROCK'S "Crystal Palace" FIREWORKS

AN APOLOGY
SORRY, GUY, BUT WE CAN'T SPARE YOU ANY FIREWORKS THIS YEAR WE ARE USING OUR POWDER FOR STERNER PURPOSES. BUT WHEN THE LIGHTS GO UP AGAIN – THE FIRE- WORKS WILL BE BY BROCK'S WHO WILL SEE THAT YOUR NEXT GUY FAWKES DAY GOES WITH A BANG.

C.T. BROCK & CO'S 'CRYSTAL PALACE' FIREWORKS L⁺ᵈ Hemel Hempstead, Herts

November 10th Churchill spoke at the Mansion House yesterday. He said we were in for a very grim time but that next year will see the climax of the European war with costly battles and big sacrifices in British and American lives. Germany may launch new forms of attack on Britain which would make demands on firewatching, he warned. Mr Dingle Foot told the House of Commons today that the government could not agree to send food through the blockade to occupied countries; he

DESPATCHES
FROM THE
HOME
FRONT

1943

131

said it would be a form of lend-lease to Germany. Mr Harold Nicolson said that though a little drop of benefit might accrue to Germany if food was sent to Belgium and Greece, it would be as nothing compared with the benefit which might be given not only to the Allies, but to unborn generations. The government's White Paper on 'mutual aid' shows that Britain has 'assumed a burden of £2,250,000,000 on behalf of the Allies over and above what she has received from them.' We've sent 4,490 planes to Russia.

November 15th The Free French have got all uppish in Lebanon, even firing on civilian crowds after having imprisoned the President and members of the cabinet. It seems that General de Gaulle is very annoyed that France was not invited to the recent Moscow Conference. The USAF has bombed Sofia in Bulgaria today and Nazi steel works in Norway yesterday. Sir Stafford Cripps may be a future PM. In today's paper he says: 'I refuse to admit that it is only by revolution and bloodshed that changes can be brought about in our social and economic conditions. Our future policy must not only be wisely thought out but it must also be severely practical. My guiding principles are those of the Christian ethic. The New Testament lays down in my belief the highest attainable standard of conduct not only for the individual relationships but for national and international relationships as well. Its principles should be our inspiration and by them we should test every item of our policy. No principles of capitalism or Socialism or any other "ism" need or must interfere with the complete liberty of action of the government in making certain that there is full employment. That to me is the cardinal point.' Sir Oswald and Lady Mosley were released yesterday. There is much criticism of this and many protests.

November 24th Berlin has been raided very severely for the past two nights. Tremendous damage has been reported with 5,000 tons of bombs in the last three raids and even the asphalt pavements were on fire. Sir Arthur Harris, Marshal of the RAF, says Berlin will continue to be attacked 'until the heart of Nazi Germany ceases to beat'. Grim words. Goebbels says the German Home Front is unaffected by the raids. Hitler says 'reprisals are being planned'. Mother went to a sale in aid of Prisoners of War Parcel Fund. It was packed as usual – they made over £200.

November 27th General Montgomery, in a message to the Eighth Army, says: 'The time has now come to drive the Germans north of Rome. We will hit them a colossal crack.' Goebbels is reported to be preparing 'with feverish industry to pay the British back' for the recent air raids on Berlin. He condemns Britain for fighting 'with phosphorus and fire against women and children, who in their defencelessness, are natur-

AIR CREW DIED TO SAVE VILLAGE

All but one member of the crew of a flying fortress gave their lives to save the Berkshire village of Wargrave on Saturday. They stayed in their burning plane, steered it away from the houses and accurately released their entire load of bombs along a narrow river a second before the plane blew up in mid-air. The man who survived was blown out by the explosion. He landed by parachute and escaped with a sprained ankle. It was stated yesterday that the airmen could have baled out in plenty of time, as they had previously sent a radio distress call. Their self-sacrifice and extraordinarily accurate bomb-aiming saved the village from being practically wiped out.

ally more remunerative targets than armed German soldiers. The enemy smothers Berlin with high explosive and incendiary bombs on its cultural monuments, hospitals, churches and workers' districts. The enemy wishes the war to end with unconditional capitulation. In the name of the German capital and its people, as well as in the name of the whole German nation, I can give but one reply – never.'

December 2nd   General Montgomery, who five days ago promised the Germans a 'colossal crack' has announced that the Eighth Army has broken through the German winter line in Italy.

A mild form of 'flu is ravaging the country. Luckily it's over in two days roughly. I had today off work but managed to go to the YMCA tonight. The soldiers all looked and sounded full of cold. Stalin, Roosevelt and Churchill are meeting in Teheran. In the current *British Medical Journal*, Air Commodore Symonds states that nervous disease among airmen is highest among night bomber crews but goes on to say: 'It is nevertheless widely recognised that fear, within limits, is not only a natural but a healthy emotion, stimulating attention, sharpening judgement, and evoking maximal effort. An experienced squadron leader told me that he liked a man to have enough imagination to fear the worst and hope for the best.' It was announced on German radio that owing to the lack of transport and manpower shortage, the sale of Christmas trees would be banned.

December 7th   The three leaders in Teheran have issued a statement that refers to concerting their plans for defeating Germany by attacks from East, South and West and have reached an understanding for establishing peace on a basis that will banish war for generations to come. It ends by saying: 'From these friendly conferences we look with confidence to the day when all peoples of the world may live free lives untouched by tyranny and according to their desires and their own consciences. We came here with hope and determination. We leave here friends in fact, in spirit and in purpose. Roosevelt, Stalin, Churchill.'

December 8th   One of my patients had an unexpected visit from her son she thought was still in Italy. He says thirty ships arrived in a Scottish port last week with 3,000 men on each ship. Some people think they may be back to help in the invasion of Western Europe. How unutterably wretched. A new system of local warning of the approach of hostile aircraft is to be inaugurated in Worthing – it will emit sounds similar to those of a cuckoo. Our ship losses are the lowest since May 1940 – the U-boats' activities have been curbed by our planes based in the Azores. Marjorie Carter and I had a really nice 'peace-time' afternoon. We went over to the Dome, Brighton to a symphony concert with Ida Haendel, the violin soloist. We

Marshal Stalin, President Roosevelt and Mr. Churchill photographed at their first historic meeting together in the old Imperial Russian Embassy at Teheran. This picture, and another on Page 3, arrived by air last night from Cairo. Some of their advisers are seen behind. Left to right are: Mr. Harry Hopkins; M. Molotov, People's Commissar for Foreign Affairs; Mr. Averell Harriman, United States Ambassador in Moscow; Section Officer Sarah Oliver, Mr. Churchill's daughter, and the Foreign Secretary, Mr. Eden.

Daily Telegraph, December 7th

had quite a heavy fall of snow during the night.

December 20th Pre-Christmas rush is upon us and there is no time for diary writing. Salient news features of last few days: (1) Mr Churchill's illness (pneumonia again) in the Middle East; he is going away to an 'unknown destination' in the sun to regain his strength. (2) Mr Roosevelt's safe return to the USA. (3) The Soviet winter offensive has started in good earnest. (4) Worthing had its first genuine 'cuckoo' alarm at 6 am today and bombs were dropped nearby. (5) We've started our tenth Carol singing expeditions! No moon all this week but we made £18–12–0d tonight. (6) Last Saturday Mother and I joined Kit at the Carols Concert in the Albert Hall. Well-known carols were sung by Royal Choral Society members under Malcolm Sargent and the 7,000 audience joined the choristers for such carols as 'Adeste Fideles'. The papers reported the next day that Dr Sargent's eighteen-year-old daughter Pamela had just died. She fell victim to infantile paralysis while on holiday with her parents in Italy in 1937. Dr Sargent had searched all Europe for a cure.

Christmas Eve 1943 I've counted well over 200 bombers flying south today. On the news I heard that over 1,300 had bombed occupied France. The weather has been lovely – sunny and clear. We went out carol singing again and collected over £13! So we've made in this fifth winter of war a record £34–15–0d in three nights. The Archbishop of Canterbury has said that victory will bring great responsibility and we must be ready to meet it; it will be a time for greatness and if we are to rise to the occasion we must deepen our faith and make it more secure.

Christmas, 1938 43

" And this I wish. Every day some new love of lovely things; some new forgetfulness of the teasing things, and some sweeter peace from the hurrying things. Longer stay of time when you are happy, and lighter flight of hours that are unkind."

From

Mr. & Mrs. Gordon Holman.

The Croft,
MARINE Manor Close,
West Worthing

This is a real wartime Christmas card! We've had some very nice ones but they are *very* expensive. Nothing nice under 4d.

Christmas Day 1943 The quietest one we've ever had! Our dinner consisted of liver (from the rabbit Harold Frampton gave us) and bacon, greens and potatoes and stewed fruit! We had it in the kitchen early and then set off to see a good horse film at the Odeon *My Friend Flicka*. We've been asked not to use the telephone over the holiday so we've not used it as we usually do. The King's broadcast at three o'clock was very good. In his customary message to British people throughout the world he said: 'Wherever you may be, today of all days in the year, your thoughts will be in distant places and your hearts with those you love. I hope that my words may be the bond that joins us all in one company for a few moments on this Christmas Day. With this thought in mind I wish to all who are on service away from home good luck and a stout heart; to all who wait for them to return, proud memories and high hopes to keep you strong; to all children, here and in the lands beyond the seas, a day of real happiness . . . . As we were not downcast by defeat, we are not unduly exalted by victory. We know that much hard working and hard fighting than ever before are necessary and we shall not rest from our task until it is nobly ended. So, as we see the clouds breaking on this Christmas Day, we should take comfort from our faith that out of desolation shall rise a new hope, and out of strife be born a new brotherhood. In the words of Lord Tweedsmuir (John Buchan): "No experience can be too strange and no task too formidable if a man can link it up with what he knows and loves."'

December 27th General Eisenhower is to be the Allied Commander-in-Chief in Europe with General Montgomery his deputy. The great Nazi battleship *Scharnhorst* has been sunk in north Norwegian waters. I went to the final supper party at the Mayor's Rest Home. The seven 'lovely Londoners' have had a marvellous time – parties, pantomimes, presents!

December 31st At the YMCA some of the men were rather 'jolly' tonight – one merchant navy boy we found still asleep in the writing room at 10.30. He'd been there since 3 pm! He'd not had a drop for seven months while on board, and does not think he'll have any more ever!

1944

January 1st Vth year of the war. V = for Victory. New Year speeches and newspaper articles all stress that this year promises to be 'the year of destiny'. Although an Allied victory is certain, everyone is urged not to relax their efforts. The German High Command is expecting an Allied invasion 'somewhere'. As I bought this book, the tenth, I could not help wondering if I shall ever complete it! I was tempted to buy a smaller one.

January 2nd This Sunday is the American Day of Prayer. A special service was held in St Paul's crypt. With all military preparations for the day of the liberation of Europe apparently completed, the papers have reported the day of prayer 'as a last meeting with God before the battle'. At the service in London Lt General Devers read a proclamation from Mr Roosevelt to all Americans 'in our churches, in our homes, and in our hearts, those of us who walk in the familiar paths of home, those who fight in the wide battlefields of the world, those who go down to the sea in ships, and those who rise in the air on wings.' In his sermon, Chaplain John Weaver reminded all that between the President's proclamation and Easter, their people would have to pass through a dreadful period of agony. 'This will be known as the passion of our nation, when the enemies of Christ feel the impact of our strength, our might and righteous fury. Our nation will have its Lent – its dark Thursday and its Good Friday. Whether there will be a resurrection most glorious to behold will depend on whether we keep in close touch with God.'

January 3rd The battleship *Duke of York* has sailed back after sinking the *Scharnhorst* a week ago. Only thirty out of 1,460 men were saved and taken prisoner. The Captain of the *Duke of York* is a Findon Valley man – the Honourable G. H. E. Russell. People hate the Worthing 'cuckoo' – it is lowering to morale!

January 8th I went up to London by the eight o'clock train – blackout was not over till 8.35 and it was a very dark morning. There is news today of a great new RAF invention – the 'jet plane'. Propellers are not used. In London a lot of boroughs are getting their street lights into order – a good omen. Deptford has even had a try out just before blackout. The Russians have taken Kirovograd and the breach has been widened to seventy-five miles. Nazis are in retreat on a big front and much booty and many prisoners have been taken. The collapse of Germany really does look imminent. Slow but steady progress is being made in Italy. Mr Brailsford says that food rationing here is bound to remain in force for some time and a good job too if it brings home to our people the plight of people in Europe.

January 15th Our milk boy told us today that we shall get milk on five days only for a bit – a pint each delivery. I feel sure great stocks of food and other commodities are being rapidly stored for liberated Europe. There's very little dried fruit, dried milk, leather etc. A Croydon cinema was hit last night by a lone raider – seven were killed. Over 800 of our raiders attacked Germany – thirty-eight machines are missing. Lord Woolton, Minister of Reconstruction, says that houses for returning servicemen will be 'priority number one' at the end of the war. Mr Churchill is now reported to be absolutely well again and has met General de Gaulle and General Eisenhower recently. Some time ago the newspapers reported that there would be at least one lb of oranges for everyone in Britain. Now one ship has been blown up by delayed action bombs probably placed by Spanish Nazi agents, and the other has got to be thoroughly searched and all the fruit may be ruined. A small item but typical of the times. Mr Bevin's first eighteen-year-old boys (200 selected by ballot) have started work today, ie coal mine training. Boys are from all classes – public schools, boys who have been working for some years etc.

January 20th Our road became a scene of great animation today. Hundreds of soldiers and many lorries and guns arrived. The Russians have taken by storm the very important city of Novgorod but there is still uneasiness about the dispute over the Polish frontier. Goebbels in his weekly article says: 'Invasion at any moment. We await developments with composure and calm. We have done everything that could be done to meet invasion and we are fighting for our lives.' Rather different from 1940 when they were going to invade us!

January 23rd The very large-scale landing near Rome has proved extremely successful so far, taking the Nazis by surprise (no opposition was met for over two hours by which time we'd got well established). The Russians are pushing well forward on the Leningrad front. Another U-boat attack on an Atlantic convoy, lasting four days, has been beaten off. At home miners

DESPATCHES
FROM THE
HOME
FRONT
1944

137

are to have a minimum wage of £5 a week. A good thing. Two German airmen have been washed up at East Worthing. Already there are over twenty buried up at the New Cemetery. Mother is very busy making trolley cloths from a linen sheet given her by Miss Bridges marked 1882! It's an enormous sheet and will make dozens for sales. In this case it's for a Prisoner of War sale 'something new from something old'.

January 25th   Mother phoned me at the Report Centre at 8 pm to say 'could I find a night nurse for Mrs Harris?' (my ninety-five-year-old patient). With great difficulty I did but then could get no taxi. I had to leave the centre to act as taxi driver. It seems that all taxi people are on their last week of their petrol allowance and have none except for their regular customers. I pleaded that it was a case of life and death but with no success. I was furious for the second time today as I was called to the hospital at 10 am to be a blood donor and was kept waiting for three-quarters of an hour. Most awkward. The other person there found it equally annoying. Steady progress is being made by the Fifth Army towards Rome. German reports say they have urged the Pope to leave the Vatican City for Germany but he has refused.

January 26th   I had to be a taxi driver again tonight but the blackout was horrid and I had to take Uncle Bert with an extra torch to light up the kerbstone. The Argentine has at last broken with the Axis. The siege of Leningrad is at an end.

We're out of anthracite too! (It arrived five days later. Mother felt equally jubilant and gave the man a shilling!)

SMILING THROUGH (No. 2,921) By LEE

"Lord and Lady Phipps-Toot . . . Colonel Chumpleigh-Champing . . . . the Duchess of Dough . . . the COALMAN !"

*Evening News,
January 29th*

January 29th   The British and American governments have indicated Japanese brutality to our prisoners – it is terrible. We hear General Montgomery was in Worthing three days ago inspecting troops on Broadwater Green. There are a great number of Eighth Army men here. We listened in to a lovely symphony concert, Beethoven's *Eroica*, from Germany this evening – 1700 metre band at 6 pm.

January 31st   Hitler made a speech on the twelfth anniversary of his coming to power. It was feeble and mostly referred to Germany being the only bulwark against Bolshevism in Europe. No promises this time! The long promised oranges have arrived in Worthing. I saw several queues. One lb (two oranges) each ration book is the allowance and most welcome too. There are no torch batteries anywhere – the papers say it is due to the impending invasion.

February 3rd   I tuned in to Lord Haw Haw – he had to admit some losses but most of his 'views on the news' were of the Bolshevik menace and so on. He is very boring and has a hateful voice.

February 10th   In parliament yesterday, Dr Bell, the Bishop of Chichester, stated that our bombing policy was wrong. He says that it is going beyond what we set out to do originally – it is affecting civilians and church property more than it should. Lord Cranborne said it was necessary to bring the war to an early victorious end and bombing would continue. He showed how the big Krupps works had been completely wiped out in Essen. News is not so good from Italy with fierce fighting at the Anzio beach head. I allotmented in the afternoon.

School children are collecting the books and we turned out 130 today which were removed triumphantly in two sacks. Up to today about 50,000 have been received.

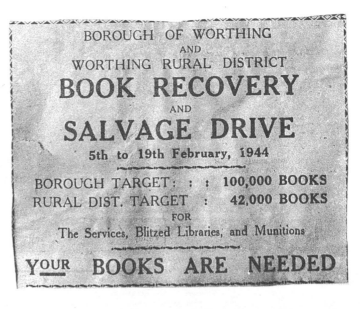

BOROUGH OF WORTHING
AND
WORTHING RURAL DISTRICT

BOOK RECOVERY
AND
SALVAGE DRIVE

5th to 19th February, 1944

BOROUGH TARGET : : 100,000 BOOKS
RURAL DIST. TARGET : 42,000 BOOKS

FOR

The Services, Blitzed Libraries, and Munitions

YOUR   BOOKS   ARE   NEEDED

February 13th The situation at Anzio in Italy is distinctly better — everyone is relieved. Mother is seventy-six today. It's very difficult to think of a present. Note paper and flowers are about the only things one can buy. There were a lot of the famous Eighth Army people in church today. Last night at midnight all the Worthing Home Guard were called out to report for duty as a test. Most were asleep as they are mostly middle-aged business men doing more work than they should. It was a success apart from their language on waking!

February 15th At one o'clock we heard that the world famous monastery overlooking Cassino, now a strongly fortified German position holding up the Allied advance, had been bombed by over 200 US bombers. Previously leaflets had been dropped and broadcasts made warning the authorities to evacuate the 10,000 refugees sheltering there.

February 18th The big German force, cut off in the Ukraine, is no more. Hitler sent orders that they were not to surrender and promised relief. Over 50,000 were killed and a few thousand taken prisoner. Our book target has been smashed. Over 120,000 were collected in Worthing for the services, blitzed libraries and for salvage. The *Worthing Herald* reports that Lieutenant Alan Toley, RAC, is missing in the Middle East. He is a former patient of mine and a very clever young fellow. He is a well known golfer and played rugby for Worthing, Bath and Sussex. There were heavy raids on Germany last night with Leipsig the main target. We lost seventy-nine planes. That's about 400 men of Alan Toley's type . . . .

February 22nd Mr Churchill gave a solemn warning to Germany today when he made his first speech in the House of Commons for five months. He said that Stalin, Roosevelt and he agreed in Teheran to 'fall on and smite the Hun by land, sea and air with all the strength that is in us in the coming spring and summer. The task is heavy, the toil is long, the trial will be severe. Let us all try our best to do our duty. Victory may not be so far away and will certainly not be denied us in the end.' He warned that the Germans may counter-attack with pilot-less aircraft or possibly rockets and he said that Stalin was resolved 'on the creation and maintenance of a strong integral and independent Poland as one of the leading powers of Europe.' A very unpleasant evening. I had just got in when the cuckoo sounded. Uncle Bert departed to the sound of gunfire. We had diving planes, and the sound of gunfire and bombs for about an hour. I was on fire-watching and went out to look for anything untoward from time to time; there was nothing except I heard shrapnel falling nearby. Mother sat in the passage working her drawn-threadwork trolley cloth. Had I been an artist I could have drawn a good picture of 'Life in 1944' with me in tin hat sitting on the stairs.

RUGBY PLAYER MISSING

A portrait of Lieutenant Alan Willoughby Toley, R.A.C., who, as reported last week, has been reported missing in the Middle East. Lieut. Toley, whose parents live at Chimneys, Fourth-avenue, is a well-known golfer. He played Rugby for Worthing, Bath and Sussex.

Worthing Herald,
February 19th

140

February 25th I picked up a piece of special paper in our garden. They are black strips with silver paper underneath. They have been dropped all over Worthing from a Nazi plane to upset our radio-location. Ken and Helen have their third son! Simon was born a few hours after last night's raid, during which Helen and the boys were in the Morrison shelter. Lemons are on sale with no restrictions. To celebrate we had pancakes for supper! I did my usual monthly swop of three eggs for some lard with Mrs Playdon and so was able to fry them in lard.

STRANGE.—On Feb. 25. 1944. at Charnwood Nursing Home, Worthing, to HELEN (née Wenban Smith) and KENNETH STRANGE, a third son (Simon Ridley).

Daily Telegraph,
February 29th

March 4th The USAF have bombed Berlin in daylight today for the first time. The RAF used their biggest bombs, 'factory busters' 5½ tons each, yesterday. If they were not certain they'd hit the target they were ordered to bring them back. They cause terrible havoc. Brigadier James Hargest, who escaped from a prisoner of war camp, has returned to Britain helped by the French underground. In France he heard a good story. When the Allied armies landed in North Africa the Germans suffered a momentary panic in France. They asked the French railway management if they could completely evacuate all the German troops from France in twenty-four hours. 'No,' they said, 'we can't do that, but we shall be *delighted* to do it in forty-eight.' I saw Simon today for the first time – he's a healthy looking baby – a good wartime effort! 90,000 Welsh miners are on strike.

March 17th The Italian front has started up again – we have flattened Cassino out with a terrific bombardment. Poor Italy. All the road signs (which disappeared in 1940 owing to possible German invasion) are up this week. It looks good to see them again. They will help all the American and other transport vehicles to find their way more easily. Kit is working flat out in Chelsea from 6 am to midnight to rehouse bombed-out families in Chelsea. Peterborough reports in the *Telegraph* that a suburban house 'Mon Abri' was blitzed recently. The occupier quickly changed the name to 'Mon Debris'.

Fritz Krausz, one of Worthing's Austrian Jewish refugees, came for the weekend. Now he is in the Home Guard he has no restrictions on travel. He is working on the 'Z' rocket guns on Hampstead Heath which are part of Britain's anti-aircraft defences.

March 22nd Hitler has occupied all Hungary and set up a puppet government. A ban is to be in force on all coastal districts from the Wash to Lands End from April 1st for 'operational reasons'. Other 'Home Front' news is that in future we have to

TRUNK CALLS RECORD

TELEPHONE

LESS

Above is a reproduction of the Post Office appeal to the public to telephone less.

But the latest figures show that: Long-distance calls are increasing and recently reached a record of over 1,000,000 in one week; Seventy per cent. are estimated to be directly or indirectly connected with the war, 29 per cent. being on Government work; Many of the remaining 30 per cent. are thought to be business calls.

The rationing of calls to six minutes is said to be causing people to make more calls. Other reasons given for the increase were: Difficulty of travelling; Movement of troops; and the Large number of " telephone-minded " Allied troops in Britain.

DESPATCHES
FROM THE
H☉ME
FRONT

1944

141

fetch our bread (we've fetched grocery rations for a long time). Some laundries can only collect and deliver once a month in future! I took the Cooks some sprout-tops from the allotment. Mr Cook is in the Pioneer Corps and is working on a food storage depot – more like a town – where hundreds of tons of all sorts of food are being stored for the occupied countries directly the Allies get to them. Rather encouraging.

April 2nd Civil Defence personnel attended a Naval Security film at the Odeon this morning. It was excellent. Makes you feel you'll never mention the war to anyone in case an enemy agent gets to hear the remark! I almost wondered if I'd make it the excuse for discontinuing this diary! The film was called *Jigsaw*. One thing that made the whole audience gasp: a convoy

London night sky during a recent raid

of thirty-eight merchant ships bound for Russia in August 1942 with frightfully important stores on board was attacked and only two ships reached port. News had leaked out and the largest packs of U-boats were ready to do their fell deeds. It was a 'pre-invasion' show . . . . And it's Palm Sunday . . . . There are serious coal mining strikes in England. It is thought that enemy agents are at work among the men, thousands are affected. Better news tonight – many men are returning to the pits.

April 9th   Easter Sunday. The big Nazi battleship, the 50,000 ton *Tirpitz*, has been very badly damaged while in its hideout in a Norwegian fjord – twenty-four hits from our bombers were recorded. It has been recently repaired and only just sea-worthy again! The Russians have now reached the Czechoslovak border. The RAF and the USAF are out in full strength all over Europe. Everyone is getting tuned up for the final and we hope swift blow.

April 16th   A lovely day of April rain and seedlings are doing very well. Mollie sent us a lovely piece of cold ham through the post yesterday! We are not allowed to forget the impending invasion. But when will it be? April or May? France? Low Countries? Balkans? We shall know soon no doubt. Canadians, REMEs, RAs, Commandos and others are here in Worthing. US troops are nearby. General Giraud has been dismissed and General de Gaulle, a much younger man, is the new Fighting French Commander-in-Chief.

April 23rd   The London bus strike and the Manchester gas strike were of short duration – about two days. Kit came for the weekend; she'd had a free ride on a bus run by soldiers. My German measles are over, worse luck! I enjoyed the rest. Uncle Bert and I went for an all day walk near Arundel – many scenes of military and air activity! The Downs near Worthing are almost all taken over by the military and are forbidden to the public.
   Gottfried Ritter was released on Friday – he's been interned since May 1940! Some people think the invasion will take place tonight – tides and weather are good. From Uncle Bert's *Church Times*: 'The state of the world today is the consequence of crimes committed in the name of patriotism. Nations and individuals have yet to learn that love of one's country finds its truest expression in good neighbourliness, not only towards one's friends and fellow citizens, but also towards one's fellow men on the other side of the street or frontier . . . '

April 30th   I went up to London to meet Gottfried Ritter and hear about his plans after internment. His experiences would fill a book. He looks well and seems happy once again.

Raider's Incendiary Container

Salvaged from the wreckage of a German plane brought down in the Home Counties after yesterday's raid on London was this incendiary-bomb container. The plane which carried it blew up as it crashed.

May 1st   Jock, our dog, ate our week's ration of cheese (2 oz each a week!). Mollie sent us about 5 lb of pork – part of the share out from Jack's National Fire Service Pig Club. It happens about twice a year. Everyone is keyed up to concert pitch over the invasion. The Germans say May 25th now! We've thousands of the troops and vehicles in the town. We've got some of the 'Desert Rat' lorries here in Langton Rd, very decent Eighth Army men in charge. All Allied Expeditionary Force vehicles carry a large white, five pointed star.

May 10th   The Russians have captured Sebastopol and the Allies have opened an 'all-out' attack in Italy. Britain, USA and Russia have jointly broadcast to the satellite countries of Finland, Rumania and Bulgaria to get out of the war as quickly as possible.

Mr de Valera's government was defeated by one vote yesterday and there is to be a general election in Eire at the end of May. A Dutch naval officer has bet a patient of mine a shilling he will be in Holland by June 20th! Two Home Guards were killed when some tank shells went astray in Steyning.

May 16th   Still no invasion. To the Report Centre and all quiet. Four of us got permission to watch the dance at the Assembly Hall and we thoroughly enjoyed a couple of hours there. It was an Eighth Army dance and the men looked very

144

well and behaved themselves. Quite a lot of drink about too. Such a lot of the dances end up rowdily.

May 20th There is distressing news from Sweden. Apparently about fifty prisoners of war who were trying to escape en masse from Stalag Luft III about 100 miles southeast of Berlin have been shot dead. The Swiss government has been asked to make a full enquiry. We had a *very* nice Eighth Army man in to tea and supper – Milner, a Regimental Sergeant Major. I'd met him on the allotment last week. He's seen service in North Africa and is expecting to do so again on the second front. He says it may be any time from now until the middle of August!

May 26th Mr Churchill announced to the House of Commons yesterday that after the war the victorious Allies would form an armed world council. It would prevent war 'at least in the time of our children and grand children'. He also said that justice will have to be done and retribution will fall on the wicked and the cruel. 'The miscreants who set out to subjugate first Europe and then the world must be punished.'

May 28th Some typical war time sights: (1) You never see a woman without a shopping basket. (2) Many Grannies push the grand children out while Mother works. If a Mother pushes the child herself she is *very* young. (3) Very many bicycles. (4) Paving stone kerbs and walls often broken down by heavy tanks. (5) Early morning queues at confectioners. If there are no queues it means the cakes are poor. (6) Greengrocers' shops are very dull – no fruit usually. (7) Marked civility shown to milkmen and butchers. (8) Numerous lorries, tanks etc in private roads. During the campaign that ended triumphantly in Tunis, the Eighth Army's own weekly paper *The Crusader* held a poetry competition. This is the start of one of them entitled 'A Soldier – His Prayer'.

> Stay with me God. The night is dark,
> The night is cold: my little spark
> Of courage dies. The night is long;
> Be with me God, and make me strong.
> I love a game. I love a fight.
> I hate the dark; I love the light,
> I love my child; I love my wife,
> I am no coward. I love life,
> Life with its change of mood and shade.
> I want to live. I'm not afraid,
> But me and mine are hard to part;
> Oh, unknown God, lift up my heart.

June 5th Rome is in Allied hands. This is of paramount importance. There is very little material damage and the two-million inhabitants are hysterical with joy at their liberation:

A local cutting from the Gazette.

PRINCESS ELIZABETH arriving yesterday on a visit to the Grenadier Guards, of which regiment she is Colonel-in-Chief.

flowers, kisses, shouts of joy, flags, cups of wine (in spite of food shortage). The Nazis blew up the gas, electricity and water before retreating. The Allies are in hot pursuit beyond the Tiber.

June 6th　Today has proved to be D-Day. We awoke at 5 am to hear peculiar sounding planes flying over – gliders apparently. On the 8 am news it was reported that the Germans had broadcast that we'd dropped paratroops in France. By midday everyone seemed to know *it* had happened at last. We'd had large convoys of troops in all sorts of vehicles passing through Worthing for the last two days and planes had been very active. We listened in at the Report Centre and heard that 4,000 ships had taken part and many thousands of small ones. Normandy was the chosen spot and Mr Churchill made a statement that the first landings had been successful. He wanted to go himself but was dissuaded. Funnily enough it's been quieter in the air over here today and there was 'nothing to report' on duty at the Report Centre.

June 8th　General Eisenhower has visited the beachhead in Normandy. It is believed that General Montgomery is already established over there. The bridgehead is twenty-five miles wide and we have captured Bayeux – the first French town to be liberated. The inhabitants were hysterical with joy and thankfulness.

THE SUNDAY TIMES, JUNE 11, 1944

Gen. Montgomery saw among the booty British vehicles of the Morris make, which the Germans apparently captured at Dunkirk.

The two foremost German prisoners betray astonishment when they realise that the officer perched on top of the Jeep watching them go past is Gen. Montgomery. He had just driven up to the road from the beach, where he landed in a " duck "

Sunday Times, June 11th

146

June 13th Mr Churchill, General Smuts and Sir Alan Brooke visited the beachhead yesterday! Fighting is bitter but General Montgomery is well satisfied with the progress so far. The beachhead is sixty miles long now. We had a report at the Report Centre that the enemy is now using PAC (pilotless aircraft). This is the first time this has happened. King Leopold of Belgium has been removed to Germany – the Nazis fear he might rally his people. US 'Super Fortresses' have bombed Tokyo.

June 17th The dreaded 'pilotless aircraft' were over Southern England last night. Nothing landed on Worthing though several people saw the things and we certainly heard them. Mr Brendan Bracken, Minister for Information, said in Parliament: 'No one can deter the PM from taking risks if he feels that by doing so he can do something to save the precious blood of our fighting men who are our saviours and, I hope, our redeemers.' Mr Bracken concluded on a lighter note: 'Nothing said here today will make me take the unnecessary risk of trying to persuade the Prime Minister not to take risks.' We *know* the end is in sight. *The King visited Normandy yesterday.* I bought a new dress today, with Ma's coupons!

June 18th Kit phoned to say she couldn't possibly come for her godson's christening. She said the night had been 'unspeakable' which for Kit is very strong. Simon was duly christened at Tarring Church today and we had a nice tea later – no godparents could come so I had to be the proxy. We've gone back to 1940 days again. Preparing for the night is quite a performance. Gas turned off at main, tea tray ready, chairs, knitting and books in hall, suitcase packed with spare clothes and money! Nevertheless all news is good from the war fronts and many of these pilotless planes are being shot into the sea before they reach us. Our English Channel is a great boon.

June 23rd The battle of Cherbourg has entered a violent stage and Americans have got as far as the outskirts. The planes we saw by the hundreds yesterday were going off there to help prepare the way for the infantry. General Eisenhower has called on the dock and rail workers there to stop sabotage and be prepared to help Allied forces directly they arrive there. Fishermen off the French, Belgian and Dutch coasts are advised to stop fishing for a further (third) week. Dairy farmers in parts of Southern England are attributing a drop in milk yields to the flying bombs. During the day most animals are indifferent to the noise but night gunfire is another proposition. Owners of ducks also report that night firing at flying bombs reduces their egg output. Pilots have nicknamed these things 'doodle bugs'. One has wrecked a Worthing allotment holder's potato crop. Within an hour or two he was phlegmatically replacing it with winter greens. Some MPs want the British government to appeal to the Pope about these 'flying bombs' but the government does not propose doing so.

PILOTLESS PLANE SHOT DOWN OVER ENGLAND BY R.A.F. FIGHTERS

One of the pilotless planes, which has been shot down by R.A.F. fighter aircraft over Southern England, lying with its tail in the foreground. Fighter pilots from a neighbouring airfield examine the wreckage to discover, if possible, more about its vulnerability.

July 2nd   The *Sunday Times* editorial today talks about the flying bombs: 'The Germans, who never understand the people of another country, perhaps think they will, by this new weapon, destroy British morale. There could be no greater blunder. The killing of women and children by this robot will not intimidate our people. It will move them to a righteous anger. It will harden their resolution to prosecute the war with the utmost energy and the remorseless use of the whole resources of the nation.' It is reported that gold bars from Germany have been received in Portugal and arrangements have been made for high Nazis to leave Germany by plane for Japan! This is not official! Progress is reported on all Allied fronts and more people feel the war may be over very soon. I've got a bet of £1 with Christine Linfield that it will be over by August (she to give me the £1 for our physiotherapy van!). Miss Green had her sale for the van and it brought in £80! All from her toy animals. The Mayor opened the sale and said that the van will be used to give physiotherapy to patients in nearby villages.

July 8th   Everybody's still talking about the V1 flying bombs. On the wireless tonight was an old cockney talking about them. 'Do these bombs frighten me? Oh no, look at it this way. When it's got to England, it's got to find London. When it's

148

found London, it's got to find Bethnal Green. When it's found Bethnal Green, it's got to find Widow's Walk. Then it's got to find No 5 and chances are I'd be at the pub anyway.'!

July 10th The victory at Caen is the main topic of news. Germany is considering taking her troops away from Norway to help her manpower situation. She is beaten and knows it. It has been divulged that only one ship was lost on D-Day. The Guards' Chapel in Wellington Barracks near Buckingham Palace received a direct hit from a flying bomb during a Sunday morning parade service yesterday. Many were killed including a nurse from Gladys Mills' hospital (King's College) – only her wrist watch was found. Murray Clifford, a Worthing boy and friend of the Carters who is just nineteen and is in the Guards had the job of seeing to thirty bodies of dead Guardsmen – they all died from blast – their heads were fractured and their eyes blown out. This is awful to write but it has a purpose – to show how utterly vile and terrible is this modern war.

Worthing is getting plans together already through the League of Nations Union to help in a nationwide effort to banish war for ever. We are to have a big conference in October with Lord R. Cecil as speaker. Harold Frampton is the prime mover.

July 11th The bacon ration is to be increased from 4 oz to 6 oz a week each! Stalin announces still another offensive. The *Times* says there is no doubt that the Russians will be in Germany first and that in a few days probably. The Nazis have lost nineteen generals in the last nineteen days – either killed or captured, mostly by the Russians. The coastal ban has been lifted from Cornwall to Hampshire. In Germany no-one is allowed to travel anywhere without permission.

July 14th There is a vile report of the complete wiping out of a whole French village – the men shot, women and children burned alive in a church by SS troops.

Typical conversation at the YMCA tonight among the helpers: 'Every German building should be laid low', 'We should retaliate with flying bombs', 'You can't trust the French', 'When this war is over we shall have to fight the Russians', 'Jews cheat you'. It looks as if it's high time public opinion was re-educated. The League of Nations Union hopes to do something towards it with the conference to be held here in October.

July 15th Kit came home for the first time in three months. The flying bombs are certainly abating she says. London's had five quiet nights this week. She says four weeks ago there was no-one in Battersea Park on Saturday afternoon; today it looked normal. Theatres are re-opening again too.

July 21st   F. Allen read the 8 am news and started by saying: 'This is the 8 am news . . . and very sensational news it is too.' It seems Hitler was in conference with some of his military chiefs when one of them threw a bomb at him. He got burns and bruises on his face and others were killed or injured. The papers think it is 'the beginning of the end'. There have been rumours for some time of dissatisfaction among military men with Hitler's régime.

July 22nd   Himmler has been put in charge of the Home Front. He is hated by everyone. Hitler has ordered the Nazi salute (Heil Hitler) and not the military salute to be used in the future. Trains full of children passed through Worthing today. I hear they are from Hastings and Bexhill. The flying bombs are very numerous over those towns. We had a cuckoo and doodle bug about 11.30 tonight. As the war must be ending soon I decided I ought to see one so looked out and had a good view for about a minute then it disappeared and there was a sudden tremendous red glow, but it was too far off for me to hear the explosion.

July 30th   Very busy week preparing for our three-week holiday. Mother doesn't expect the war to last until we return on August 26th so has got the flags ready for Mr Tyler to hang out if it ends when we are away! The Russians are pushing the German Army back faster and faster in the East. In Normandy, despite bad weather, the Americans and the British troops are making steady progress. The Nazis say they're getting ready something much worse than the beastly flying bomb menace for use against Britain and they claim it can even reach New York. Let's hope the war's over before they can try it out. Considerable damage was done to London Zoo by a flying bomb but only two sulphur-crested cockatoos were killed. Many of the animals were unperturbed by the explosion but the inmates of the monkey house were upset for several hours.

July 31st   In today's paper the editorial said that the war was not won yet: 'A stranglehold succeeds on one condition – that one never lets go. We need on our side to cultivate cheerfulness without slackness, courage without presumption, criticism with knowledge, not nagging. In short what the Romans called "equanimity" – a high temper at once energetic and well-balanced.' It is strongly rumoured that Rommel was killed recently when the RAF bombed his HQ.

August 2nd   A glorious day at last and the Worthing Anglo-Soviet Friendship Committee had a good fete at Broadwater. A sum of £375 is required for an x-ray unit for Russia – a Russian colonel (who fought at Stalingrad) was here to open the fete with his interpreter – both very nice looking men. Mr Churchill reported that the Nazis had launched 5,340 flying bombs on southern England; 4,735 persons had been killed and 14,000 seriously wounded. About 17,000 homes had been totally destroyed and about 800,000 damaged. Nearly 1,000,000 people had been encouraged and assisted to leave London. But he also said: 'I no longer feel bound to deny that victory may perhaps come soon.'

August 3rd Freddie Grisewood started the nine o'clock news by saying that everything, everywhere is going from bad to worse for the Germans. US tanks have reached Brest, the Allies are into the suburbs of Florence, the Russians are pushing on, the Japs are leaving Dutch New Guinea.

August 13th I am helping at the Harvest Camp at Breacham Green which has twenty-five boys from fourteen to seventeen, and eight helpers in twelve tents. There is an Italian Prisoners' Camp nearby and the Hertford War Agricultural Committee use the prisoners. Only non-Fascists are used, ie the 'collaborators' and they seem very decent and friendly. There are seventy-one men with one British sergeant in charge who can speak a little Italian. They've all been over in Bombay for four years having been taken prisoner in Abyssinia in 1940! They roam about the roads after work. One of the boys is trying to learn a little Italian from them and one of the prisoners has offered to help us cook. We were given a hare by one of the farmers and the Italians took it off and made a delicious dish – with olive oil, onions and cocoa! A typical menu for the day is 6.30 cup of tea. Breakfast at 8 consisting of porridge (or flakes), rasher (or sausage) and potato, bread and marg and marmalade ad lib, tea. The boys have six large sandwiches which they take to their farms (four savoury – cheese, meat, fish – and two jam). Tea is bread and butter and jam and tea. The evening meal is the meal of the day with a joint, potatoes and one other vegetable, plums and custard or rice. All the boys agree the food is excellent but one group wanted two more sandwiches at lunchtime!

Sunday Times,
August 27th

THE SUNDAY TIMES, AUGUST 27, 194

Citizens parading through the streets of newly freed Paris bearing "Liberation" banners and placards acclaiming Gen. de Gaulle and the Allies.

August 25th The really great news is the liberation of Paris. Back home from our holiday, the ban has been lifted from coastal areas. Parts of the beach are free again for the first time for over four years.

September 3rd Fifth anniversary of the outbreak of war. American forces entered Belgium yesterday and British forces have done the same today. General Eisenhower has issued his orders to all the Belgians – 'the hour they have waited for for over four years has struck'. Some are to assist the Allied troops, others are to protect factories etc and those in unliberated areas are to do nothing till they are told. In South France Allied troops have captured Lyons. In Italy the strong Nazi defences known as the 'Gothic Line' have been breached by our troops. German troops are leaving Finland. The Russians are thrusting up through Bulgaria, Rumania and Hungary. In Britain the King has ordained that today be recognised as the National Day of Prayer and Dedication. Buses have been allowed to run in the morning – the first time for two years. Churches were more than full in Worthing. No flying bombs have been over since Friday afternoon, the longest lull yet. In today's *Sunday Times* the editorial says: 'When the full record is known it will be found that no nation has ever achieved so high a degree of organised output for war, has been more efficiently active in such a great number of directions as the British people in adversity. We, who at first had underrated the scale of the war, rose to its full challenge.'

September 6th 'The Battle of Germany' has begun – American patrols have penetrated into the Reich territory. Canadian forces have reached the sea on either side of Calais – 'The Battle of the Channel Ports' is in progress. Russia has declared war on Bulgaria – one can scarcely keep up with events. In Worthing, corporation workmen are getting all the street lamps into working order. The blackout is to be lifted after five years on September 17th – Mother has already scraped off some of the black paper strips! Holiday makers are making the most of the lifting of the travel ban – Worthing is very full indeed. Mr Duncan Sandys MP, chairman of the War Cabinet Committee has declared: 'Except possibly for a few last shots, the flying bomb Battle of London is over.' He said during the eighty days of the bombardment, over 8,000 bombs were launched and some 2,300 got through to London which had about 92% of all the casualties.

4 Years Ago To-day

Hitler said: "If the R.A.F. attack our cities we will simply erase theirs. The hour will come when one of us two will break up, and it won't be Nazi Germany."

2 Years Ago

Rommel, in Egypt, withdrew his forces westward after failure to penetrate British defence positions.

1 Year Ago

Eighth Army secured firm foothold on Italian mainland and held at least 40 miles of coast.

Free Kick

A COLONEL in the Home Guard received a severe kick a tergo from the sergeant who opened the door of his car for him. A private, who was passing by, promptly followed suit.

At the subsequent court-martial the sergeant pleaded that the colonel had stepped down on his pet corn, and that he had lost control of himself.

The private, in his turn, explained that on seeing the sergeant's action he naturally thought that the war was over.

PETERBOROUGH

"Look Adolf, I don't care whether Sweden or the whole world won't have you—I STILL say there isn't a clause about a 'safe haven' in OUR agreement."

152

September 9th   The Victoria Cross has been awarded to Wing-Commander Geoffrey Leonard Cheshire DSO and two bars, DFC. He is twenty-seven and has flown over 100 missions in four years. The citation says he displayed courage and determination of an exceptional leader against strongly defended targets. Mrs Wenban-Smith is quite thrilled with the news as Wing-Commander Cheshire is her Australian airman Max's senior officer. Hilda and I went to East Worthing canteen for the last time today; it's been open for four years. There are only very few soldiers left in Worthing now. Despite the authorities warning them not to, people are flocking back to London even though there are still explosions from V2s. These 'rocket bombs' travel over silently so there is no warning beforehand. Kit says there is so little available accommodation left for those returning.

September 16th   I took the boys on the beach at East Worthing today. It was my first visit to the beach since May 1940. There were crowds of people there. Tonight we put the clocks back an hour and tomorrow we have 'dim-out' instead of 'blackout' conditions. Curtains must be drawn but suffused light is allowed. There is to be modified street lighting too. General Montgomery says we have captured 400,000 prisoners in France, so far. They are brought over here and then sent overseas to Canada and America. Today US 'flying fortresses' flew to Poland and dropped food and ammunition.

September 20th   A big revolt has broken out in Denmark. Finland has accepted Russian terms and is already fighting *against* the Germans – what a war. I helped at a 'United Aid to China' sale today. The distress in China is beyond the imagination, millions of homeless, millions of orphans. In Kit's letter today she confirms the arrival of the V2s – she says they hear occasional terrific explosions. Some say it's bombs dropped from very high planes – others that it's the dreaded 'rocket'. Worthing fire watchers have been officially notified that fire watching ceases after tonight but there is one proviso: in the event of 'anything happening' we are expected to report to our posts. The biggest robot rocket assembly plant has been captured. The papers say this vast tunnelled underground factory could have produced 700 flying bombs a day. Over 15,000 forced labourers were eventually to have worked there. It was situated in a disused French iron mine. Everyone realises what a dire plight London and Southern England would have been in if the Nazis could have got all these 'secret weapons' going earlier.

September 22nd   Some of the British paratroopers who were dropped five days ago at Arnhem in Holland to secure the bridge across the Rhine are having a terrible time awaiting our Second Army which is struggling to reach them. The government has published a white paper on how demobilisation will take place; age and length of service will decide priority. Pay for servicemen is to be raised considerably too. The War Memorials Advisory Council of the Royal Society of Arts says monuments to this war should not be standardised commercial products, but created by individual artists to suit the sentiments of the community and the memorial's location.

September 24th We found a *Daily Telegraph* of 1936 today – it consisted of twenty pages (against the present four) and was most interesting. There were photos of the Spanish Civil War and of the PM Mr Baldwin. Even then there was a lot of talk about rearmament on the continent. General Eisenhower has called on the twelve million foreign workers in Germany to rise against the Gestapo – 'the hour has struck'.

September 28th Everyone is talking about our withdrawal from Arnhem. Of 8,000 troops, over 2,000 have managed to get back with some 1,200 wounded having to be left in enemy hands. It is our first set back for many, many months. Even so the stand our men made has helped the progress of our Second Army in Holland. Our troops were sent to capture three very important bridges – we captured two but couldn't manage the third at Arnhem. After all it is only natural the Nazis will put up increasing resistance the nearer we draw to the German frontiers.

ANOTHER RECONNAISSANCE PHOTOGRAPH of the scene in Holland during the Allied airborne invasion: Gliders are lying at the end of the tracks they have made while landing.

Daily Telegraph, September 19th

September 29th The PM made a comprehensive war report to Parliament yesterday. He's afraid the war may go on into the spring of next year and even then there may be guerrilla warfare in Germany for some time. He acclaimed the Arnhem heroes and was optimistic about both the European and Pacific wars.

October 1st Calais has fallen and there is dancing in the streets in Dover. They are to have a thanksgiving service conducted by the Archbishop of Canterbury next Sunday following their liberation from the guns across the Channel. Dover has had a terrible time, especially just lately. In all more than

2,000 shells of all types and 464 bombs as well as parachute mines, flying bombs and hundreds of incendiaries have landed on the town. The first German shell fired across the Strait burst in Dover shortly before noon on August 12th, 1940. Children there cannot remember sleeping in their beds.

October 4th   The Polish defenders of Warsaw who revolted against the Nazis have surrendered. This is bad news following on so soon after the epic of Arnhem. The lights are up in Worthing streets! They are not very bright but they are a help.

October 8th   In Greece things are going very well — the Nazis are preparing to evacuate completely rather than be cut off by Russians advancing through countries to the north. On the BBC it was divulged that plans for the liberation of Greece were formed in 1942 — British personnel were dropped by parachute and brought by ships and contact was made with the patriot forces. Mr Wendell Wilkie has died suddenly in the US; he opposed Mr Roosevelt in the last Presidential elections. I went out early to collect the bread and meat — a joint of lamb this week (the usual 1/2d amount per person) but on it there was enough suet for two puddings! Meat has been rather scarce this week as we have a good many commandos in town and they are allowed double the civilian ration. I managed to get half lb of liver though (offal — not rations). I got a jam sandwich at the baker's. They waited till the other customer had gone out as they'd told her they had no cakes — they keep them for their bread customers only! The cheese ration is up to 3 oz a week next week instead of 2 oz but milk is still very short. Twice a week we get half a pint which does not go far especially if visitors come to tea. Golden syrup is very difficult again. I bought a pair of 'utility' gloves 11/- plus three coupons, two pairs of winter underwear 5/3d and 4/9d plus six coupons and a length of dress material at 8/9d a yard. No paper is allowed to wrap things with and everyone takes a basket or a string bag. We've had no coal for a week and there is talk of another strike. Ivy came to tea and spent the evening with us recently — she brought away with her two bags — one containing bones (for the bone bin) and the other containing six biscuits. Unfortunately she absent-mindedly put the biscuits in the bin and brought us the bones!

October 15th   Athens is liberated — the British Navy and US planes have landed British and Greek troops. Hungary has asked for an armistice — the last of Germany's Balkan allies.

October 18th   Himmler has ordered every male from sixteen to sixty to have military training to help in the defence of Germany against the Allied invaders. American wounded have

How Worthing Took It

The following are the official A.R.P. statistics of all the bombing incidents that have occurred in Worthing from September 3rd, 1939-September 29th, 1944, inclusive :—

Number of air raid "Alerts,"—1,028.

Number of bombing "Incidents,"—65.

Number of bombs dropped.—
205   50 kg.
20   250 kg.
28   500 kg.
4   1,000 kg.
5   Phosphorus.
4   Fire Pots.
1   Parachute Mine.
1   Flying Bomb.

Number of people killed.—41 + 3 missing, believed killed.

Seriously injured and detained in hospital.—72.

Minor casualties.—134.

Houses demolished or to be demolished.—97.

Number of houses seriously damaged.—554.

Number of houses, minor damage.—6,169* (excluding window damage).

*Including damage caused by sea and land mines.

Worthing Gazette,
October 4th

DESPATCHES
FROM THE
HOME
FRONT

1944

155

SURRENDER ULTIMATUM CARRIED INTO AACHEN

The "Surrender-or-die" ultimatum to Aachen is taken to the German commander of the city. The dangerous mission was carried out by Lt. William Boehme (left) and Lt. Cedric A. Laffey (right), accompanied by Pte. Kenneth Kading, who is seen bearing a sheet tied to a pole as token of their rôle of envoys.

arrived at Worthing Hospital. The weather is simply *awful*, terrific gales and downpours — the worst October weather for forty years. The Minister of Food, Colonel Llewellin, said in the Commons yesterday: 'At Christmas we think first of the children and everyone between the ages of six months and eighteen shall be entitled to an extra ration of half a pound of sweets this year.' He also announced that 80,000,000 packets of Iraqi dates totalling 9,000 tons will be sold at 3d a packet and one point. These dates were prepacked for the forces and are no longer required.

October 21st Over 100,000 men from 600 American ships have landed as an invasion force under General MacArthur in the Philippines. He says 'it's going like clockwork'. Not one ship was lost. Mr Churchill has left Moscow after a successful meeting with Stalin and relief ships have already reached Greece with over 5,000 tons of food. The Allies have at last recognised General de Gaulle's government. In Paris today the treason trials have started. There are over 100,000 people accused of collaboration with the enemy. The death sentence has been passed on one pro-German editor of a paper who worked whole-heartedly with the Nazis. In today's paper were pictures of the prefabricated dock parts nicknamed 'Mulberries' that were manufactured in this country in great secrecy, towed across to the coast of Normandy and assembled there after D-

156

DUTCH APPEAL FOR PRAYER

"FAMINE IMMINENT"

The Dutch Prime Minister, Prof. Gerbrandy, has sent a telegram of appeal to the Archbishop of Canterbury, Dr. Temple, the Archbishop of Westminster, Dr. Griffin, the Moderator of the General Assembly of the Church of Scotland, Dr. Hagan, the Free Church Federal Council, and the Chief Rabbi, Dr. Hertz. In this he says:

By unsurpassed trials, murder, robbery, arson and destruction the enemy threatens the people of the Netherlands with a terrible fate. Famine is also imminent.

In all churches in Holland our people undoubtedly will implore the aid and mercy of the Almighty. Many millions of Dutch people will be greatly comforted by the knowledge that others elsewhere will join them in prayer.

May I, therefore, for the sake of the people of the Netherlands, so sorely tried, appeal to you to lead the faithful under your care in a special prayer to the Almighty, imploring His aid and succour in their special plight.

Famine Peril—P6

Day. It simplified greatly the problem of supplying the invasion forces with every form of support in great quantities and a short time. It was a remarkable feat involving civilian contractors; many building workers lost their lives while making them.

October 26th Russia has started the liberation of Norway from the north and King Haakon has broadcast a message to his people to help the Russians to the utmost.

The sudden death of the Archbishop of Canterbury, Dr William Temple, was announced this evening. Also Princess Beatrice, the last surviving daughter of Queen Victoria.

October 30th Worthing is shedding her battle dress and gradually returning to normality. The deep ditches to trap tanks that criss-cross the Downs and the valley behind the town are being filled in. The *Worthing Herald* says that in its editorial view growing cabbages on the Manor County Cricket Ground was a panic measure that should never have been permitted. Robert Riskin, the brilliant writer-producer who left Hollywood in 1941 to work for America's Office of War Information has come to London to confer with the Ministry of Information on film plans for liberated Europe. He considers documentary films a tremendously important means of spreading information and suggesting a point of view. He says films like *In Which We Serve* and *London Can Take It* helped Americans to a wider understanding of Britain's experience in the war. 'American film people have found the documentary technique new and fascinating and I'm sure their experience will profoundly affect commercial film-making. Far more fictional films will have a factual basis and background,' he said in today's paper.

November 8th President Roosevelt was elected for still another term of four years making sixteen in all — unprecedented. On the 8 am wireless news it was announced that everyone will be entitled to 4 lb of oranges between now and January and *one* egg between now and Christmas!! Lord Moyne our resident Minister in the Middle East was killed in Cairo last Sunday by two terrorists belonging to the 'Stern Gang' of Jewish Zionists.

November 12th Himmler made excuses today for Hitler not broadcasting three days ago on the anniversary of the Nazi rise to power. But still Hitler does not broadcast – many think he's dead or mad. Weather is awful on the battle fronts and progress is slowed down in consequence. Mr Churchill has received the freedom of the city of Paris. He delivered a speech in schoolboy French which was received with acclamation and laughter. In today's paper a correspondent says that both the flying bomb and the V2 rocket will have serious influence on our strategic thinking and security planning in the years to come, particularly if in, say, ten years we may expect ranges of 2,000 to 3,000 miles and explosive war heads of 10 tons or more. The best news of the day is that the great Nazi battleship *Tirpitz* has been sunk by RAF bombers in Norwegian waters. The Germans originally believed that this ship and the *Bismark* were unsinkable. She was a constant and formidable menace to Allied convoys taking war material to Russia.

November 17th After the frost a terrible and continuous gale and rain for the last twenty-four hours. Just as the whole 400 mile front has launched an offensive from Holland to Switzerland too. The weather has been against the Western Allies ever since D-Day. We were very quiet at the YMCA tonight. It was nice to have a real milky cup of coffee-Hough, civilians only get two pints of milk now. Chemists are short of quite a lot of things too. I went into Astons to exchange a 3/- elastoplast and I said I'd have 3/- worth of Dettol — unobtainable. Then I'll have a toothbrush — unobtainable! Saccharines — nil. Quinine — nil and so on. Couldn't seem to think of anything they'd got, so took some other antiseptic and some change!

November 22nd Mr P G Wodehouse — the English humorist novelist has been imprisoned by the French in Paris. He was in France in 1940 and was taken to Germany. He broadcast five times to the USA and everyone was disgusted with him. The French General le Clerc (who marched his troops up from Lake Chad in Central Africa to join our troops in the Eighth Army African campaign) has entered Strasbourg. General Eisenhower seems to be making an all out effort to force a decision by Christmas but the weather continues awful and makes fighting very difficult. Mother has made me a very nice smocked overall out of a green blackout curtain! I've just made seventeen calendars out of old Christmas cards for a sale. Should bring in about 30/- having spent just 4/-.

November 28th A terrible explosion at Burton-on-Trent yesterday when an RAF underground ammunition store blew up. Terrible devastation and the vibration was felt sixty miles away and the death roll is heavy.

November 29th The government's White Paper on Britain's Prodigious War Effort was published. It's now possible to form a quantitative picture of Britain's achievement in total mobilisation for war. Between June 1939 and June 1944, the total number of men aged fourteen to sixty-four and of women aged fourteen to fifty-nine in the Services or in industry rose from 18,500,000 to 22,000,000. The increase was achieved by the absorption of 1,250,000 unemployed and of 2,250,000 persons, mainly women, not previously engaged in industry. In June 1939 there were 477,000 men and no women in the Armed

Forces and 80,000 men and no women in the Civil Defence. In June 1944 there were 4,502,000 men and 467,000 women in the Armed Forces and 225,000 men and 56,000 women in the Civil Defence. Fifty-seven per cent of the whole male population between the ages of eighteen and forty have served or are serving in the Armed Forces. In addition part-time voluntary service has been rendered by 1,750,000 men in the Home Guard and 1,250,000 men and 350,000 women in the Civil Defence and over 1,000,000 in the WVS and several hundreds of thousands more in salvage groups, savings groups etc as well as several million men and women giving forty-eight hours a month to fire watching. The total strength of the British Empire Forces in June 1944 was 8,713,000 and of these 48% belonged to other countries than the UK. The total output of tanks amounts to 25,116, rifles 2,001,949, machine guns 317,000, aircraft 102,609.

November 30th The Americans continue to press their attack in the Philippines; if successful the Japs will have no chance of reinforcing their forces south of the islands. In China the position of our Allies is bad. General Chiang Kai-Shek seems to be more concerned with getting rid of the Chinese Communists than fighting the Japs. His opponents say he is holding up supplies granted by US and Britain for this purpose. General Stilwell's recall to the US is obviously because of General Chiang's attitude. Other problems in China: there is a steady increase in inflation and there is a strong Communist movement in the north, as against the Nationalists in the south. The civilian population is in a dire plight. The US press has acclaimed our White Paper on Britain's War Effort. Quite a large part of the US press has had a surprise and what is more has owned up to it. From some American papers one might think the British took the role of spectators on the occasion of the Normandy invasion! The *San Francisco Chronicle* says: 'The statement of sacrifices in manpower, tangible things and surplus wealth made in the White Paper does not touch on the one essential asset of national health by which we mean the capacity of a people to endure an ordeal, stick to the job, and maintain a reasonably even keel. In the long run the loss of man power and wealth is grievous, but not ruinous to the British people while they have the essential ingredient out of which their wealth has been created.' Other details emerging from the White Paper are that imports of foodstuffs fell from 22,000,000 tons pre-war to 11,500,000 tons last year, a fact that reflects the extraordinary effort of British farming to feed the population of 46,750,000. The supply of newsprint, home produced and imported, has fallen by 82%. The number of private cars licensed has fallen from 2,000,000 to 700,000 and their petrol consumption by 84%. To help pay for the war Britain has sold £1,065,000,000 in overseas assets and in addition has incurred overseas liabilities to the amount of

£2,300,000,000. Out of 13,000,000 houses in the UK, 4,500,000 have been destroyed or damaged by enemy action. Three months of flying bomb attacks this summer were responsible for one-quarter of all houses damaged. Wing Commander Guy Gibson who won the VC when breaching the Mohne Dam in 1943 failed to return last night from an attack on strongly defended positions behind the Siegfried Line.

December 3rd Britain's Home guard is officially 'stood down' as from today. The King broadcast a nice message to them tonight: 'The Home Guard has reached the end of more than four years of duty under arms. But I know that your devotion to our land, your comradeship, your power to work your hardest at the end of the longest day, will discover new outlets for patriotic service in time of peace. History will say that your share in the greatest of all our struggles for freedom was a vitally important one. You have given your service without thought of reward. You have earned in full measure your country's gratitude.'

December 5th There is terrible trouble in Athens: the Communists are trying to seize power — British troops have had to go into action to separate the warring factions.

—by Illingworth.

December 17th   Thirteen of us went to the Albert Hall to hear the carol concert. It was wonderful and we wondered if in any other capital in Europe such a concert could be held. The choir numbered about 400 and the audience about 5,000. Dr M Sargent conducted the entire audience for several of the carols. We'd been told we might expect rockets (the Germans are said to be preparing 'vengeance weapons' or V3s to be launched from Norway), fogs, unwarmed trains, over-crowded restaurants etc but nothing untoward happened and we all, Mother included, thoroughly enjoyed the day. Yesterday I saw a big flash through the curtains and this was followed by terrific explosions which lit up the sky for several minutes. Today we learned that it was one of our planes and that the pilot held on to the controls to the last and crashed on the beach to avoid plunging into the heart of the town. His self-sacrificing heroism averted a major tragedy. No-one knows what happened to the rest of the crew. The plane caused a lot of devastation along the Marine Parade but one feels that to be a very minor detail.

December 21st   The news is bad and the weather is bad. The Nazis have undoubtedly broken through the US lines to a depth of thirty miles into Belgium and Luxembourg. They are using fifteen divisions, mainly panzers, and so far there seems little chance of a halt in the enemy advance. But better news in the Philippines – all Jap resistance on Leyte Island has ceased.

December 31st   It's very difficult to keep up a war diary in the Christmas season! I've been out carol singing – £43 this year, a record. The money is to be divided between the ex-Servicemen of Gifford House and the local blind. We had a lovely Christmas, all the family being present, the first time since 1941. With the extra Christmas rations, presents from abroad and Mollie's home-reared turkey we did very well. Some things were non-existent, eg crackers, oranges, currants. Christmas cards were a wicked price. We had a very nice British soldier in for the day: he'd offered to come with our carol party, having heard us talking about it in the YMCA. I listened to a New Year's Eve concert on the Home Service and later I switched on to Germany and heard Hitler giving his people a New Year message: 'In the coming year we will ward off the enemy's attacks and in the end we shall break him by our counter-strokes. Where our enemies enter a country, chaos sets in. Democracy is incapable of solving even the smallest problem. This continent can only survive if all its energies are used in a planned scheme and if the egotistic instincts are utterly suppressed. Only two leaders in Europe have ever honestly tackled this problem – the Nazis in Germany and the Fascists in Italy.'

1945

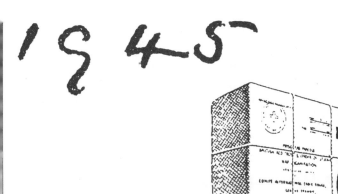

January 1st Little did I think I should still be writing in this book when I bought it last September. However things do seem to be hastening to the end of the war. In the West the Allies have regained about a third of the ground lost to the Nazis' counter-offensive. Their real plan, to reach Antwerp, has not materialised. Only once a month now to the Report Centre, instead of once a week — good! Lemons are on sale in the town and the last of the barbed wire on the Worthing Parade is being removed by soldiers. It's been there for more than four years and looks very rusty. The cold spell has ended.

January 4th Sir Stafford Cripps, Minister of Aircraft Production, outlined his policy of 'practical Christian idealism' for the post-war treatment of Germany when he addressed the Baptist Board in London yesterday. He advocated no revenge against the German people but protection for their frightened neighbours — 'The Germans are to be regarded as human beings like ourselves, equally brothers in the human family and sharing the Fatherhood of God but we must attempt to wean them from Nazi leadership and ideas and by dignified and just methods we must bring the worst wrong doers to account,' he said. 'To the German people, we, as Christians would say: "We are not your judges — God alone can judge of human actions and motives — but we shall take what practical steps we can to provide a safe period of absence of war, during which we can start to build the more permanent structure of lasting peace." ' Sir Stafford added that we must beware of exercising our Christianity in one direction only — towards the evildoer — and overlooking the plight of the victim. He ended by saying: 'A new range of fears has been created in the world — the fear of new weapons, each more ghastly and terrible than the last, each carrying its destruction farther and farther into the territories of other nations. No-one knows — or ever can — the climax of the terrors of this unending exhibition of human ingenuity or how frightful will be the weapon of another war if it should come.'

January 10th   Petrol can be bought at any garage again. Field Marshal Montgomery has been given command of *all* the Allied armies (including two US armies) on the north side of the German salient. He has re-established confidence. The Germans are doing their best to split the Allies with broadcasts purporting to come from the BBC which contain high praise for Monty and reviling the American troops in the Ardennes battle.

January 21st   Mrs Wenban-Smith has sawn up her air-raid shelter wood supports as there is no coal. Another difficulty: owing to having to expend five coupons on a pair of shoes everyone has their foot gear mended until the end. I shot into Watts today to retrieve a pair and to leave behind those I was wearing! I had to queue up! Watts had over 500 pairs brought in last week. Unfortunately I queued behind a woman who had taken in six pairs and each pair had to be ticketed separately! Shopping is difficult. So far newspapers are delivered in this road but many people have to collect theirs. The Burma Road has been re-opened.

January 24th   We had a Refugee Committee meeting today to discuss plans for coping with hundreds of war-shocked, badly nourished Dutch children. It looks as if the German children are in a similar plight. These are the children who will be forming the post-war world — will their experiences make for better international relations or will their terrible times hinder friendly overtures? Mother made some real Seville orange marmalade today — the first for several years. Many people can't spare any sugar for it so the oranges still look plentiful in the shop windows even though the supply arrived two days ago.

January 25th   Mr Bevin, Minister for Labour, has estimated that the artificial ports used in the Normandy landings must have saved between 100,000 and 150,000 British and American casualties. He also disclosed in today's paper that between the Teheran Conference and D-Day his Ministry transferred more than one million people from one occupation to another to prepare for the invasion of France. 'About 60,000 men had to be provided so that the railways could move that great force,' he said. 'We closed down steel works, took men earning £10 a week and made platelayers and goods guards of them for D-Day. They never grumbled and did a great job, although some of them lost as much as half their wages by being transferred.'

January 30th   The Russians are only ninety miles from Berlin. Terrible conditions reign in Germany — millions evacuating *out* of Berlin and millions trekking *into* the capital from invaded German territory. Intense cold worsens the conditions for these wretched civilians — Nazi authorities continu-

GERMANY STAND FAST!

EAST

EAST

BERLIN

SPLITZKRIEG

Pressure in the West : Driving Through in the East

STEMPE

0 50 100 150
MILES

BORNHOLM

KOENIGSBERG MEMEL

KIEL

PEENEMUNDE

HAMBURG DANZIG ELBING CHERNIAKHOVSKI

BREMEN POMERANIA DIRSCHAU MARIENBG

STETTIN SCHNEIDEMUHL CHOJNICE

ARNHEM KREUZ

HANOVER DRIESEN TORUN ROKOSSOVSKY

BERLIN LANDSB'G

NIJMEGEN FRANKFURT POZNAN WARSAW

VENLO BRANDENBURG ZHUKOV

ROERMOND GERMANY ODER

COLOGNE GLOGAU VISTULA

AACHEN LEIPZIG STEINAU KONIEV

ST.VITH COBLENZ

R.OUR DRESDEN BRESLAU

RHINE OPPELN

TREVES NEISSE GLEIWITZ BEUTHEN

PRAGUE RATIBOR HINDENBERG

SAARBRUCKEN MUNICH KATOWICE CRACOW

KARLSRUHE PILSEN M.OSTRAVA KETY NOVY TARG PETROV

STRASBOURG STÜTTGART CZECHOSLOVAKIA TESCHEN

COLMAR BRUNN POPRAD KOSICE

ally beg their people not to harass them by asking the whereabouts of relatives. The cold has been intense in Britain too. We ran out of fuel four days ago and I had to accept offers of logs and a bucket of coal from patients! We swopped the logs for two eggs and a packet of mixed fruit from Australia! Ivy got frozen out of her flat and came here. We phoned the coal merchant and explained our plight and the girl said if I could go to the coal dump with two sacks I could collect the stuff — which I did with speed. A commando raid on a prison camp on Luzon freed 513 Allied prisoners captured by Japs three years ago. Langton Rd street lights were alight tonight for the first time since 1939.

February 3rd   The Framptons and I went to the Albert Hall today to hear *The Dream of Gerontius* conducted by Malcolm Sargent. It was lovely. We saw some emergency fuel transport in London – a soldier driving a small coster barrow with logs! We heard one distant rocket bomb. After the concert we had tea with Kit and ices – the first time in three years now that the ban is off!

February 5th   The Americans have liberated the first capital held by the Japs – Manila in the Philippines. My patient, Brian Farrel, has two elder brothers there; they teach in a school. Their parents have heard nothing of them for three years.

We had a 'Famine Relief' Committee tonight and tempers rose. Roger Wilson, serving with the Friend's Relief Society, says odd food parcels (as advocated by Pacifists) are impracticable. People were furious at finding it's not necessary to give up some of their rations! Money and clothes are desperately wanted.

February 11th   The Black Sea Conference has ended and the points agreed on by the three leaders have been broadcast. Germany is to be totally occupied and totally disarmed. The declaration ends: 'Our meeting here in the Crimea has reaffirmed our common determination to maintain and strengthen in the peace to come that unity of purpose and of action which has made victory possible and certain for the United Nations in this war. We believe that this is a sacred obligation which our governments owe to our peoples and the people of the world. Only with continuing and growing co-operation and understanding among our three countries and among all the peace-loving nations can the highest aspirations of humanity be realised – a secure and lasting peace which will, in the words of the Atlantic Charter "afford assurance that all the men in all the lands may live out their lives in freedom from fear and want". It is considered that victory in this war and the establishment of the proposed International Organisation will provide the greatest opportunity of all to create in the years to come the essential conditions of such a peace.'

February 15th   One of the greatest assaults of the war was launched against Germany by the Allied air forces in the last twenty-four hours to last evening. Over 2,750 heavy bombers smashed at strategic targets, mostly in support of the advancing Russian armies. Over 650,000 fire bombs were dropped on Dresden alone.

February 20th   A really spring-like day – very welcome after the cold and wet, especially as we've still no coal. Allied forces have smashed through the Siegfried Line and are at the entrance to the Rhine Plain. Casualties are high on both sides. US planes have given Tokyo its biggest raid yet; parts of the city were still seen to be blazing from earlier raids. It looks as if the world will be a mass of ruins if the war goes on much longer. V2s are still coming over here – chiefly in and around London.

February 24th   Dr Benes is going to return to Czechoslovakia. In a broadcast last night he expressed the gratitude of all Czechoslovaks who had found a home in Britain during the past terrible years. Every single one of them had seen with deep admiration the magnificent British resistance to the German aggressor. 'You gave us friendship, understanding, moral support,' he said. He was profoundly convinced that his people would never abandon their democratic way of life. Their own bitter experience had taught them that government divorced from the consent of the governed, became tyranny. 'I am leaving these unconquerable islands convinced that victory is absolutely certain and not far distant, and I am leaving you with gratitude in my heart,' he said. 'I am proud to have lived in Britain during her darkest and most glorious hour.' Turkey declared war on Japan and Germany yesterday and Egypt has done the same today! Hitler has sent a message to his people on the twenty-fifth anniversary of the birth of the Nazi political party. He promises them victory!

February 25th   Tokyo is continually being bombed. It looks as if the European and Pacific wars will end at the same time. This book stops at the ceasefire in Europe! May it be soon. Berlin has had its worst raid of the war – over half a million incendiaries and over 1,100 tons of high explosives. It must be terrible there. The Egyptian premier was assassinated shortly after he'd announced his country's entry into the war on the Allied side.

March 6th   The BBC have just reported that Mr Churchill has returned safely from a visit to *Germany*! He's the first British statesman to set foot there since Mr Chamberlain went

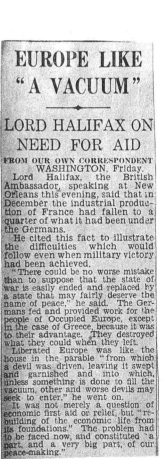

EUROPE LIKE "A VACUUM"

LORD HALIFAX ON NEED FOR AID

FROM OUR OWN CORRESPONDENT
WASHINGTON, Friday.

Lord Halifax, the British Ambassador, speaking at New Orleans this evening, said that in December the industrial production of France had fallen to a quarter of what it had been under the Germans.

He cited this fact to illustrate the difficulties which would follow even when military victory had been achieved.

"There could be no worse mistake than to suppose that the state of war is easily ended and replaced by a state that may fairly deserve the name of peace," he said. The Germans fed and provided work for the people of Occupied Europe, except in the case of Greece, because it was to their advantage. They destroyed what they could when they left.

Liberated Europe was like the house in the parable "from which a devil was driven, leaving it swept and garnished and into which, unless something is done to fill the vacuum, other and worse devils may seek to enter," he went on.

It was not merely a question of economic first aid or relief, but "rebuilding of the economic life from its foundations." The problem had to be faced now, and constituted 'a part, and a very big part, of our peace-making."

to Munich six and a half years ago. The crossing of the Rhine in strength will be a difficult task but nothing will stop the Allies now. There is to be a World Security Conference in April in San Francisco – thirty-nine countries have been invited. The lifting of wartime restrictions continues in Worthing: corporation workmen are helping sappers remove the beach mines near the pier, the Town Hall clock is now illuminated, concrete anti-invasion devices are being smashed up. The chief difficulties remaining are the scarcity of fuel, queuing for fish etc, lack of good domestic help, lack of accommodation – all hotels are booked up fully for months ahead and some have dismissed their 'permanent' guests even, to make room for more. The ration of fat is rather small and people try all sorts of dodges like using liquid paraffin for cake making – quite good too – and some choc and sweet shops have such short supplies they only open so many days a week and shut early. MPs have found that housing is of greater concern to their constituents than any other post-war problem.

March 13th The Americans have thrown a pontoon bridge over the Rhine and troops are streaming across both the permanent and temporary bridges. The Germans have attacked the Remagen Bridge several times but only slight damage has been done. All the same, things are pretty hot there – Peter Lawless, a *Telegraph* reporter, was killed yesterday while crossing in a jeep. Today's paper, in the 289th week of the war, pointed out: 'It is difficult not to ask what the feelings of our fighting men in Germany and Burma are likely to be when they hear of some of the recent strikes that have disfigured the home front. In London 9,000 dockers, on Tyneside 4,000 transport workers, in Manchester several hundred gas workers, in Birmingham 3,000 aircraft workers, at a Durham colliery 1,600 miners; in all these diverse industries and places men have been deliberately sabotaging the nation's business while their comrades at the front are laying down their lives.'

March 14th We had a good WEA meeting tonight and discussed the future of Germany concerning reparations and of re-educating the youth. Both subjects are fraught with almost insoluble answers! The German Commander-in-Chief of Berlin has ordered Berliners 'to fight to the last bullet'. Why the Nazis don't surrender we can't understand.

March 17th Worthing Refugee Committee announced they were looking for holiday accommodation for young Dutch children. Within three days over twenty families had applied. We heard that the children are proving rather difficult as they are all young and some cannot remember their country not being occupied. Hence what was right then – lying to Nazis etc – is *wrong* now! A bit difficult for young minds to get accustomed to the right way of living. The relentless forward movement

QUEEN WILHELMINA of the Netherlands among a group of Dutch children who have been evacuated from Holland to a camp near Coventry. The visit was informal, and her Majesty had lunch and conversations with many of the boys and girls.

by the Allies into Germany continues. General Eisenhower has warned the inhabitants of Mannheim and Frankfurt to leave immediately as the two places are to be 'mercilessly bombarded' until utterly destroyed. Lord Mountbatten has announced the British capture of Mandalay – the Japs had been told to hold on till the last man.

Mother bought two grapefruit today – the first for five years – *lovely*. The butcher sent two small tongues too, so we are in luck's way.

March 24th *Field Marshal Montgomery's army is crossing the Rhine in strength*. I felt we should hear this great news today – the leading article in yesterday's paper was titled: 'The Eve of the Heave'! Mr Churchill is over there too, at Monty's HQ. I went to buy a cake this morning; it was a lovely sunny morning and the queue was in a good mood. Mr Ashford, the owner of the cake shop, came along and spotted me (to his surprise) and asked what I was doing there. A little later on he called me over to his car and presented me with a jam sponge 'for Mother'. It is most uncomfortable to be shown preference in this manner and I felt like a worm as I hurriedly cycled out of sight!

March 26th The British forces have secured the east bank of the Rhine to a depth of seven miles. Mr Churchill and Field Marshal Montgomery have had a short cruise up the river! Earl Lloyd George, the First World War PM, died today.

March 30th Good Friday. No papers today but everyone is listening to every wireless bulletin, just as we did in 1940. The great advance goes on. The Americans are closing the Ruhr trap on thousands of Nazis. It looks as if the Germans are clearing out of Holland – no rockets have come over for two days. Russians are crossing into Austria. The Polish flag is flying over Danzig once again. The end *is* near!

April 2nd   In the Far East there's been a big US landing, with the British Navy helping, on islands between Formosa and the mainland. Okinawa is only 370 miles from Japan. We had the first weather report on the wireless tonight since August 1939! Worthing is *packed* for the first Easter since then too! The Germans are trying to whip up a 'Resistance Movement' in their occupied territories, calling themselves 'werewolves'. Mrs Churchill has arrived in Moscow by plane for a month's stay. Her 'Aid to Russia' Fund has raised over £7 million.

April 6th   This book is not proving to be my last war diary after all and there are no more exercise books to be found in the whole of Worthing. There are no envelopes either! All I can find is a poor little 3d one. However the war is definitely on its last legs. All goes well everywhere. The Russians are in sight of Vienna.

April 7th   War Diary Number Twelve. Positively the last. The news is excellent. British troops are only twenty miles from Hanover. Russian troops are in the outskirts of Vienna. American troops are only 135 miles from Berlin. But the Luftwaffe came up in force today in an attempt to stave off a big attack by over 1,300 USAF and RAF planes on munitions works, railyards and oil depots in North Germany.

April 9th   The Krupps' huge munition works has surrendered to US troops. British paratroops, dropped in Holland two days ago have linked up with Canadian forces today. Now Holland is almost entirely cut off and there are about 80,000 Germans virtually imprisoned there. The Russians are in Vienna. The Soviet Union has pledged Austria's independence. Although thousands of Germans are surrendering all up and down the Western front it looks as if there will not be a clean-cut end to the war when there are young Germans like the one quoted in today's paper. He is a twenty-year-old lieutenant of the 741 Jager Regiment recently captured in Italy: 'Germany is going to win this war, if not immediately and glamorously, at least in the long run. A master-race born to govern cannot be held down eternally. Militarism and domination are the two avocations of Germany and we Germans shall not rest content until we have fulfilled Germany's mission. We shall never capitulate.' Food really is a bit difficult and a lot of swopping goes on – lard for washing soap, dripping for sugar. I swopped some custard powder for seed potatoes with a patient.

April 12th   All goes well with the Allied 'concentric attack'. It looks like they will all arrive in Berlin at the same moment. Nazi plans to hit London with *ten V3 shells a minute* have been discovered.

RAPH AND MORNING POST, WEDNESDAY, APRIL 11, 19

Telegraph and Morning Post, April 11th

WHEN GEN. PATTON'S TROOPS found the German gold hoard, estimated at 100 tons, in a salt mine at Merkers, near Mulhausen, they took into custody three Reichsbank officials left to guard the treasure. One of them, assisted by Finance Corps men of the American Third Army, is seen checking the bags of currency in a tunnel of the mine.

April 13th There was terribly sad news on the 8 am BBC news – the death of President Roosevelt. He was resting at his country house and appeared in reasonable health. It came as a personal shock to everyone in Britain. In the USA it must be devastating. Mr Churchill has sent a message to Mrs Roosevelt: 'I have lost a dear and cherished friendship which was forged in the fire of war. I trust you may find consolation in the glory of his name and the magnitude of his work.'

April 19th Everyday brings news of POW camps freed by Allied troops – also the Nazi concentration camps. The tales are very terrible. I had quite an affair with a patient today who is full of most vicious hatred for all Germans. I told her I realised the ghastliness of the Nazi atrocities but it was *not* typical of all the nation. I nearly walked out: she realised how angry I was and apologised. Nevertheless the tales are very ugly. Wing Commander Douglas Bader, the thirty-five-year-old legless air ace, who was captured in August 1941 when he baled out over France has been freed by the American First Army from a prison camp at Colditz.

April 23rd Hitler is reported to be staying on in Berlin!? We hope he is! Every day come eye witness disclosures of the ghastly Nazi concentration camp horrors. The re-education of

170

Germany is a problem that at present evades the best brains. How and where to begin? Here is a letter from the *New Statesman*; it's a letter written by Douglas Dickens, a war correspondent. 'War correspondents in Germany are showing bewilderment at the discovery of numbers of Germans who appear to welcome us as liberators and a still greater number who are completely apathetic. Where is the mystery? Did anyone seriously expect peasants, women and children and the working classes to go a "heiling" when the Gestapo were removed? If the mass of the people were really behind Hitler, would he have still needed, after 12 years in power, the huge Gestapo organisation and concentration camps, torture chambers and regular execution of opponents? As to the apathetic; they have their counterpart in the millions of English men and women who are politically unconscious and interested in nothing but their own affairs. What these "new" discoveries really demonstrate is the error of "Vansittartism", of clumping all Germans together. We are finding out now that there are two Germanys. The war has an ideological basis and unless we substitute a positive and active philosophy of democracy for the Fascism we are exterminating, the danger of a nation of 80 millions left in a moral, political and economic vacuum, will be extreme . . .'

*Telegraph and Morning Post,
April 24th*

RAPH AND MORNING POST, TUESDAY, APRIL 24, 1945

M.P.s, INVITED by Gen. Eisenhower to the concentration camp at Buchenwald, near Weimar, gaze with horror and nausea at the evidence of Nazi crimes. All the emaciated corpses piled in front of them bear signs of unspeakable maltreatment.
Left to right: Sir Henry Morris-Jones (Lib.-Nat.), Lt.-Col. E. T. R. Wickham (Cons.), Mr. Graham White (Lib.), Mrs. Mavis Tate (Cons.), and Mr. Ness Edwards (Soc.).

DESPATCHES
FROM THE
HOME
FRONT
1945

171

April 25th   Marshal Stalin has announced that Berlin is completely surrounded. Nazi radio still asserts the 'beloved Fuhrer' is in the capital personally conducting the impregnable defence. British soldiers are inside Bremen and house-to-house fighting is taking place. Over a million prisoners have been taken this month. The Burgermaster of Leipsig, his wife and eighteen-year-old daughter, committed suicide when Leipsig fell to US troops. Chaos is spreading throughout the whole country but captured Nazi generals state that only a proclamation from General Eisenhower will end the war: the Nazis will never admit it. Pétain, the eighty-nine-year-old Vichy leader gave himself up and will be tried soon. Great Allied gains are reported from Italy.

April 26th   Tonight we heard that Field Marshal Goering has asked Hitler to relieve him of his position as head of the Luftwaffe because he's got heart trouble . . . RAF Lancasters bombed Hitler's bunker with 12,000 pound bombs. The end must be near. I seem to have said that before! President Truman has welcomed the delegates to the San Francisco Conference 'Not isolated in war, we dare not be so in peace'. Mussolini and some Fascist thugs have been captured by Italian patriots!

One of the MPs who visited Buchenwald Camp, Mr S S Silverman, has addressed the British section of the World Jewish Congress at Toynbee Hall in London: 'If I had been a German citizen who knew the facts, and who knew too that a protest would have meant that my children would have been in Buchenwald next morning, I would not have had the courage to do anything. There was greater blame on those who could have protested in safety, and did not, than on those who could only protest at the risk of sharing the same fate. One ounce of practical assistance to the survivors would be worth several tons of indignant speeches.'

April 28th   We can't miss a news bullétin now. Increasing and rapid progress continues everywhere. At 5 pm it was reported that Himmler had made an 'unconditional surrender' to the US and Britain through a Swedish source. Russia was not mentioned.

April 29th   Rumours of surrenders are still rife. Mussolini has been tried and shot today. Hitler is supposed to be dying from cerebral haemorrhage. Berlin is nothing but a mass of rubble but terrible fighting continues there. Today's editorial says the only purpose of resistance has been to gratify the Nihilism of the Nazi chiefs, anxious that, if they must perish, their country shall perish with them. British bombing planes have dropped 600 tons of food to the Dutch in occupied Holland.

May 1st   It is reported that Count Folke Bernadotte, the head of the Swedish Red Cross, has seen Himmler again about the

BADER PHONES WIFE: "FREED, COMING HOME"

LEGLESS AIR ACE

Wing Cmdr. Douglas Bader, D.S.O., D.F.C., the 35-year-old legless air ace, who was captured in August, 1941, when he baled out over France, has been freed by the American First Army from a prison camp at Colditz, near Leipzig. He is on his way to England by air.

At Red Wells, the Ascot house where she has been living with her mother and stepfather, Mrs. Bader said yesterday that the first news she had of her husband's liberation came from Wing Cmdr. Bader himself. She was told that someone wished to speak to her on the telephone, and when she picked up the receiver she heard her husband's voice.

"I can't remember our first words," said Mrs. Bader. "It was such a complete surprise to me and we could only speak for a few moments. I had received no official telegram or communication of any kind.

"His voice sounded exactly the same as ever," she continued. "I recognised it immediately. All he could tell me was that we should be meeting within the next few days."

The camp where Wing Cmdr. Bader was imprisoned was Oflag IV.C. At the same time as he was freed, 500 British and American officers were liberated.

Wing Cmdr. Bader lost both his legs following a flying accident in 1931. After the loss of his limbs he taught himself to fly again, to play golf, drive a car and to take part in dances with the aid of artificial legs. He rejoined the R.A.F. when war broke out.

HISTORIC PICTURE of the first meeting of the two Dictators at Venice in June, 1934. Mussolini was reported yesterday to have been shot by Italian patriots, and two British war correspondents were officially stated to have seen his body in Milan. When Himmler made his unconditional surrender offer to Britain and America he said that Hitler might not live another 24 hours.

No. 1,224 and last

BRITAIN'S air sirens will sound no more—not even to signal victory.

London, which had 1,224 alerts, heard the last on the morning of March 28.

Yesterday the Ministry of Home Security ended the air-raid warning system at noon.

But hooters may now be sounded, and mills and factories can use their sirens again.

surrender plans but nothing definite has been disclosed. The papers are full of Mussolini's death. He was strung up head downwards with his mistress on meat hooks in a petrol station – it all sounds medieval.

May 2nd The news is most extraordinary, the Nazi radio late last night announced the death of Hitler: he died a 'hero's death at his post in Berlin'. What can we make of this? Admiral Doenitz takes his place. Himmler seems to have vanished! Likewise Goering, Goebbels, and Ribbentrop. Mr Churchill has announced that *all resistance in Italy has ended* – a magnificent achievement. At 10.30 our wireless was interrupted to tell us that *Berlin has fallen to the Russians today*. What will happen next? British troops have taken Lubeck and cut off the Nazis in Denmark. Civil Defence has come to an end officially today. No more Tuesday nights at the Report Centre! I collected my sheets etc today.

May 3rd It seems that the 'unconditional surrender' terms signed by the Germans in Italy mean that over a million Germans are out of the war and that the whole of Austria has been lost by the Nazis. In Berlin over 70,000 Germans have been taken prisoner by the Russians. Apparently both Hitler and Goebbels committed suicide. British and Russian troops have met in North Germany. Our troops have captured both Hamburg and Rangoon today.

May 4th There is a tremendous feeling of repressed excitement as today may be V-Day! Soldiers and helpers all listened in at 9 pm at the YMCA canteen to hear the news that all organised resistance by the Nazis in north-west Europe, Denmark, Holland, Heligoland and the Frisian Isles ceases tomorrow at 8 am. At 10.30 the BBC broke into the programmes to give a recording of the surrender by the Germans to Field Marshal Montgomery this evening at 6.20 pm. According to today's paper the Nazis are trying a 'Dunkirk' and some ships and U-boats are endeavouring to get to Norway, but are being harried by the RAF. Queen Wilhelmina is in Holland and there are great scenes of rejoicing already both in Holland and Denmark tonight.

May 5th Not quite VE-Day yet! London is in a terrific state of excitement and expects the announcement at any minute. Over a million Germans were concerned in last night's surrender. Fighting continues still in the South but Russians and Americans are rushing ahead into Czechoslovakia. Sweden seems to think that the Nazis will capitulate in Norway very soon. There seems to have been a Czech rising in Prague today. The seventy-nine passenger stations on the Tube systems of London Transport which have been used as air-raid shelters ever since the first London raids in 1940 will be closed as shelters after tomorrow.

May 6th The leader in today's paper is titled: 'Long Night Ended' and, now that Hitler and Mussolini are dead, ends: 'So pass from the scenes of their crimes two baleful enemies of mankind. The monstrous fabric of their wicked ambitions had shrivelled up, and at the end they were fugitives from justice: the world's justice and – let it be said with reverence – the justice of God. Would that the evil they did could be interred with their bones! It lives after them and will long live: the ruin of their own countries; the destruction and desolation spread over Europe and far beyond its borders; the legacy of hate and things abominable which they bequeathed to their own people.'

May 7th At last the pronouncement has come! All day long everyone has been listening to the wireless and on the six o'clock news it was reported that tomorrow will be the official VE-Day although the surrender terms were signed by the Germans at 2.41 am this morning in General Eisenhower's headquarters at Rheims. The only Germans still fighting are those in Prague but that will cease soon. Allied ships are sailing into Oslo Fjord today. The bodies of Goebbels and his family have been found in Berlin: he poisoned his six children and ordered an SS guard to shoot himself and his wife. Hitler's body has not been found. Many important people have been liberated from Nazi prison: three former French premiers

Goebbels suicides

GOEBBELS.
The shouting and the tumult dies.

Says deputy seized by Russians

HITLER and Goebbels committed suicide, Hans Fritzsche, director of Nazi radio propaganda, has told the Russians.

This was announced in Marshal Stalin's communiqué early to-day.

Fritzsche was taken prisoner with a number of other German military and political chiefs when Berlin was captured, said the communiqué.

(Daladier, Blum and Reynaud), the Generals Gamelin and Weygand, Princess Mary's son and Pastor Niemöller, the anti-Nazi German pastor. He was held in Italy and was rescued by the Fifth Army; he'd been seven years in concentration camps. A few hours after his release he held a service in the lounge of an hotel. His text was the words of Isaiah: 'For the mountains shall depart, and the hills be removed: but my kindness shall not depart from thee, neither shall the covenant of my peace be removed, saith the Lord that hath mercy on thee.'

We've heard that Nevill is in Allied hands at last and Lionel Blake is back home after five years as a POW. Here in Worthing some flags have appeared in preparation for tomorrow, also a platform for the mayor to make his speech from outside the Town Hall (quite a number of people were sitting there from early afternoon waiting hopefully!). Aeroplanes have been doing their 'victory rolls' over the town and I'm sitting here at 11 pm without the curtains being drawn!

VE-DAY
VICTORY EDITION

May 8th It's come at last. I woke up at 7 am to hear the sound of Mother wrestling with the flags (rather moth-eaten and patched, relics of Queen Victoria's Jubilee!). But we weren't the first in the road after all as we were when Mussolini was captured in July 1943. The weather's been good for the first of the two VE holidays. It's been a queer sort of day, the highlights being the Prime Minister's short broadcast at 3 pm and the King's at 9 pm. The Prime Minister told huge crowds that gathered in Whitehall: 'This is your victory. In all our long history we have never seen a greater day than this.' Hostilities cease officially at one minute past midnight tonight when it's hoped that any fighting against the Russians will cease. Mother and I listened in to the thrilling broadcasts on the European victory. There were services in all churches and cinemas at 12 pm today.

May 9th The papers are full of yesterday's rejoicings. Today is still being celebrated as a public holiday – it's Russia's V-Day today. At 8 pm Marshal Stalin broadcast his victory message to his peoples. The other items of news are: (1) Quisling has given himself up in Norway. (2) Goering (the head of the Luftwaffe) and Kesselring (the General in charge of all German forces in the south) have been captured. (3) Prague is now entirely in Czech hands. (4) The King and Queen have made a 'victory' tour of London's badly bombed, but much beflagged East End. (5) The German garrisons in the Atlantic French ports of Dunkirk, Lorient, St Nazaire and La Rochelle have surrendered to the French.

May 10th The Channel Islands are free again today and U-boats are arriving at British ports to give themselves up. Godalming had a very gay V-night and Michael and Roger were allowed to stay up and see the fun. They were just sitting down to a V supper – red, white and blue flowers, asparagus, tinned peaches etc when Kit cycled up! There were bonfires in the recreation ground and dancing in the streets, searchlights etc up on Charterhouse Hill. Nevill is home again after five years as a POW. Eighty-four of the Defence Regulations which have controlled our lives in wartime have been swept away by an Order in Council: it is no longer illegal to communicate with any person in enemy territory – except Japan – nor to keep or liberate any racing or homing pigeon without a police permit. Looters of bombed buildings can no longer be sentenced to death – they will now be dealt with under the ordinary civil code. Some of the British POWs came into the YMCA canteen tonight – they are from the camp at Sompting, which is the largest of its kind in the country. Over a thousand servicemen a day are repatriated and the time elapsing between their entry and re-joining their families is less than two days. They can then spend fifty-six days with their families before reporting back to their regiment, ship or squadron. Figures just released show that Allied casualties between D-Day and VE-Day were: Americans killed 89,477, wounded 367,180, missing 57,877, total 514,534 – British and Canadian killed 39,599, wounded 126,545, missing 18,368, total 184,512 – French killed 11,080, wounded 45,966, missing 4,201, total 61,247 – Polish killed 1,189, wounded 4,029, missing 375, total 5,593. The casualty figures were regarded officially as surprisingly low in view of the tremendous operation involved. They were said to be far under the figures estimated before the invasion. One of the

CEASE-FIRE ORDER TO U-BOATS

Adml. Doenitz has ordered all U-boats to cease activity, the German Flensburg radio reported yesterday.

The cease-fire order to U-boat commanders was given in an Order of the Day on Saturday, the radio said.

chief reasons for the comparatively low casualties was General Eisenhower's strategy, executed by his field commanders, of creating pockets, sealing off enemy forces within the pockets, and forcing surrender rather than attempting to steamroller opposition and spend Allied lives.

William Joyce has been captured by the British Forces in North Germany. He is Lord Haw Haw who broadcast 'Jairmany Calling' propaganda for the Nazis.

May 13th Thanksgiving Sunday all over Britain. All Worthing churches are full and there was a huge victory procession up South Street and Chapel Road to Broadwater Green where an open air service was held. The air war against Japan continues with great force. Mr Churchill made his speech to the nation tonight – it was rather sober.

One man signs for millions 2.40 a.m

IN a red schoolhouse at Rheims, headquarters of General Eisenhower, unconditional surren made. General Jodl, representing Grand-Admiral Doenitz, signs. On his right, his aide. grim, on his left, General-Admiral von Friedeberg, C-in-C German Navy.

SURRENDER SCENE AT ALLIED H.Q.

DRAMATIC 15 MINUTES THAT ENDED WAR

HUMBLED GERMANS

From *DOUGLAS WILLIAMS,*
Daily Telegraph Special Correspondent
RHEIMS, Tuesday.

Daily Telegraph

T TEA PARTY in King-street on Saturday was also a practice run for a real monster
⬩lanned for the day Japan is beaten.   Preparations for it are already being made in the
street.

CONCLUSION

As I reread this diary after fifty years, I hoped that our obvious
thankfulness for final victory would not obscure the yearning
for peace and justice which had been uppermost in our minds
throughout six terrible years of war. Intense sorrow was felt
for the loss of life of both victors and vanquished and we all
prayed that never again would mankind resort to the evil
of war.

In Britain at the end of hostilities, thirty-one churches and
co-operating societies united to form the Organisation of Christian Reconstruction in Europe. The appalling devastation found
throughout Europe, especially in Germany, immediately resulted in a magnificent response from Christians of all
denominations.

He shall judge between the nations, and shall decide for
many peoples; and they shall beat their swords into plough-
shares, and their spears into pruninghooks; nation shall not
lift up sword against nation, neither shall they learn war
anymore (Isaiah 2: 4).

ST. PAUL'S HAS ITS V SIGN

THE golden cross surmounting St. Paul's was still shining after midnight. Golden arcs within the balcony bathed the dome in soft light. The twin towers were silver against a purple sky. And, behind the Cathedral, searchlights wrote a giant "V."